ULTRA VIRES

Why the IRS Lacks the Jurisdiction and Authority to Regulate Nonprofit Governance

ULTRA VIRES

Why the IRS Lacks the Jurisdiction and Authority to Regulate Nonprofit Governance

BRUCE R. HOPKINS

TALBOT PUBLISHING
Clark, New Jersey

ISBN 978-1-61619-386-7

TALBOT PUBLISHING
AN IMPRINT OF
THE LAWBOOK EXCHANGE, LTD.
33 Terminal Avenue
Clark, New Jersey 07066-1321

Please see our website for a selection of our other publications and fine facsimile reprints of classic works of legal history:
www.lawbookexchange.com

Library of Congress Cataloging-in-Publication Data

Names: Hopkins, Bruce R., author.
Title: Ultra vires : why the IRS lacks the jurisdiction and authority to regulate nonprofit governance / Bruce R. Hopkins.
Description: Clark, NJ : Talbot Publishing, an imprint of The Lawbook Exchange, Ltd., 2017. | Includes bibliographical references and index.
Identifiers: LCCN 2017003404 | ISBN 9781616193867 (hardcover : alk. paper)
Subjects: LCSH: Nonprofit organizations--Law and legislation--United States. | United States. Internal Revenue Service. | Administrative agencies--United States.
Classification: LCC KF1388 .H67 2017 | DDC 346.73/064--dc23
LC record available at https://lccn.loc.gov/2017003404

Printed in the United States of America on acid-free paper

Dedication

This book is dedicated to those at the Department of the Treasury and the Internal Revenue Service who are seeking, with respect to IRS regulation of nonprofit governance, an exit strategy, to enable the IRS to abandon this form of regulation as part of a larger effort to return the tax-exempt organizations function to the tasks it is supposed to be undertaking.

Table of Contents

Preface xi

1 Opening Perspectives 1
A Tale of Two Developments 1
Role and Function of the IRS 7
Treasury/IRS Regulatory Guidance 13
Concept of Nonprofit Governance 21

2 Government Agency Law Basics 27
Introduction as to Agency Jurisdiction and Authority 27
Scope of Government Agencies' Authority 31
Scope of Government Agencies' Jurisdiction 33
Law as to Scope of Government Agencies' Authority 49
Factor of Agency Expertise 68
Factor of Relevance 71

3 Relevant Basic Tax-Exempt Organizations Law 75
Organization of IRS 75
General Federal Tax Law Rules 76
Nonprofit Governance 87
Federal Tax Law as to Nonprofit Board Composition 88

4 Nonprofit Organizations' Governance Standards 105
Governance Philosophy in General 105
Sarbanes-Oxley Act 106
Watchdog Agencies' Standards 107
Philanthropic Advisory Service Standards 107
Better Business Bureau Wise Giving Alliance Standards 111
Evangelical Council for Financial Accountability Standards 113
Standards for Excellence Institute Standards 121
American Institute of Philanthropy Standards 127
Other Watchdog Agencies 128
California's Nonprofit Integrity Act 129
Senate Finance Committee Staff Paper 131
US Treasury Department's Voluntary Best Practices 134

Committee for Purchase Proposed Best Practices 136
Panel on Nonprofit Sector Recommendations 137
American National Red Cross Governance Modernization Act Principles 139
Panel on Nonprofit Sector Good Governance Principles 140
Perspective 151

5 Evolution of IRS Policy as to Nonprofit Governance 155
IRS Officials' Speeches 156
Revamped Annual Information Return 159
Exempt Organizations Division 2009 Annual Report 164
Draft IRS Good Governance Principles 164
IRS Agents' Training Materials 168
IRS Agents' Governance Check Sheet 170
Data as to Correlation 171

6 IRS Private Letter Ruling Policy 175
Board Size 176
Related Boards 195
Lack of Governance Policies 205
Discrepant IRS Rulings 208

7 IRS Lacks Jurisdiction to Regulate Nonprofit Governance 211
Application of Law 212
Singular Governance Case 217
IRS's Lack of Expertise 230
IRS' Demonstrated Lack of Expertise to Regulate Nonprofit Governance 232
Summary of Analysis 250

8 IRS Lacks Authority to Regulate Nonprofit Governance 255
Application of *Chevron* Standard 256
Application of *Skidmore* Standard 259
Analysis of *Skidmore* Factors 259
IRS Policy is Arbitrary and Capricious 261
Summary of Analysis 266
Concept of the Extraordinary Case 267

9 Concluding Thoughts 269
Review of Central Issue 269
Review of Central Arguments 270

Review of Reasons in Support of Arguments 270
IRS Guidance Document Types 272
Unanswered Issues 275

Bibliography 281
Table of Cases 283
Index 293

Preface

I am fond of the Internal Revenue Service. I love to tell clients how much I enjoy interacting with representatives of the IRS. They look at me strangely, of course, yet there is also a glimmer of relief – a giving of thanks for those like me so they can (or try to) avoid the experience. I have been dealing with the IRS for nearly 50 years, liking it now more than ever. Sure, there are occasional ugly episodes but overall it is and continues to be rewarding.

The exempt organizations component of the IRS – my minuet partner -- is going through rough times. Capitol Hill and the courts are battering that part of the agency, in part for good reason. The events that unfolded beginning in the Spring of 2013 – whether you think it mismanagement, brouhaha, scandal, or too much over too little – started with some inexcusable and foolish decisions. (If you don't know what I am referencing, see Chapter 5, note 60.)

Notwithstanding the extent of the blame, I feel sorry for the agency – it is understaffed and underfunded. The IRS can't do much under these circumstances. I miss the initiatives that were in play before the collapse, although my clients do not. They were intellectually stimulating projects, plus they gave me material for presentations, newsletters, and books. I long for the pre-2013 days.

I suppose the exempt organizations function of the IRS is currently doing the best it can with the resources it has. It puzzles me, nonetheless, why a government agency, in such throes, would persist in a regulatory effort that is clearly beyond the scope of its jurisdiction and authority, when it is so far behind in what it should be doing and under such siege. (If you don't know what I am referencing, see Chapter 8, notes 43 and 44.) I am referring, of course, to the IRS's misguided decision to leap into the realm of nonprofit governance, and keep thrashing around there when it should be focusing on matters that are within the bounds of its authority -- and demanding its attention.

The IRS lacks the jurisdiction and authority to regulate nonprofit governance. Explaining why this is as a matter of law is the point of this book. The agency should cease doing what it is doing in the context of nonprofit governance. That move would free up resources to do what the law and good policy demands. This is not an IRS-bashing book (well, maybe to a little extent) but a paean to the IRS to abandon its antics with respect to nonprofit governance and get on with its true responsibilities.

Point of personal disclosure: This book is based on research I undertook in writing a dissertation as part of my pursuit of an SJD degree at the University of Kansas School of Law. (A magnificent experience, by the way; see Chapter 1, note 16.) Books based on dissertations can be potentially numbing. I have tried my best to convert from that genre to a more suitable one.

Bruce R. Hopkins
2017

1

Opening Perspectives

> The role of the IRS is to "administer, manage, conduct, direct, and supervise the execution and application of the *internal revenue laws* or related statutes and *tax* conventions to which the United States is a party" (emphasis supplied)
>
> *Internal Revenue Code*

Two developments in nonprofit law in recent years are indelibly embedded in my mind. One haunts me; the other delights me to this day.

A Tale of Two Developments

The first of these developments was, of all things, a speech.

The IRS Speaks – and Stuns

One of the most dramatic and consequential events in the development of contemporary nonprofit law occurred on April 26, 2007. On that occasion, Steven Miller, then the Commissioner of the Tax Exempt/Government Entities Division of the Internal Revenue Service,[1] was the opening speaker at the annual Georgetown University Law School's conference on Representing and Managing Tax-Exempt Organizations. He stood at a podium in a huge hotel ballroom in Washington, DC, filled to capacity with individuals (mostly lawyers) interested in nonprofit law. A quiet and respectful

---

[1] The Internal Revenue Service is referenced throughout as the IRS.

audience awaited Mr. Miller's comments, no doubt anticipating merely a staid summary of recent doings at the TE/GE Division. At the outset, they were not surprised at the tenor of the talk. But, about midway into his remarks, he announced, to an uncomprehending, then quickly stunned audience, that the IRS was contemplating entry into the realm of governance of tax-exempt organizations, principally public charities.[2]

When the TE/GE Commissioner began addressing the IRS's role in nonprofit governance, on this occasion, he conceded that, for the IRS to propound and enforce good governance principles, the agency would have to go "beyond its traditional spheres of activity." He revealed that he was pondering the question of "whether it would benefit the public and the tax-exempt sector [for the IRS] to require organizations to adopt and follow recognized principles of good governance."[3] He asserted that there is a "vacuum" that needs to be filled in the realm of education on "basic standards and practices of good governance and accountability."

The TE/GE Commissioner, that day, made the best case that can be asserted for intertwining the matter of governance law and nonprofit, tax-exempt organizations' compliance with the federal tax law. Mr. Miller said that a "well-governed organization is more likely to be compliant [with the tax law], while poor governance can easily lead an exempt organization into trouble." He spoke, for example, of an "engaged, informed, and independent board of directors accountable to the community [that the tax-exempt organization] serves."

Mr. Miller's positions as to the IRS's involvement in the regulation of nonprofit governance became clearer, and hardened, as the ensuing months wore on.[4]

I remember, once having recovered from my Miller-induced shock, thinking that this is absurd: The IRS has no business getting into nonprofit governance. More legally (not to mention elegantly)

---

[2] See Chapter 5, text accompanied by note 1.

[3] In fact, there are no "recognized principles of good governance" for nonprofit organizations, at least not in the sense of uniformity of and consensus on these principles. There are ample sets of principles to choose from; they are, however, often inconsistent. See Chapter 4.

[4] See Chapter 5, text accompanied by notes 3–7.

stated, my view was that the agency lacked the jurisdiction and the authority, let alone the competence, to regulate in the sphere of governance of public charities and other tax-exempt organizations.

As matters unfolded, they worsened. I became more appalled. The Commissioner gave another speech in the fall of 2007; his attitude and tone had dramatically changed.[5] No more pondering, musing, and speculating. Rather, the Commissioner stated that, "[w]hile a few continue to argue that governance is outside our jurisdiction, most now support an active IRS that is engaged in this area." (No evidence was provided then or since in support of that observation.) He expressed his view that the IRS "contributes to a compliant, healthy charitable sector by expecting the tax-exempt community to adhere to commonly accepted standards of good governance."[6] He continued: "We are comfortable that we are well within our authority to act in these areas." And: "To more clearly put our weight behind good governance may represent a small step beyond our traditional sphere of influence, but we believe the subject is well within our core responsibilities." (A year later, at the Georgetown Law School conference, Mr. Miller stated that the "question is no longer whether the IRS has a role to play in this area, but rather, what that role will be."[7])

My ire increased when the IRS began issuing private letter rulings in this area, in part because the agency's views were (and continue to be) based on application of the private benefit doctrine. That is, the IRS started ruling that small nonprofit boards and nonprofit boards comprised of related individuals were inherent manifestations of private benefit, precluding tax exemption. This was (and remains) nonsense; the doctrine does not support that view. In fact, the law is nearly the opposite.

There is one court opinion on point, which is often cited by the IRS (and sometimes misconstrued by the agency); it is a 1980 Tax Court opinion involving an organization by the name of the

---

[5] See Chapter 5, text accompanied by note 2.

[6] There are no "commonly accepted standards of good governance." See *supra* note 3.

[7] See Chapter 5, text accompanied by note 7.

Bubbling Well Church of Universal Love.[8] This church had a board of three family members. The organization was not forthcoming in providing factual information to the IRS as to its eligibility for tax exemption, which ultimately ruled that the entity was organized and operated for private benefit, and thus was not tax-exempt. The court agreed with the IRS that this entity was not entitled to exemption but did so on the ground that the organization did not meet its burden of proving it qualified for exemption. It certainly did not base its finding on the private benefit doctrine. Quite the contrary. The court wrote that the "domination" of the organization by this trio "alone may not necessarily disqualify it for exemption, it provides an obvious opportunity for abuse of the claimed tax-exempt status."[9] The court added that this set of facts "calls for open and candid disclosure of all facts bearing upon [this] organization, operations, and finances so that the Court, should it uphold the claimed exemption, can be assured that it is not sanctioning an abuse of the revenue laws."[10] Obviously, then, the test is not an automatic denial of exemption but a strict scrutiny approach. (Distortions of this opinion by the IRS include a 2013 ruling citing the opinion for the proposition that "undue control of the organization by a related board causes the organization to serve private interests"[11] and a 2014 ruling stating that a "small group of individuals ... have [sic] exclusive control over the management of [the entity's] funds and operations" and "as a result of this exclusive control [the entity's] founders benefit."[12])

Thereafter, the IRS began issuing rulings, denying recognition of exemption to nonprofit organizations that did not adopt certain governance policies, most frequently conflict-of-interest policies. That was also contrary to the law; there is nothing in the federal tax

---

[8] Bubbling Well Church of Universal Love, Inc. v. Commissioner, 74 T.C. 531 (1980), *aff'd*, 670 F.2d 104 (9th Cir. 1981). The opinion in this case is detailed in Chapter 3, text accompanied by notes 92–100.

[9] Bubbling Well Church of Universal Love, Inc. v. Commissioner, 74 T.C. at 535.

[10] *Id.*

[11] IRS Private Letter Ruling (Priv. Ltr. Rul.) 201325017 (March 28, 2013).

[12] Priv. Ltr. Rul. 201421022 (February 27, 2014). Other distortions and misconstructions of the *Bubbling Well* opinion are inventoried in Chapter 7, text accompanied by notes 108–113.

law mandating policies of this nature. Indeed, the principal annual information return filed with the IRS by tax- exempt organizations explicitly states, at the outset of a section asking questions about various governance policies, that the IRS is "requesting information about policies not required by the Internal Revenue Code."[13] For that matter, these policies are not required by any other statute, regulation, or formal rule.

Not only was I upset with the IRS's obviously incorrect basis in law for justification of its entry into nonprofit governance, I was appalled with the audaciousness of the agency's act in launching this regulatory initiative in violation of the principles of the Administrative Procedure Act.[14] A federal government agency is not empowered to undertake a wholly new program, absent congressional authorization, without first explaining its position in some formal way (such as a proposed regulation or even a revenue ruling) and seeking comments from the public. Few federal agencies could get away with what the IRS, which views itself as above the requirements of administrative law applicable to other federal agencies,[15] has done.

I railed against this IRS policy every chance I got, in my newsletter and in the course of speeches. (As to the latter, I would review all of the IRS's private letter rulings on governance – the members of the audience had my current developments outline before them, with the list of these rulings in it – then call out: "What do these rulings have in common?" Following a brief, surprised silence, I would yell: "They're all wrong!" I heard lots of chuckles, some applause.) I wanted to write an article on the subject of the IRS and nonprofit governance but could not find the time. Then I decided to go back to law school for a doctoral degree;[16] my dissertation was on that subject.[17]

---

[13] Form 990, Part VI, Section B.

[14] See Chapter 8, text accompanied by notes 27–41.

[15] See Chapter 2, text accompanied by notes 160–165 (discussion of *tax exceptionalism*).

[16] My adventures in that regard are chronicled in Hopkins, *SJD: What's the Point of Three (Law Degrees)?* (BookFuel 2016).

[17] The title of the dissertation is "The Federal Tax Law Aspects of the Governance of Public Charities and Other Nonprofit Organizations: Arguments That the Internal

The Supreme Court Proclaims the Framework

The second of these two developments came in 2003, when the US Supreme Court issued an interesting – and quite pertinent – opinion concerning the scope of jurisdiction of government agencies, recognizing the dichotomy between an "assertion of authority not conferred" and an "incorrect application of agency authority."[18] In either instance, an agency's action is "ultra vires."[19]

There is, nonetheless, occasional confusion as to this matter of agency *jurisdiction* and *authority*.[20] In a sense, the distinction has little meaning, in that, in either instance, an agency is permitted (by the judicial branch) to do what it wants to do or it is not.[21] As the Supreme Court stated: "The reality, laid bare, is that there is *no difference*, insofar as the validity of agency action is concerned, between an agency's exceeding the scope of its authority (its 'jurisdiction') and its exceeding authorized application of authority that it unquestionably has."[22] The "question in every case is, simply, whether the statutory text forecloses the agency's assertion of authority, or not."[23]

The Supreme Court has admonished the judiciary to "tak[e] seriously, and apply[] rigorously, in all cases, statutory limits on agencies' authority."[24] The Court added: "Where Congress has

---

Revenue Service Lacks Jurisdiction and Regulatory Authority, and a Critique of the IRS Ruling Policy on Nonprofit Governance" (January 2016).

[18] City of Arlington, Texas v. Federal Communications Commission, 133 S. Ct. 1863, 1869 (2013).

[19] *Id.*

[20] This confusion (or disagreement) is manifested in, e.g., the differences in analysis found in the majority and dissenting opinions in City of Arlington, Texas v. Federal Communications Commission, 133 S. Ct. 1863 (2013). Indeed, the overlap in this area is inherent in the Administrative Procedure Act, which empowers courts to "hold unlawful and set aside agency action [that is] in excess of statutory *jurisdiction*, *authority*, or limitations (5 U.S.C. § 706(2)(C)) (emphasis added).

[21] Thus, the Supreme Court stated: "To exceed authorized application is to exceed authority. Virtually any administrative action can be characterized as either the one or the other, depending on how generally one wishes to describe the 'authority'" (Mississippi Power & Light Co. v. Mississippi ex rel. Moore, 487 U.S. 354, 381 (1988)).

[22] City of Arlington, Texas v. Federal Communications Commission, 133 S. Ct. 1863, 1870 (2013).

[23] *Id.* at 1871.

[24] *Id.* at 1874.

established a clear line, the agency cannot go beyond it; and where Congress has established an ambiguous line, the agency can go no further than the ambiguity will fairly allow."[25]

This opinion gave me the basic framework for my assessment as to whether the IRS has the jurisdiction and authority to regulate in the realm of nonprofit governance. Thus, this analysis will explore whether the IRS has the jurisdiction to regulate in the realm of nonprofit governance.[26] Thereafter, the analysis will shift its focus to whether, in the exercise of its authority, the IRS has exceeded the scope of it.[27]

Preliminarily, however, there needs to be a discussion of the role and function of the IRS, the nature of the regulatory guidance issued by the Treasury Department and the IRS, and the concept of nonprofit governance.

Role and Function of the IRS

The essence of this book is that the IRS is, in regulating nonprofit governance, exceeding the boundaries of its jurisdiction and authority. This position is predicated on an understanding of the appropriate (that is, lawful) role and function of the IRS.

The IRS is of the view that it has the jurisdiction and authority (and capacity) to articulate and enforce a federal law version of governance rules for tax-exempt organizations, principally public charities, and to regulate the operational affairs of these entities, with denial of recognition of tax-exempt status or revocation of tax exemption as the sanction. This matter of nonprofit governance has historically and traditionally been almost exclusively the province of state law regulation.[28]

---

[25] *Id.*

[26] See Chapter 7.

[27] See Chapter 8.

[28] The agency is implicitly of this view, as demonstrated by its various actions referenced throughout this dissertation, including massive revision of an annual information return (Form 990), promulgation of a draft of "good governance" principles, and issuance of dozens of private letter rulings.

This view of the IRS has never been explicitly stated by the agency; it may be extrapolated from its actions.[29] The distinction between agency jurisdiction and agency authority, presented in core court opinions, is discussed in detail below.[30] Generally, however, at the federal level, determination of the jurisdiction of a government agency normally starts with review of actions by Congress, which by statute creates federal government agencies, and defines their purposes and responsibilities. The matter of agency authority usually entails judicial review of an agency's guidance, most frequently in the form of a regulation, to determine if it has engaged in rulemaking that is beyond the boundaries of what Congress has permitted it to do. When a government agency has undertaken a form of regulation that is an ultra vires act because of a lack of jurisdiction, it is what the Supreme Court has termed an "assertion of authority not conferred."[31] When there is such an ultra vires act because of a lack of authority, it is what the Court has called an "incorrect application of agency authority."[32]

Thus, as to the matter of jurisdiction, the beginning point of the analysis is the role and function of the IRS. The US Supreme Court declared that it is important to "tak[e] seriously, and apply[] rigorously, in all cases, statutory limits on [government] agencies' authority."[33]

All federal government agencies are created by Congress, with their purposes, duties, and responsibilities articulated in one or more statutes. Usually, there is a statute sketching the overall authority of an agency; the Supreme Court has referred to this type of law as an "organic" statute.[34] This fact is reflected in the foregoing quotation from the Supreme Court, referencing "statutory limits" on the authority of government agencies. Normally, then, the starting point for this type of an analysis is the content of the statute creating the agency and describing its authority.

---

[29] See Chapter 5.

[30] See Chapter 2, text accompanied by notes 30–193.

[31] City of Arlington, Texas v. Federal Communications Commission, 133 S. Ct. 1863, 1869 (2013).

[32] *Id.*

[33] *Id.* at 1874.

[34] E.g., United States v. Southwestern Cable Co., 392 U.S. 157, 168 (1968).

As it happens, however, in this context there is no such statute. That is, there is no statute creating the IRS. As will be discussed, nonetheless, there is statutory law concerning the role and function of the IRS. This statutory law conveys one specific sense of the IRS's overarching role, as stated by an eminent authority on the subject: "[T]he role and requisite authority of the IRS is simply stated: to enforce the federal tax laws."[35]

The IRS is a "subordinate agency within the Treasury Department."[36] The Department of the Treasury was created by an act of Congress in 1789.[37] A provision of the Internal Revenue Code[38] is captioned "Authority of the Department of the Treasury" but in actuality that statute creates and authorizes the Secretary of the Treasury.[39] The general role of the Department of the Treasury is to collect taxes.[40] Thus, the Secretary of the Treasury is authorized to pay such sums as he or she deems necessary for detecting underpayments of tax or detecting and bring to trial and punishment persons guilty of violating the internal revenue laws or conniving to do so.[41]

Although there is no statute explicitly creating the IRS, the Internal Revenue Code contains a provision authorizing "in the Department of the Treasury a Commissioner of Internal Revenue."[42] The duty of this Commissioner is to "administer, manage, conduct,

---

[35] Owens, "Charities and Governance: Is the IRS Subject to Challenge?" 60 *Exempt Org. Tax Rev.* (no. 3) 287, 289 (June 2008) (Owens Article). The author of this article, Marcus S. Owens, was the Director of the IRS's Exempt Organizations Division (see Chapter 3, second paragraph) for ten years.

[36] Loving v. Internal Revenue Service, 742 F.3d 1013, 1015 (D.C. Cir. 2014).

[37] 31 U.S.C. § 301.

[38] The Internal Revenue Code of 1986, as amended, 26 U.S.C., is referenced throughout, in footnotes, as the IRC.

[39] IRC § 7801(a)(1).

[40] IRC § 7601(a), which provides: "The Secretary [of the Treasury] shall, to the extent he deems it practicable, cause officers or employees of the Treasury Department to proceed, from time to time, through each internal revenue district and inquire after and concerning all persons therein who may be liable to pay any internal revenue tax, and all persons owning or having the care and management of any objects with respect to which any tax is imposed."

[41] IRC § 7623(a).

[42] IRC § 7803(a)(1)(A).

direct, and supervise the execution and application of the internal revenue laws or related statutes and tax conventions to which the United States is a party."[43] This authority in the Commissioner has subsequently been obliquely assigned to the IRS, in that the statute authorizing the Internal Revenue Service Oversight Board provides that the general responsibility of the Board is to "oversee the Internal Revenue Service in its administration, management, conduct, direction, and supervision of the execution and application of the internal revenue laws or related statutes and tax conventions to which the United States is a party."[44] This provision is the closest one there is to being a statutory authorization of – an organic statute for – the IRS.[45]

There are other provisions of the Internal Revenue Code that support the conclusion that the IRS is essentially the tax collection and tax law enforcement agency for the federal government. The Department of the Treasury and the IRS are accorded authority to issue "all needful rules and regulations" for enforcement of the internal revenue laws.[46] The Code requires the filing of returns and maintenance of records, to facilitate the authority in the Treasury Department authority to design return to collect information for the "purpose of carrying out the internal revenue laws." [47] A Code provision providing federal district courts with jurisdiction as to IRS summons matter makes reference to summonses "under the internal revenue laws."[48]

Certainly, this is the function of the IRS from the standpoint of the Treasury Department. Thus, a tax regulation states: "The Internal Revenue Service is a bureau of the Department of the Treasury under the immediate direction of the Commissioner of Internal Revenue. The Commissioner has general superintendence of the

---

[43] IRC § 7803(a)(2)(A).

[44] IRC § 7802(c)(1)(A).

[45] The federal agency created (in 1862) to collect taxes for the national government was named the Bureau of Internal Revenue. The name was changed in 1953 to the Internal Revenue Service (Treasury Decision 6038, 1953–2 C.B. 443) to emphasize the "service" element of the agency's efforts on behalf of taxpayers.

[46] IRC § 7805(a).

[47] IRC §§ 6033(a), 6001, respectively.

[48] IRC § 7402(b).

assessment and collection of all taxes imposed by any law providing internal revenue. The Internal Revenue Service is the agency by which these functions are performed."[49] The IRS's Office of Chief Counsel has stated that the exempt organization return requirements have as their primary purpose provision of information to the IRS to enable that agency to "enforce the tax laws."[50]

The IRS states that its mission is to "provide America's taxpayers with top quality service by helping them understand and meet their tax responsibilities and by applying the tax law with integrity and fairness to all."[51] The mission of the Tax Exempt/Governmental Entities Division, as stated in the Internal Revenue Manual, is "to provide its customers top quality service by helping them understand and comply with applicable tax laws and to protect the public interest by applying the tax law with integrity and fairness to all."[52]

The foregoing summary of the purpose, mission, role, and function of the IRS, statutorily based or otherwise, makes it clear that the agency primarily exists as the nation's tax-collection agency. It has collateral functions, such as the issuance of rulings, conducting educational and other outreach efforts, and administering the law of tax-exempt organizations but these are undertaken from the standpoint of administration of the federal *tax* law.

At his confirmation hearing on December 10, 2013, Commissioner of Internal Revenue John A. Koskinen stated that "it is

---

[49] Department of the Treasury Tax Regulation (Reg.) § 601.101(a).

[50] General Counsel Memorandum (Gen. Couns. Mem.) 36506 (Dec. 8, 1975).

[51] This mission statement is on the IRS website and is reproduced weekly in the Internal Revenue Bulletin. It appears in the Internal Revenue Manual (Part 1, Chap. 1 § 23.1). The statement further appears in the IRS Strategic Plan for fiscal years 2014–2017, as noted in a US Government Accountability Office report issued in July 2015 ("IRS Examination Selection: Internal Controls for Exempt Organization Selection Should Be Strengthened" (GAO-15-514)). This statement also was referenced by the GAO in a report issued in September 2016, at p. 2 ("Regulatory Guidance Processes: Treasury and OMB Need to Reevaluate Long-standing Exemptions of Tax Regulations and Guidance" (GAO-16-720)) ("Regulatory Guidance Processes Report"). Also Lederman and Mazza, *Tax Controversies: Practice and Procedure, Third Edition* (LexisNexis: 2009) § 1.02.

[52] This Division is the primary component of the IRS with the responsibility of administering and enforcing the federal law of tax-exempt organizations. See Chapter 3, second paragraph.

clear that the responsibility of the Commissioner is to make sure that the agency fairly, efficiently and effectively *collects the taxes* owed by every business and individual, that the agency provides *taxpayer* services, in the form of easily understandable information and prompt answers to questions, to make it as simple as possible for people and firms to *pay their taxes*."[53]

The Senate Finance Committee conducted a two-year bipartisan investigation of the IRS, concluding, in a report published on August 6, 2015, that from 2010 to 2013, IRS management was "delinquent" in its responsibility to provide "effective control, guidance, and direction" over the processing of applications for recognition of tax-exempt status filed by political advocacy organizations.[54] This report stated that, during that period, the IRS "failed to fulfill its obligation to administer the *tax law* with 'integrity and fairness to all.'"[55] The report observed that this investigation "uncovered serious shortcomings in how the IRS exercised that authority when it processed applications for [recognition of] tax exemption from organizations that were engaged in political advocacy – shortcomings that raise public doubt about whether the IRS is a neutral *administrator of the tax laws*."[56]

The IRS stated, in late 2015, that the Exempt Organizations Division's "overarching compliance strategy is to ensure [that] organizations enjoying tax-exempt status comply with the requirements for exemption and adhere to all applicable federal *tax* laws."[57]

During the period the Treasury Department and the IRS were developing proposed regulations concerning the regulation of political campaign activities by tax-exempt social welfare organizations, the Republican commissioners then serving on the Federal Election Commission wrote to the Department and the IRS,

---

[53] Emphasis added. The Commissioner's statement is at http://www.finance.senate.gov/imo/media/doc/JAK_Opening_statement_FINAL.PDF.

[54] Committee on Finance, United States Senate, "The Internal Revenue Service's Processing of 501(c)(3) and 501(c)(4) Applications for Tax-Exempt Status Submitted by 'Political Advocacy' Organizations from 2010–2013" 6 (S. Rep. No. 114–119, 114th Cong., 1st Sess. (2015)).

[55] *Id.* at 141 (emphasis added).

[56] *Id.* at 142 (emphasis added).

[57] IRS TE/GE Report on FY 2016 Priorities (October 1, 2015) (emphasis added).

observing that the IRS "administers the Internal Revenue Code and *focuses on tax revenues and fiscal policy*" and that the "sole purpose of the IRS is *revenue collection*."[58]

One commentator wrote: "Because the [C]ode, including the provision regarding summons enforcement jurisdiction (arguably, the place at which the enforcement power of the agency is starkest), links IRS authority to the need for enforcement of the internal revenue laws, *the agency' authority regarding administration of the tax laws applicable to tax-exempt organizations is limited by the requirements of that very task*, however it might be defined by particular provisions of the [C]ode and Treasury regulations."[59]

Treasury/IRS Regulatory Guidance

For over 100 years, the Department of the Treasury and the IRS have issued guidance documents to help taxpayers comply with the federal tax law. These documents include tax regulations, revenue rulings and revenue procedures, notices, announcements, technical advice memoranda, and private letter rulings. This guidance is based on the statutory authorization extended to the Secretary of the Treasury to "prescribe all needful rules and regulations for the enforcement of" the federal tax law.[60]

---

[58] Letter dated February 27, 2014, reproduced at Bloomberg BNA, *Daily Tax Report*, p. G-2 (Mar. 3, 2014). These commissioners added that, because of the scope of the IRS's mission (as defined), "it would be prudent for the IRS to defer to FEC regulations and relevant court precedents when its rules venture into politically sensitive areas, absent a compelling policy reason to change."

[59] Owens Article at 289 (emphasis added). Among the many other illustrations of this point is an article about the IRS's role in administering the earned income tax credit, which provides benefits irrespective of tax liability. This article states that the National Taxpayer Advocate "recommended that the Service change its mission statement to identify that it has dual roles, one as revenue collector and the other as benefits administrator" (Book, "Bureaucratic Oppression and the Tax System," 69 *Tax Law.* (No. 3) 567, 569 (Spring 2016)). Nothing said there (or anywhere else outside the IRS) about a third role for the agency: Federal regulator of nonprofit governance.

[60] IRC § 7805(a).

Some of this tax law guidance is published in the weekly *Internal Revenue Bulletin*. The US General Accountability Office estimated that annually about 2,000 pages of regulations and other forms of guidance are published in the *Bulletin*.[61] Indeed, "Treasury and IRS are among the largest generators of federal agency regulations and they issue thousands of other forms of taxpayer guidance."[62] It is the view of the IRS that only guidance published in the *Bulletin* states the IRS's authoritative interpretation of the law.[63]

In addition to the guidance published in the *Internal Revenue Bulletin*, thousands of other documents that provide information to taxpayers are available on the IRS's website. Some IRS guidance written by its Office of Chief Counsel provides detailed and technical explanations of the federal tax law for professional return preparers as well as taxpayers generally. Other IRS sources of information that explain the tax law in "plain language" include (1) forms, instructions, and publications for taxpayers to use in preparing their returns; (2) news releases, fact sheets, and tax tips to the news media; (3) online interactive tools by means of which taxpayers can receive answers after asking general or taxpayer specific questions; and (4) instructional audio and visual presentations.[64]

It remains a mystery as to why, when the IRS decided to embark on its efforts to regulate nonprofit governance, the agency chose the document guidance approach that it did. This was a decision with enormous economic significance to public charities and other types of tax-exempt organizations, affecting the composition and functioning of their governing boards, the management of these entities (including adoption of various governance policies), and their use (and need for use) of legal counsel, accountants, management consultants, and others. Yet none of the guidance issued by the IRS at that time and since is authoritative. All the exempt community has seen to date is the text of a few speeches and dozens of private letter rulings.

---

[61] Regulatory Guidance Processes Report, at 3.

[62] *Id.* at 2.

[63] *Id.* at 7.

[64] *Id.* at 3.

There are five statutory authorities for the IRS to follow when drafting and issuing regulations: the Administrative Procedure Act,[65] the Paperwork Reduction Act,[66] the Regulatory Flexibility Act,[67] the Congressional Review Act,[68] and a section of the Internal Revenue Code.[69] The APA generally requires that federal agencies notify the public about, and solicit comments on, proposed regulations via a notice of proposed rulemaking published in the *Federal Register*. The CRA requires agencies to submit each rule to Congress and to the Comptroller General before it can take effect.[70] All agencies are required, by the CRA, to specify whether the rule is *major*; yet, the Office of Information and Regulatory Affairs, within the Office of Management and Budget, is responsible for determining whether a rule is major based on certain criteria. [71] The US General Accountability Office issues reports to Congress on major rules, summarizing and assessing the agency's compliance with required procedural steps.

Presidents have issued executive orders to centralize review of executive branch agency rulemaking within the OMB, and to require executive branch agencies to prepare additional assessments and analyses of the potential costs and benefits of rules that are

---

[65] 5 U.S.C. §§ 551–559.

[66] 44 U.S.C. §§ 3501–3520. This Act requires federal agencies to minimize the paperwork burden they impose on the public and submit certain proposed information collections to the OMB for approval.

[67] 5 U.S.C. §§ 601–608. This Act generally requires federal agencies to consider the impact of their regulatory proposals on small businesses and other small entities, analyze effective alternatives that minimize the impact on small entities, and make their analyses available for public comment.

[68] 5 U.S.C. §§ 801–808.

[69] IRC § 7805. See the text accompanied by *supra* notes 46 and 60.

[70] Inasmuch as the IRS has never proposed a "rule" as to its involvement in the regulation of nonprofit governance, Congress has never been formally apprised as to what the IRS is up to in this regard.

[71] The CRA defines a "major" rule as one that the OIRA determines has resulted in or is likely to result in (1) an annual effect on the nation's economy of at least $100 million; (2) a major increase in costs or prices for consumers, individual industries, federal, state, or local government agencies, or geographic regions; or (3) significant adverse effects on competition, employment, investment, productivity, innovation, or the ability of US-based enterprises to compete with foreign-based enterprises in domestic and export markets.

significant and *economically significant.*[72] The OIRA is responsible for the coordinated review of regulatory actions by federal executive agencies. This coordinated review is necessary to ensure that, among other outcomes, regulations are consistent with applicable laws, the President's priorities, and the principles set forth in executive orders, and that decisions made by one agency do not conflict with the policies or actions taken or planned by another agency. Executive agencies provide the OIRA with lists of planned regulatory actions when drafting rules, including assessments about whether the rules are significant, to determine if additional OIRA review is required. If so, agencies provide the text of the draft regulation and any required analyses (including information on estimated costs and benefits) to OIRA before issuing the rule. The OIRA staff reviews the rule and related documents and may request changes or additional analyses. The OIRA can notify the agency that it has separately determined that a planned regulation is a significant regulatory action.[73]

The OIRA is also responsible for reviewing certain non-regulatory guidance issued by executive branch agencies. The OMB issued a bulletin in 2007 to establish policies and procedures for the development, issuance, and use of significant guidance documents by executive branch agencies.[74] This bulletin's definition of a *significant* guidance document is similar to the definition of a significant regulatory action under the executive order.[75] The bulletin

---

[72] Pursuant to Executive Order No. 12866 (Oct. 4, 1993), a regulatory action is "significant" if it is likely to result in a rule that (1) has an annual effect on the economy of at least $100 million or adversely affects the nation's economy, a sector of the economy, a sector of the economy, productivity, competition, jobs, the environment, public health or safety, or state, local, or tribal governments or communities; (2) creates a serious inconsistency or otherwise interferes with another agency's actions taken or planned; (3) materially alters the budgetary impact of entitlements, grants, user fees, or loan programs or the rights and obligations of recipients thereof; or (4) raises novel legal or policy issues. A rule that meets the first of these criteria is colloquially referred to as "economically significant" and further assessments of the rule's costs and benefits are required.

[73] Regulatory Guidance Processes Report at 4–5.

[74] OMB Bulletin No. 07-02 (Jan. 18, 2007).

[75] The bulletin's definition of *guidance document* does not include many types of documents, including speeches.

requires that agencies establish procedures to allow the public to view and comment on significant guidance documents after they are released and, for any economically significant guidance documents, also make a draft available for public comment and announce its availability in the *Federal Register*. Consistent with an OMB memorandum implementing the bulletin, OIRA has the opportunity to review some significant guidance documents prior to issuance.[76] Guidance that is not significant, as defined by the OMB bulletin, is not subject to policies and procedures in the bulletin; guidance procedures are, in these circumstances, left to agency discretion.[77]

Tax regulations are Treasury's and the IRS's official interpretation of the federal tax laws. These regulations are the most authoritative source of published guidance, inasmuch as they are binding on the IRS and taxpayers, having the force and effect of law. Other guidance in the *Bulletin* – revenue rulings, revenue procedures, notices, and announcements – do not have the same "force and effect" as Treasury regulations but taxpayers can still rely on it as authoritative. Written determinations are Chief Counsel letters to, or memoranda regarding, individual taxpayers; the IRS cautions that only the taxpayer addressed by the guidance can rely on it as precedent. This fact is embodied in a statute.[78] Again, the weekly *Internal Revenue Bulletin* is the "authoritative instrument" for publishing official IRS rulings and procedures, and tax regulations.[79]

The GAO discovered an anomaly: The IRS has extensive policies and procedures for producing guidance but these procedures do not include selection of a type of guidance. The IRS's detailed procedures for identifying guidance projects, designating guidance projects as priorities, and issuing guidance are in the *Internal Revenue Manual*, in a section of it known as the Chief Counsel Directives Manual. The IRS also has detailed policies and procedures to determine when to add a guidance topic to each year's Priority Guidance Plan and designate it as a priority for the

---

[76] OMB Memorandum No. M-07-13 (April 25, 2007).
[77] Regulatory Guidance Processes Report at 5–6.
[78] IRC § 6110(k)(3).
[79] Regulatory Guidance Processes Report at 9.

year.[80] By contrast, according to the GAO, the IRS "does not have documented procedures for selecting the type of guidance product to issue."[81]

Treasury and IRS officials told the GAO that it may not be "practical or feasible" to develop clear-cut procedures for selecting guidance types because "determining the appropriate type is not always a straightforward process." That is, "sometimes the most appropriate type of guidance may not be known at the start of a project, and the choice of guidance type may change as the project develops." The GAO did not relent on this point, observing: "According to internal control standards, agencies should use techniques and processes to identify and manage risk."[82]

The GAO concluded that "few" tax regulations are deemed significant by the OIRA, and subject to additional rulemaking requirements and analysis under the executive order. For example, between 2013 and 2015, merely one of more than 200 tax regulations issued was determined to be significant;[83] this rule was determined to not be economically significant. Likewise, few tax regulations have been deemed by the OIRA to be major under the Congressional Review Act.[84]

Treasury and IRS policies and procedures state that the notice and comment procedures under the APA do not apply to most tax regulations because these regulations are almost always *interpretative*, as opposed to *legislative*, in nature. The thought behind this is that the underlying tax code provision being implemented by the regulation contains the necessary legal authority for the action taken; that is, any effect of the regulation flows directly from the code. Nonetheless, according to Treasury and IRS officials, the IRS provides for notice and comment on nearly every tax regulation.[85]

Treasury and IRS officials told the GAO that they rarely recommend to OIRA that tax regulations are *major* under the CRA

---

[80] Internal Revenue Manual §§ 32.1.1.4.3 and 32.2.2.6.4. See Chapter 8, notes 42 and 43.
[81] Regulatory Guidance Processes Report at 16–17.
[82] *Id.* at 17.
[83] See *supra* note 72.
[84] Regulatory Guidance Processes Report at 18–21.
[85] *Id.* at 21.

or *economically significant* under the executive order because of their view that any economic impact of a tax regulation generally is derived from the underlying statute, not the regulation.[86] Also, some tax regulations are exempt from OIRA review that would otherwise be required under the executive order based on a long-standing agreement between Treasury and the OMB. This agreement, entered into in 1983, exempts regulations issued by the IRS from further analysis and review unless the regulations are legislative in nature and major under an executive order. This agreement also exempts from OMB review documents such as revenue rulings and revenue procedures. The effect of this agreement has been that few tax regulations and none of other types of tax guidance are subject to OMB review. This agreement was reworked in 1993.[87]

The GAO is of the view that this agreement should be reconsidered. One historic rationale for the agreement has been to insulate the Executive Office of the President from a charge that it was using OMB's review of the IRS for political purposes. Another such reason was that historically the OMB lacked staff expertise on tax policy. One reason for the GAO's view is the "importance of increasing the transparency of the rulemaking process." Another reason lies in the nature of tax regulations subsequently being issued, namely, that the tax regulations are "related to social and economic objectives rather than traditional tax collection or administration issues." For example, recently, 20 percent of the tax regulations were related to the implementation of the Patient Protection and Affordable Care Act.[88]

OMB's 2007 bulletin on agency good guidance practices and the accompanying memorandum establish executive branch policies and procedures for federal agencies to follow when they develop and issue significant guidance documents. This bulletin excludes tax guidance documents from the definition of economically significant guidance. The effect is that non-regulatory tax guidance is exempted from centralized review and additional analysis. Nonetheless, the

---

[86] *Id.* at 24–25.

[87] *Id.* at 25–27. The 1983 version of this agreement was made public, on September 26, 2016.

[88] Regulatory Guidance Processes Report at 26–28.

IRS "routinely provides opportunities for the public to comment on non-regulatory guidance documents that address topics that are likely to be covered by future regulations."[89]

The GAO recommended that the Commissioner of Internal Revenue take the following actions: (1) "Communicate more clearly the limitations of information not published in the IRB to taxpayers," (2) amend current policies and procedures for drafting guidance to include factors to consider when deciding what type of guidance to issue and procedures for documenting those decisions internally, (3) develop policies and procedures to help guidance-drafting teams assess whether non-regulatory guidance should be considered a rule for purposes of the CRA, and (4) take action to ensure that required steps are consistently documented during key phases of the non-regulatory guidance process.

The GAO recommended that the Director of the Office of Management and Budget and the Secretary of the Treasury examine the relevance of the long-standing agreement that exempts certain IRS regulations from executive order requirements and OIRA oversight, and, if relevant, make publicly available any reaffirmation of the agreement and the reasons for it. Another recommendation was that these two officials develop a process to ensure that the OIRA has the information necessary to determine whether IRS rules are major under the CRA and significant under the executive order. Consideration should be given to ways to solicit public comments on the potential effects of proposed regulations and non-regulatory guidance, including measures of economic impacts, and on how to document internally the consideration of significant comments by both the IRS and the OIRA.[90]

---

[89] *Id.* at 28–31.

[90] *Id.* at 34–35. A commentary on some of these recommendations is in Chapter 9, text accompanied by notes 1–3.

Concept of Nonprofit Governance

Many elements converge to encompass the concept of governance of nonprofit organizations, usually public charities.[91] Fundamentally, of course, the governance of nonprofit organizations focuses on the manner in which they are governed (from a structural standpoint), who does the governing, and the duties and responsibilities of those doing the governing. These elements of nonprofit governance are essentially a matter of state law, principally the states' nonprofit corporation statutes.

This structure is normally provided for in an organization's articles of organization.[92] This document, for a nonprofit corporation, will be its articles (or certificate) of incorporation; for a trust, its declaration of trust or trust agreement; for an unincorporated association, its constitution; and for a limited liability company, its operating agreement.

The articles of organization will likely stipulate the nature of the governing board – board of directors or board of trustees (collectively, directors), how the directors are selected, the size of the board (that is, the number of its members), the terms of the directors and whether they can be reelected, any term limits, and the manner of their removal (if necessary) from office. The selection of directors can involve innumerable possibilities and combinations; common models include the self-perpetuating board, boards comprised of members who serve in an ex officio capacity, board members elected by the organization's membership (or comparable constituency), or combinations of the foregoing. State law usually addresses the matter of board size. Most states require a minimum of three directors. A few states permit one-director boards.

---

[91] This concept is often expressed in the shorter phrase "nonprofit governance."

[92] A tax-exempt organization's *articles of organization* is the document by which the organization was established. In the case of a nonprofit corporation, the document is the articles of incorporation; in the case of an unincorporated association, the document is a constitution; in the case of a trust, the document is the trust agreement or declaration of trust; in the case of a limited liability company, the document is the articles of organization. Reg. § 1.501(c)(3)-1(b)(2).

A set of articles of organization should state the purpose of the organization, perhaps including one or more statements as to how that purpose is to be advanced, and contain a provision decreeing how the organization's assets and net income will be distributed in the event of the entity's dissolution or liquidation (known as a "dissolution clause").

Another governance document is important, particularly in the case of a nonprofit corporation or a nonprofit unincorporated association – an organization's bylaws. This document should spell out the nature of the organization's officer structure (including description of positions), its committees, the holding of meetings (directors' and, if there are members, members'), and a statement limiting the liability of directors and officers. The bylaws may expand on the organization's purposes and programs, although the bylaws ought not be broader than the organization's articles in this regard. The bylaws may have something to say about the qualifications of directors and/or their compensation by the organization.

A nonprofit organization may have several other documents pertaining to its governance, such as a mission statement, a code of ethics, an employees' manual, and a collection of board resolutions. Plus, of increasing importance are board-approved "policies." These are separate documents; the IRS has identified over 30 of these policies for nonprofit entities. Not all policies are suitable for all organizations, of course.

The basic policies that a nonprofit organization, particularly a public charity, would be likely to consider are a conflict-of-interest policy, a whistleblower policy, a document retention and destruction policy, an investment policy, and a travel expense and reimbursement policy. Charitable organizations that engagement in considerable fundraising might consider a gift acceptance policy. Organizations that accept gifts of conservation easements might have a policy as to that practice. Organizations that engage in joint ventures with for-profit entities may have a policy pertaining to those arrangements. Nonprofit hospitals are required to have various policies, including a community needs assessment policy, a financial assistance policy, and a billing and collections policy.

Nonprofit governance, however, embraces far more than organizational structure and documentation. Also encompassed by that concept is the matter of board duties, responsibilities, and liability. For charitable organizations, this is a wide-ranging matter of fiduciary duties and responsibilities for board members and officers. Today, this is almost completely the realm of state law, both statutory and case law.

Historically, overall, the matter of nonprofit governance has been nearly exclusively the province of state law.[93] Congress has narrowly legislated on this topic on two occasions; the Department of the Treasury and the IRS have, in four instances, formally provided guidance on the topic.[94]

Nonprofit governance law thus – at least not until 2007 – involved little federal tax law. In general, the law concerning the governance of nonprofit entities is not tax law. Tax-exempt organizations are, as discussed, subject to a variety of tax law requirements but they do not relate directly (or, usually, even indirectly) to governance. For example, the federal tax law imposes rules concerning private inurement, private benefit, self-dealing, and excess benefit transactions.[95] By contrast, although the IRS usually insists that public charities have conflict-of-interest policies, there is nothing in the federal tax law concerning conflicts of interest[96] and thus the IRS has no jurisdiction with respect to them.[97]

What the IRS did, as a consequence of its sudden plunge in 2007 into nonprofit governance regulation,[98] is immediately create a huge body of agency-mandated requirements. The IRS quickly,

---

[93] E.g., Hopkins, *Legal Responsibilities of Nonprofit Boards, Second Edition* (BoardSource: 2009).

[94] See Chapter 3, text accompanied by notes 65–82.

[95] IRC §§ 501(c)(3), 4942, and 4958, respectively.

[96] A "conflict of interest" arises when an individual, in a position of authority in connection with an organization, is in a position where he or she is on both sides of an actual or potential transaction or other situation and can personally benefit financially from a decision made with respect to the situation. A conflict-of-interest position may lead to a self-dealing transaction or the like but it is not inherently such and thus is not inherently a transgression of law.

[97] An instance where Congress granted authority to a federal agency to resolve conflicts of interest in connection with entities it regulates is noted in Chapter 7, note 65.

[98] See Chapter 5.

largely by revamping the annual information return,[99] created the equivalent of a massive federal regulation. The agency exponentially expanded the annual return, in considerable part by adding many questions and other references to various aspects of nonprofit governance. Embedded in this return are references to over 30 types of policies, procedures, practices, and protocols. Compliance with all of these rules, which the IRS mandated by inserting "yes" or "no" boxes to be checked as to whether the policies and the like had been adopted, knowing that the return is a public document and understanding that exempt organizations would want to check the "yes" boxes (where applicable) to demonstrate, to their constituencies, the media, and the public, their compliance with the new federal law governance requirements. These developments sparked the formation of a new industry, with lawyers, accountants, and various other types of consultants clambering to prepare these documents and advise their clients as to the meaning and use of them. It is difficult to estimate the expense of money and time associated with compliance with these IRS requirements, both from 2008 to the present and also going forward.[100]

It is hard to believe that somehow Congress intended to invest the IRS with this new reach as to jurisdiction. As the Supreme Court said in one of its agency jurisdiction cases, there was no "directive" to the IRS from Congress to embark on this new element of tax law jurisdiction. [101] Then-IRS TE/GE Commissioner Miller was surely correct when he conceded that, in its quest to formulate and enforce good governance principles, the IRS would have to go "beyond its traditional spheres of activity."[102]

---

[99] See *id.*, text accompanied by notes 12–47.

[100] It is a question of judgment as to whether all of this is the equivalent of considerable "economic or political significance," which is an element of the *Chevron* analysis. Federal Drug Administration v. Brown & Williamson Tobacco Corp., 529 U.S. 120, 160 (2000). See Chapter 7, text accompanied by note 162; Chapter 8, text accompanied by notes 21 and 22.

[101] National Association for the Advancement of Colored People v. Federal Power Commission, 425 U.S. 662, 669–670 (1976).

[102] See the text accompanied by *supra* note 3. The Owens Article cites an instance in early 2007 when a top official in the Exempt Organizations Division

Reference is made throughout this book to the regulation of nonprofit governance by the IRS. This mode of regulation has several manifestations, principally dictating the size of public charities' governing boards and/or the composition of them (either as part of the process of reviewing applications for recognition of exemption or during an examination); imposition of a requirement that one or more policies or procedures be adopted, as a condition of tax exemption; and annual reporting to the IRS on various aspects of nonprofit governance, by means of the annual information return.[103]

"acknowledged that the IRS has no enforcement authority regarding charity governance" (at 287).

[103] In general, Hopkins & Gross, *Nonprofit Governance: Law, Practices & Trends* (John Wiley & Sons, Hoboken, NJ: 2009).

2

Government Agency Law Basics

> The judiciary is to "tak[e] seriously, and apply[] rigorously, in all cases, statutory limits on agencies' authority." "An agency's "assertion of authority not conferred" or an "incorrect application of agency authority" is an "ultra vires" action.
>
> *City of Arlington, Texas v. Federal Communications Commission (Sup. Ct., 2013)*

This chapter summarizes federal law as to government agencies' jurisdiction and authority, which usually involves the question as to whether an agency's actions are lawful. Much of this analysis is the subject of the *Chevron* doctrine, including its specific application to the federal tax law by reason of the *Mayo Foundation* case. Two recent cases regarding the IRS's efforts to expand its regulatory authority are explored, including their ramification with respect to the matter of IRS involvement in the regulation of nonprofit governance. The chapter closes with an analysis of agency expertise and the law implications of inclusion by the IRS of questions that are not required by the federal tax law.

Introduction as to Agency Jurisdiction and Authority

A court, when considering the legality of a government agency's action, will either directly confront the issue of the agency's jurisdiction[1] or, more likely (and collaterally), assess the lawfulness of a rule promulgated by the agency, with that exercise usually leading the court to an evaluation of the scope of the agency's regulatory

---

[1] See Chapter 7.

authority.[2] The US Supreme Court recognized this dichotomy, in a case pitting the City of Arlington, Texas against the Federal Communication Commission. The *City of Arlington* opinion is highly significant in connection with this matter of the lack of IRS jurisdiction or authority with respect to nonprofit governance, inasmuch as the opinion frames the distinction between an "assertion of authority not conferred" (that is, lack of jurisdiction) and an "incorrect application of agency authority."[3] An agency's action is, absent jurisdiction or authority, "ultra vires."[4] That is why the IRS's involvement in the regulation of nonprofit governance is ultra vires action on two counts: lack of jurisdiction and lack of authority.

These ultra vires acts by the IRS are strikingly similar to comparable attempts by the Federal Energy Regulatory Commission, which undertook to regulate the activities of public utilities that are under its jurisdiction, including their personnel and the structure of their corporate governance. In a grand and sweeping opinion from the US Court of Appeals for the District of Columbia, decided nine years before the Supreme Court's *City of Arlington* decision, it was held that the FERC had "no authority to do such a thing," that is, dictate the composition of governing boards of nonprofit organizations that are within the scope of its regulation.[5] The appellate court deemed the FERC's interpretation of the scope of its jurisdiction "breathtaking,"[6] found the agency to have engaged in "overreaching" and "stretching" of its authority,[7] held the FERC to have committed an "absurdity,"[8] and concluded that the implications of what the FERC tried to do were "staggering."[9] The DC Circuit thus strongly slapped down what it portrayed as an "unprecedented

---

[2] See Chapter 8.

[3] City of Arlington, Texas v. Federal Communications Commission, 133 S. Ct. 1863, 1869 (2013).

[4] *Id.*

[5] California Independent System Operator Corporation v. Federal Energy Regulatory Commission, 372 F.3d 395, 398 (D.C. Cir. 2004). This opinion is discussed in Chapter 7, text accompanied by notes 39–95.

[6] *Id.* at 401.

[7] *Id.* at 402.

[8] *Id.*

[9] *Id.* at 403.

invasion of internal corporate governance."[10] The IRS today is doing precisely the same thing. The DC Circuit did not invoke the phrase *ultra vires* but it is amply clear from its opinion that that is what it found the FERC to be doing: engaging in acts that are ultra vires. So too is the IRS.

The *City of Arlington* case is about a federal agency's interpretation of a statutory ambiguity that concerned the scope of its regulatory authority (that is, its jurisdiction).[11] This case involved an element of federal communications law.

Wireless telecommunications networks require towers and antennas; proposed sites for these towers and antennas must be approved by local zoning authorities. In the Telecommunications Act of 1996, Congress imposed limitations on the traditional authority of state and local governments to regulate the location, construction, and modification of these facilities. These limitations were incorporated into the Communications Act of 1934. A section of the latter Act empowers the FCC to "prescribe such rules and regulations as may be necessary in the public interest to carry out [its] provisions." Pursuant to Supreme Court precedent, that rulemaking authority extends to subsequently added portions of the Act.

The Act imposes five limitations; one of them was at issue in the case. That provision requires state or local governments to act on wireless siting applications "within a reasonable period of time after the request is duly filed." The provision also makes it clear that nothing in the Act, other than the five limitations, "shall limit or affect the authority of a State or local government" over siting decisions (a savings clause), and authorizes a person who believes a state or local government's wireless-siting decision to be inconsistent with any of the limitation to file a lawsuit in a court of competent jurisdiction (a judicial review clause).

---

[10] *Id.* at 399.

[11] A fundamental difference between a case of this nature and what the IRS is doing in connection with nonprofit governance is that usually a governmental agency is interpreting the scope of its authority in relation to a *statutory* mandate that ostensibly is ambiguous. With respect to the IRS, however, there is no statute that the IRS is relying on, ambiguous or not, and the IRS has never laid claim to any basis in statutory law for its "unprecedented invasion" into the realm of nonprofit governance. See the text accompanied by *infra*, note 31.

Despite the statutory mandate, wireless providers often faced long delays. An association representing wireless service providers petitioned the FCC to clarify the meaning of the reasonable-period-of-time rule. The FCC responded with a ruling, finding that the "record evidence demonstrates that unreasonable delays in the personal wireless service facility siting process have obstructed the provision of wireless services" and that these delays "impede the promotion of advanced services and competition that Congress deemed critical in the Telecommunications Act of 1996." A "reasonable period of time" in this context, the FCC determined, is presumptively (but rebuttably) 90 days to process an application to place an antenna on an existing tower and 150 days to process all other applications.

Some state and local governments opposed adoption of the ruling on the ground that the FCC lacked authority to interpret ambiguous provisions of the statute. They contended that the savings and judicial review clauses display a congressional intent to withhold from the FCC the authority to interpret any of the five limitations. Asserting that ground of objection, the City of Arlington and another Texas city petitioned for review of the FCC's ruling in the US Court of Appeals for the Fifth Circuit.

The Fifth Circuit held that the *Chevron* framework[12] applied to the threshold question as to whether the FCC possessed the authority, under the statute, to adopt the 90- and 150-day timeframes. This appellate court found the statute's effect on the FCC's authority to administer the limitations ambiguous. It held that the FCC's interpretation of its statutory authority was a permissible construction of the statute and thus that the FCC's deadlines were entitled to *Chevron* deference. The US Supreme Court, in the *City of Arlington* case, affirmed the Fifth Circuit's decision.

The Supreme Court admonished the judiciary to "tak[e] seriously, and apply[] rigorously, in all cases, statutory limits on agencies' authority."[13] The Court added: "Where Congress has established a clear line, the agency cannot go beyond it; and where

---

[12] See the text accompanied by *infra* notes 94–120.

[13] City of Arlington, Texas v. Federal Communications Commission, 133 S. Ct. 1863, 1874 (2013).

Congress has established an ambiguous line, the agency can go no further than the ambiguity will fairly allow."[14]

Thus, the analysis in this book will first explore whether the IRS has the jurisdiction to regulate in the realm of nonprofit governance.[15] Thereafter, the analysis will shift its focus to whether, in the exercise of its authority, the IRS has exceeded the scope of it.[16]

Scope of Government Agencies' Authority

Every government department or agency in the US has boundaries as to the reach of its authority. At the federal level, for example, some agencies are sprawling and seemingly all-powerful, such as the National Security Agency and the Transportation Safety Administration. Other federal agencies are more narrowly focused, such as the Consumer Products Safety Commission and the Commission for the Preservation of America's Heritage Abroad. Each agency, however, formidable or tiny, has limits in terms of the scope of its jurisdiction.

The legislative branch of a government has the initial responsibility (within the bounds of its constitutional authority) for defining the purpose and duties of an agency in the context of the overall governmental system. This is done by statute or ordinance. This task may be augmented by actions of an executive branch or independent agency, by means of promulgation of a regulation, rule, and the like. The ultimate determiner of the contours of an agency's jurisdiction is the judicial branch. As the Supreme Court stated, the "question a court faces when confronted with an agency's interpretation of a statute it administers is always, simply, *whether the agency has stayed within the bounds of its statutory authority*."[17]

---

[14] *Id.*

[15] This is the subject of Chapter 7.

[16] This is the subject of Chapter 8.

[17] City of Arlington, Texas v. Federal Communications Commission, 133 S. Ct. 1863, 1868 (2013).

The Court wrote that, as to agencies charged with administering congressional statutes, their "power to act and how they are to act is authoritatively prescribed by Congress."[18] When these agencies "act improperly, no less than when they act beyond their jurisdiction, what they do is ultra vires."[19] With respect to either type of ultra vires act – an incorrect application of agency authority or an assertion of authority not conferred – the question "is always whether the agency has gone beyond what Congress has permitted it to do."[20]

This approach is reflected in the language of the Administrative Procedure Act, which permits a reviewing court to set aside an agency action that is "(A) arbitrary, capricious, an abuse of discretion, or otherwise not in accordance with law" or "(B) contrary to constitutional right, power, privilege, or immunity."[21] As one court construed this provision, the statutory law "allows courts to right two types of agency wrongs: procedural missteps and substantive transgressions."[22] This court added that "compliance with the law is the true touchstone of legality" (as contrasted with "procedural correctness").[23]

The beginning point of analysis of the matter of the scope of a government agency's regulatory authority or jurisdiction lies in the fundamental constitutional law principle of the separation of powers. That principle "flow[s] from the scheme of a tripartite government,"[24] as the US Constitution dictates. As the Supreme Court wrote, "[s]eparation-of-powers principles are intended, in part, to protect each branch of government from incursion by the others."[25] Article III of the Constitution is an "inseparable element of the constitutional system of checks and balances" that "both defines the power and protects the independence of the Judicial Branch."[26]

---

[18] *Id.* at 1869.

[19] *Id.*

[20] *Id.*

[21] 5 U.S.C. § 706(2)(A), (B).

[22] March for Life v. Burwell, 128 F. Supp. 3d 116 (D.D.C. 2015).

[23] *Id.*

[24] United States v. Nixon, 418 U.S. 683, 704 (1974).

[25] Bond v. United States, 131 S. Ct. 2355, 2365 (2011).

[26] Northern Pipeline Construction Co. v. Marathon Pipe Line Co., 458 U.S. 50, 58 (1982).

Thus, the role of the Supreme Court and, within the bounds of its guidance, the other courts is this famous proclamation (the standard of judicial review): "It is emphatically the province and duty of the judicial department to say what the law is."[27]

Two additional cases provide examples of comparable reasoning by the Court. In one decision, the Court wrote that "[w]e give binding deference to permissible agency interpretations of statutory ambiguities *because* Congress has delegated to the agency the authority" to interpret those ambiguities "with the force of law."[28] In that case, the Court said that deference rests on a recognition that Congress has delegated to an agency the interpretive authority to implement a "particular provision" or answer a "particular question."[29] In the other decision, the Court stated that deference "is not accorded merely because the statute is ambiguous and an administrative official is involved; more is needed: the regulation advancing the interpretation "must be promulgated pursuant to authority Congress has delegated to the official."[30]

Scope of Government Agencies' Jurisdiction

At the federal level, determination of the jurisdiction of a government agency normally starts with review of actions by Congress (subject to applicable limits imposed by the US Constitution), which by statute creates federal government agencies, and defines their purposes and responsibilities. Once created, an agency usually has the authority to promulgate rules and regulations to implement its operations; occasionally another government department or agency will participate in this process.[31] The federal

---

[27] Marbury v. Madison, 5 U.S. (1 Cranch) 137, 177 (1803).

[28] United States v. Mead Corporation, 533 U.S. 218, 229 (2001).

[29] *Id.*

[30] Gonzales v. Oregon, 546 U.S. 243, 258 (2006).

[31] An example of this type of in-tandem federal department/agency rulemaking is implementation of various provisions of the Patient Protection and Affordable Care Act by means of regulations promulgated jointly or in close coordination by the Department of Health and Human Services (particularly the Center for Medicare and Medicaid Services) and the Department of the Treasury (particularly the IRS).

judiciary, culminating with the US Supreme Court, ultimately determines the boundaries of a federal agency's jurisdiction and, having done so, ascertains whether rulemaking, enforcement action, or similar undertaking by the agency has transgressed the scope of its authority.

Four Supreme Court opinions form the core of the body of federal law concerning government agencies' jurisdiction.

FCC Case

A case concerned the Federal Communications Commission, which has, *inter alia*, the authority to approve or deny license renewals regarding television stations. A petition to deny license renewals to seven commercial television stations and one public television station was rejected by the FCC. The complaint, as to the public television station, was that the station had failed to discharge its obligations under the Communications Act of 1934 to ascertain the problems, needs, and interests of the deaf and hearing-impaired population within its service area, and had violated the Rehabilitation Act of 1973, which provides that no otherwise handicapped individual shall, solely by reason of a handicap, be excluded from participation in, be denied the benefits of, or be subjected to discrimination under any program or activity receiving federal financial assistance.

This complaint asserted that the public station failed to carry enough programming with special captioning or other aids to benefit the hearing-impaired members of the audience. In its opposition to the petition, the licensee recounted in some detail its efforts to ascertain the problems of the community it serves, including the deaf and the hearing-impaired, by a community leader survey and a public survey. It denied that it had violated the Rehabilitation Act and averred that the FCC was not an appropriate forum for the adjudication of claims pertaining to that Act.

The FCC consolidated the eight proceedings and ruled on them in a single opinion. The Commission reviewed its efforts to encourage the industry to serve the needs of the hearing-impaired, consisting of a notice as to special needs to all licensees, grant of authority to the

Public Broadcasting System as to a closed-captioning program, and adoption of a rule requiring television licensees to broadcast emergency information visually. It also, however, concluded that, because of unanswered questions about improving television service for the hearing impaired that each licensee had the responsibility to determine how it could meet these needs. The FCC said that there is no requirement that a licensee, commercial or noncommercial, provide any form of special visual program material other than for broadcasting emergency information.

The FCC approached the question as to whether the eight renewals would serve the public interest, convenience, and necessity from three perspectives: ascertainment, programming, and the requirement of the Rehabilitation Act. The Commission determined that the licensees' efforts to ascertain the special needs of the community were adequate, the facts alleged by the complainant did not give rise to a substantial and material question as to whether any of the licensees had abused its discretion in its selection of programming, the Rehabilitation Act did not apply to the commercial licensees (because they did not receive federal financial assistance), and that, while the public television station might be governed by that Act, the allegations against that station were premature unless and until the federal agency with authority to enforce compliance determined that the station had violated the Act. As to the first two of these determinations, the FCC explained that it is more difficult to provide special programming for the hearing impaired than for other segments of the community and that, in the absence of any Commission requirement for specialized programming techniques, there was no basis for faulting a licensee for failure to provide these options for the deaf and hearing impaired in the station service area.

The court of appeals involved in this case affirmed the portion of the FCC's order relating to the commercial stations but vacated the renewal of the public station's license. The appellate court held that the public station, a recipient of federal finance assistance, was under a duty to comply with the Rehabilitation Act and thus that a stricter "public interest" standard should be applied by the FCC, including an inquiry into the efforts of the public station to meet the programming needs of the hearing-impaired. Its narrow holding was that the Commission could not find the service of public stations to be adequate to justify renewal of a license without at least inquiring specifically into their efforts to meet the programming needs of the hearing impaired.

The Supreme Court reversed on the point. [32] It was not persuaded that Congress intended the Rehabilitation Act to impose any new enforcement obligations on the FCC. "It is clear," the Court wrote, that the FCC "is not a funding agency and has never been thought to have responsibility for enforcing" the Rehabilitation Act. [33] The Court noted that there is "not a word" in the Act's legislative history suggesting that it was intended to alter the FCC's standard for reviewing the programming decisions of public television licensees.[34] The Court observed that, if a licensee should be found guilty of violating the Rehabilitation Act, or indeed of violating any other federal statute, the Commission would certainly be obligated to consider the possible relevance of such a violation in determining whether or not to renew the "lawbreaker's" license.[35] The Court said, however, that in the absence of a direction in the Rehabilitation Act and without any expression of this type of intent in the legislative history, it was "unwilling to assume that Congress has instructed the Federal Communications Commission to take original jurisdiction over the processing of charges that its regulatees have violated" the Act.[36]

The Court in this case stated that the fact that a public television station has a duty to comply with the Rehabilitation Act does not support the "quite different conclusion" that the FCC must "evaluate a public station's service to the handicapped community by a more

---

[32] Community Television of Southern California v. Gottfried, 459 U.S. 498 (1983).

[33] *Id.* at 509.

[34] *Id.* at 509–510.

[35] *Id.* at 510.

[36] *Id.* The Court, on this point, summarized its earlier observation that an agency's general duty to enforce the public interest does not require it to assume responsibility for enforcing legislation that is not directed at the agency (National Association for the Advancement of Colored People v. Federal Power Commission, 425 U.S. 662, 671 (1976)).

stringent standard than that applicable to commercial stations."[37] The Court added that the "interest in having all television stations – public and commercial – consider and serve their handicapped viewers is equally strong."[38] And: "By the same token, it is equally unfair to criticize a licensee – whether public or commercial – for failing to comply with a requirement of which it had no notice."[39] It observed that both the majority and the dissenting judge below agreed that "rulemaking is generally a better, fairer, and more effective method of implementing a new industry-wide policy than is the uneven application of conditions in isolated license renewal proceedings."[40]

The Court speculated that the federal agency providing financial assistance to a public station might attach conditions to its funding or the FCC may determine that "extraordinary efforts," placing "heightened responsibility on certain stations," by that agency are required.[41] But, the Court continued, "unless and until such a differential standard has been promulgated," the FCC did "not abuse its discretion in interpreting the public interest standard ... when it decline[d] to impose a greater obligation to provide special programming for the hearing impaired on a public licensee than on a commercial licensee."[42] The Court reversed the judgment of the court of appeals insofar as it vacated the order of the FCC pertaining to the public television station.

The import of this opinion in relation to the IRS's efforts to regulate nonprofit governance is obvious. To paraphrase the Court, in the absence of a direction in a statute and without any expression of intent in legislative history, it should be likewise unwilling to assume that Congress has instructed the IRS to take original jurisdiction (at the federal law level) over regulation of the governance of public charities and other tax-exempt organizations. Rulemaking is a better, fairer, and more effective method of implementing a new industry-wide policy than in the uneven

---

[37] Community Television of Southern California v. Gottfried, 459 U.S. 498, 511 (1983).
[38] *Id.*
[39] *Id.*
[40] *Id* (internal quotation marks omitted).
[41] *Id.* at 512.
[42] *Id.*

application of conditions in isolated situations where nonprofit organizations are seeking recognition of exemption. It is unfair to criticize a putative exempt organization for failing to comply with requirements as to which it had no notice – other than by means of a speech at a lawyers' conference.

CSC Case

Another case considered by the Court concerned the validity of a regulation promulgated by the Civil Service Commission, which is responsible for adopting and enforcing regulations which will best promote the efficiency of the federal civil service.[43] In this case, resident aliens brought an action against the CSC, challenging the validity of a policy, adopted and enforced by the CSC and other federal agencies, which excluded all individuals except American citizens and natives of Samoa from employment in most positions of federal service.

Prior to an analysis of the validity of this regulation, the Court discussed at some length the policy reasons underlying the position taken in the regulations. It was noted that the legislation creating the commission (enacted in 1883) specifically did not include a limitation on civil service appointment or employment to citizens; the legislative history showed that it was assumed that the commission would impose such a requirement by regulation, which it did immediately following its creation. The Court stated that its inquiry was "whether the national interests which the Government identifies as justifications for the Commission rule are interests on which that agency may properly rely in making a decision implicating the constitutional and social values at stake in this litigation."[44] In short, the question was whether this CSC regulation was valid.[45]

---

[43] 5 U.S.C. § 3301(1).

[44] Hampton v. Mow Sun Wong, 426 U.S. 88, 113–114 (1976). The "national interests" referenced in this quotation are essentially those referenced in the text accompanied by *infra* note 47.

[45] *Id.* at 114. The Court noted that Congress has never repudiated, or even considered the desirability of repudiating the CSC's policy (*id.* at 108). Congress,

The Court, in this case, stated: "It is the business of the Civil Service Commission to adopt and enforce regulations which will best promote the efficiency of the federal civil service."[46] The Court continued: "That agency has no responsibility for foreign affairs, for treaty negotiations, for establishing immigration quotas or conditions of entry, or for naturalization policies. Indeed, it is not even within the responsibility of the Commission to be concerned with the economic consequences of permitting or prohibiting the participation by aliens in employment opportunities in different parts of the national market."[47] The Court added that, "[o]n the contrary, the Commission performs a limited and specific function," which is the "promotion of an efficient federal service."[48]

The Court stated that, with one exception, the interests advanced in support of the regulation "are not matters which are properly the business of" the CSC. [49] The exception was administrative convenience, namely, the desirability of having one simple rule excluding all noncitizens when it is manifest that citizenship is an "appropriate and legitimate requirement" for some important and sensitive positions. [50] The justification for the regulation on the ground of administrative convenience, however, was found by the Court to be "unacceptable."

As to why this justification was unacceptable, the Court wrote that the CSC, "like other administrative agencies, has an obligation to perform its responsibilities with some degree of expertise, and to make known the reasons for its important decisions."[51] For example, there was nothing in this case's record, or as to which the Court may properly take judicial notice, to indicate that the CSC made

in various appropriation acts, has imposed various limitations on the classes of employees who may be compensated by the federal government; the Court concluded that these acts "cannot fairly be construed to evidence either congressional approval or disapproval" of the CSC rule at issue (*id.* at 110). The Court essentially so held in connection with various executive orders (*id.* at 112–113).

[46] *Id.* at 114.

[47] *Id.*

[48] *Id.*

[49] *Id.* at 115.

[50] *Id.*

[51] *Id.*

any "considered evaluation" of the relative desirability of a simple exclusionary rule on the one hand, or the value to the service of enlarging the pool of eligible employees on the other.[52] Of "greater significance" was the "quality of the interest at stake."[53] The Court stated: "Any fair balancing of the public interest in avoiding the wholesale deprivation of employment opportunities caused by the Commission's indiscriminate policy, as opposed to what may be nothing more than a hypothetical justification, requires rejection of the argument of administrative convenience in this case."[54]

The Court wrote, "assuming without deciding that the national interests identified by the petitioners would adequately support an explicit determination by Congress or the President to exclude all noncitizens from the federal service, we conclude that those interests cannot provide an acceptable rationalization for such a determination by the Civil Service Commission."[55] The Court added: "By broadly denying this class substantial opportunities for employment, the Civil Service Commission rule deprives its members of an aspect of liberty."[56] It found: "Since these residents were admitted as a result of decisions made by the Congress and the President, implemented by the Immigration and Naturalization Service acting under the Attorney General of the United States, due process requires that the decision to impose that deprivation of an important liberty be made either at a comparable level of government or, if it is to be permitted to be made by the Civil Service Commission, that it be justified by reasons which are properly the concern of that agency."[57] The Court concluded that the CSC regulation deprived the affected class of an aspect of liberty without due process of law.

The import of this decision in the context of the IRS regulation of nonprofit governance is likewise unmistakable. The CSC case requires that any federal entry into the realm of nonprofit

---

[52] *Id.*
[53] *Id.*
[54] *Id.* at 115–116.
[55] *Id.* at 116.
[56] *Id.*
[57] *Id.* (internal footnote omitted).

governance be the result of a decision made (due process considerations aside) at the appropriate level of government – by Congress or perhaps the President by executive order. Here, there are no "interests" that provide an "acceptable rationalization for such a determination" by the IRS. The only articulated interest is the amorphous thought that a well-governed organization is likely to be one that is compliant with the tax law[58] – and that interest does not even hold up.[59] Even if that interest were valid, it should be advanced at the appropriate governmental level, probably by Congress. The given interest is not one that is "properly the concern of the agency" because of lack of jurisdiction. The IRS, "like other administrative agencies, has an obligation to perform its responsibilities with some degree of expertise, and to make known the reasons for its important decisions." The IRS lacks the expertise to regulate nonprofit governance.[60] Making known the reason for this important decision must be done with a formality more substantive than a speech.[61]

FPC Case

Another case in this genre concerned the Federal Power Commission. Organizations petitioned the FPC to issue a regulation requiring equal employment opportunity and nondiscrimination in the employment practices of its regulatees. The proposed rule would have required the regulated companies to adopt affirmative action programs to combat discrimination in employment and would have given any individual who believed himself or herself to have been subjected to employment discrimination by any of these companies the right to file a complaint with the Commission.

The FPC declined to issue such a rule, on the ground that it lacked jurisdiction, inasmuch as the purposes of the Natural Gas and Power Acts are economic regulation of entrepreneurs engaged

---

[58] See Chapter 5, text accompanied by note 3.
[59] See Chapter 7, text accompanied by notes 155–159.
[60] *Id.*, text accompanied by notes 96–159.
[61] See Chapter 9, text accompanied by notes 1–3.

in resource development. The FPC did not find the "necessary nexus" between these aspects of its economic regulatory activities and the employment procedures of the entities it regulates "as would justify" adoption of the proposed rule.

A federal court of appeals, agreeing that the FPC lacked power to prescribe personnel policies in detail and act on personnel complaints, held that the FPC has the power to take into account, in the performance of its regulatory functions, including licensing and rate review, evidence that a regulatee is a demonstrated discriminator in its employment relations.[62] Because of doubt as to the Commission's recognition of any power on its part to take into account the employment practices of its regulatees, even in the narrower sense, the appellate court vacated the FPC's order.

The Supreme Court opened its analysis with this: "The question presented is not whether the elimination of discrimination from our society is an important national goal. It clearly is. The question is not whether Congress could authorize the Federal Power Commission to combat such discrimination. It clearly could."[63] Rather, the question was whether or to what extent Congress granted the FPC the requisite authority.[64] Two possible statutory bases were advanced to justify the conclusion that the Commission can or must concern itself with discriminatory employment practices on the part of the companies it regulates.

The first of these statutory bases was the legislative command to the FPC under the Power and Gas Acts to establish "just and reasonable" rates for the transmission and sale of electric energy and natural gas, and, consequently, to allow only those rates as will prevent consumers from being charged any unnecessary or illegal costs. The second and broader statutory basis advanced for Commission regulation of employment discrimination is the FPC's asserted duty to advance the public interest. From various references to the "public interest" in the Gas and Power Acts, it was argued

---

[62] National Association for the Advancement of Colored People v. Federal Power Commission, 520 F.2d 432 (D.C. Cir. 1975).
[63] National Association for the Advancement of Colored People v. Federal Power Commission, 425 U.S. 662, 665 (1976).
[64] *Id.*

that the Commission was charged with advancing the public interest in general, and that the Commission is thus authorized if not required to promulgate rules prohibiting its regulatees from engaging in discriminatory employment practices, since ending discrimination in employment is in the public interest.

The court of appeals essentially accepted the first of these statutory arguments. "Without necessarily endorsing the specific identification of the costs arguably within the Commission's range of concern," the Court agreed with the basic conclusion of the appellate court "on this branch of the case."[65] The Court stated that the FPC "clearly has the duty to prevent its regulatees from charging rates based upon illegal, duplicative, or unnecessary labor costs," adding that "[t]o the extent that such costs are demonstrably the product of a regulatee's discriminatory employment practices, the Commission should disallow them."[66]

The Court stated that the appellate court was correct in rejecting the "broader argument," which was based on congressional findings that the "business of transmitting and selling electric energy for ultimate distribution to the public is affected with a public interest" and that the "business of transporting and selling natural gas for ultimate distribution to the public is affected with a public interest."[67] The Court stated that its cases "have consistently held that the use of the words 'public interest' in a regulatory statute is not a broad license to promote the general welfare"; rather, the "words take meaning from the purposes of the regulatory legislation." [68] For example, in a case involving the Interstate Commerce Commission, which is responsible for enforcing an act "designed . . . better to assure adequacy in transportation service," the Court wrote that the term *public interest* "is not a concept without ascertainable criteria, but has *direct relation* to adequacy of transportation service, to its essential conditions of economy and

---

[65] *Id.* at 668 (internal quotations omitted).
[66] *Id.*
[67] 16 U.S.C. § 824(a), 15 U.S.C. § 717(a), respectively.
[68] National Association for the Advancement of Colored People v. Federal Power Commission, 425 U.S. 662, 669 (1976).

efficiency, and to appropriate provision and best use of transportation facilities."[69]

Consequently, in order to give content and meaning to the words *public interest* as used in the Power and Gas Acts, the Court stated that "it is necessary to look to the purposes for which the Acts were adopted." In the case of these laws, the Court wrote that "it is clear that the principal purpose of those Acts was to encourage the orderly development of plentiful supplies of electricity and natural gas at reasonable prices."[70] The Court added that the parties to this litigation "point to nothing in the Acts or their legislative histories to indicate that the elimination of employment discrimination was one of the purposes that Congress had in mind when it enacted this legislation."[71] The Court said that the use of these words in these acts "is not a directive to the Commission to seek to eradicate discrimination, but, rather, is a charge to promote the orderly production of plentiful supplies of electric energy and natural gas at just and reasonable rates."[72] Thus, the Court concluded that the FPC is "authorized to consider the consequences of discriminatory employment practices on the part of its regulatees only insofar as such consequences are *directly related* to the Commission's establishment of just and reasonable rates in the public interest."[73]

The Supreme Court thus affirmed this decision, after reviewing the duties of the Commission, including the task of preventing its regulatees from charging rates based on illegal, duplicative, or unnecessary labor costs.[74]

The relevance of the FPC case to the IRS's attempts to regulate nonprofit governance is indeed quite striking. Again, to paraphrase the Supreme Court, the question is not whether governance of nonprofit organizations should be regulated at the federal level

---

[69] New York Central Securities Corp. v. United States, 287 U.S. 12, 24–25 (1932) (emphasis added).

[70] National Association for the Advancement of Colored People v. Federal Power Commission, 425 U.S. 662, 669–670 (1976).

[71] *Id.* at 670.

[72] *Id.*

[73] *Id.* at 671 (emphasis added).

[74] National Association for the Advancement of Colored People v. Federal Power Commission, 425 U.S. 662 (1976).

(aside from questions as to preemption). It clearly can be. Likewise, the question is not whether Congress could authorize the IRS to undertake such a task. It clearly could. The question, by contrast, is whether or to what extent Congress *did* grant the IRS that authority. In the FPC case, two possible statutory bases for jurisdiction were advanced. With respect, to the IRS, a statutory basis for jurisdiction over nonprofit governance has never been advanced; the IRS has never argued that there is such as basis. There have been no "legislative commands" to the IRS to undertake nonprofit governance regulation. The FPC declined to adopt the proposed rule, on the ground of lack of jurisdiction. The IRS has never done the right thing by floating a rule before acting; in the face of such a proposal, the IRS likewise should have had the good grace to refuse it, on the ground of absence of jurisdiction.

FEC Case

Another of these cases concerned the regulatory apparatus of the Federal Election Commission. In a case challenging the constitutionality of certain federal campaign financing laws, the Court considered the contemporary FEC.[75] The opinion in this case, involving an organization by the name of Citizens United, is controversial and quite well-known for its holding that the prohibition in the Federal Election Campaign Act, as amended by the Bipartisan Campaign Reform Act of 2002, on corporations and unions from using their general treasury funds to make independent expenditures for speech that constitutes an electioneering communication is unconstitutional. Less known about the *Citizens United* opinion is its analysis of the operations and regulatory impact of the FEC.

Earlier, the Court concluded that the FEC's "business is to censor."[76] The Court stated that, when the FEC issues advisory opinions that prohibit speech, "[m]any persons, rather than undertake the considerable burden (and sometimes risk) of

---

[75] Citizens United v. Federal Election Commission, 558 U.S. 310 (2010).
[76] Freedman v. Maryland, 380 U.S. 51, 57–58 (1965).

vindicating their rights through case-by-case litigation, will choose simply to abstain from protected speech – harming not only themselves but society as a whole, which is deprived of an uninhibited marketplace of ideas."[77] Consequently, the "censor's determination may in practice be final."[78]

Most recently, the Court stated that the FEC "has created a regime that allows it to select what political speech is safe for public consumption by applying ambiguous tests."[79] It added: "If parties want to avoid litigation and the possibility of civil and criminal penalties, they must either refrain from speaking or ask the FEC to issue an advisory opinion approving of the political speech in question. Government officials pore over each word of a text to see if, in their judgment, it accords with ... [the tests] they have promulgated. This is an unprecedented governmental intervention into the realm of speech."[80]

In the FEC case, the Court wrote that "[t]his regulatory scheme may not be a prior restraint on speech in the strict sense of that term, for prospective speakers are not compelled by law to seek an advisory opinion from the FEC before the speech takes place."[81] But, said the Court, "[a]s a practical matter, however, given the complexity of the regulations and the deference courts show to administrative determinations, a speaker who wants to avoid threats of criminal liability and the heavy costs of defending against FEC enforcement must ask a governmental agency for prior permission to speak."[82] On this point, the Court concluded: "These onerous restrictions thus function as the equivalent of prior restraint by giving the FEC power analogous to licensing laws implemented in 16th- and 17th-century England, laws and governmental practices of the sort that the First Amendment was drawn to prohibit."[83]

Occasionally, a government agency will assert jurisdiction over a subject where there is no corresponding predicate statute. In place

---

[77] Virginia v. Hicks, 539 U.S. 113, 119 (2003).
[78] Freedman v. Maryland, 380 U.S. 51, 58 (1965).
[79] Citizens United v. Federal Election Commission, 558 U.S. 310, 336 (2010).
[80] *Id.*
[81] *Id.* at 335.
[82] *Id.*
[83] *Id.*

of statutory law there may be a doctrine created by the judiciary. For example, in the nonprofit tax law context, the Supreme Court created the public policy doctrine.[84] A justice, dissenting in another case, addressing the IRS's role in enforcing this doctrine, wrote separately, in part because he was "disturbingly aware of the overwhelming power of the Internal Revenue Service," expressing a "needed word of caution about governmental power."[85] He wrote of the "hazard of vesting in the Commissioner [of Internal Revenue] virtual plenipotentiary power over philanthropic organizations."[86] Noting that the Commissioner has "broad powers" to issue regulations for the "enforcement of the tax laws," he observed that "there is nothing in the Code that suggests that he must be fully insulated from challenge when effectuating social policy."[87] He stated that the "program of exemption by letter ruling ... is tantamount to a licensing procedure."[88] He wrote that, "where the philanthropic organization is concerned, there appears to be little to circumscribe the almost unfettered power of the Commissioner."[89]

As to the matter of the IRS's "unfettered power," the dissenting Justice concluded with this observation: "This may be very well so long as one subscribes to the particular brand of social policy the Commissioner happens to be advocating at the time ... but application of our tax laws should not operate in so fickle a fashion. Surely, social policy in the first instance is a matter for legislative

---

[84] Bob Jones University v. United States, 461 U.S. 574 (1983). See Chapter 3, text accompanied by notes 10–13.

[85] Alexander v. Americans United, Inc., 416 U.S. 752, 763 (1974).

[86] *Id.* at 772.

[87] *Id.*

[88] *Id.* at 774.

[89] *Id.* This justice noted that, in *Bob Jones University*, the Court suggested that as long as an action of the IRS reflects a "good-faith effort to enforce the technical requirements of the tax laws," the presence of a collateral motive does not render the Anti-Injunction Act inapplicable (416 U.S. at 740). He wrote that he did not "perceive just where the good-faith inquiry is made" (Alexander v. Americans United, Inc., 416 U.S. 752, 774, note 11 (1974)). He posed these questions: "Is innovation in effectuating social policy a good-faith effort to enforce technical requirements? Is a threat to revoke a university's exemption ruling made in good faith when it rests on the proposition that the institution does not comply with government-approved admission standards?" (*id.*).

concern. To the extent these determinations are reposed in the authority of the Internal Revenue Service, they should have the system of checks and balances provided by judicial review before an organization that for years has been favored with an exemption ruling is imperiled by an allegedly unconstitutional change of direction on the part of the Service."[90]

In a concurring opinion in the public policy case, a Justice wrote that the "balancing of the[] substantial interests [involved in the case] is for Congress to perform," adding that he was "unwilling to join any suggestion that the Internal Revenue Service is invested with authority to decide which public policies are sufficiently 'fundamental' to require denial of tax exemptions."[91] The "business" of the IRS, he stated, is to "administer laws designed to produce revenue for the Government, not to promote 'public policy.'"[92] The opinion concluded with this: "This Court often has expressed concern that the scope of an agency's authorization be limited to those areas in which the agency fairly may be said to have expertise, and this concern applies with special force when the asserted administrative power is one to determine the scope of public policy."[93]

---

[90] *Id.* at 774–775.

[91] Bob Jones University v. United States, 461 U.S. 574, 611 (1983). This Justice quoted a former Commissioner of Internal Revenue, who, in the context of efforts of the IRS to define the term *church*, wrote that questions concerning religion and civil rights "are far afield from the more typical tasks of tax administration –determining taxable income" (Kurtz, "Difficult Definitional Problems in Tax Administration: Religion and Race," 23 *Cath. Law.* 301, 301 (1978)).

[92] Bob Jones University v. United States, 461 U.S. 574, 611 (1983).

[93] *Id.* As to the reference to "expertise," the Justice cited to Community Television of Southern California v. Gottfried, *supra* note 32; Hampton v. Mow Sun Wong, *supra* note 44; and National Association for the Advancement of Colored People v. Federal Power Commission, *supra* notes 62 and 63. The factor of agency expertise in the context of IRS regulation of nonprofit governance is discussed *infra*, text accompanied by notes 203–222, and Chapter 7, text accompanied by notes 96–159. Additional cases on the subject of the law as to government agencies' jurisdiction are discussed in Chapter 7, text accompanied by notes 6–95.

Law as to Scope of Government Agencies' Authority

This section of the chapter focuses on judicial review of an agency's authority from the standpoint of evaluation of agencies' guidance, such as regulations. Several court decisions are explored, including the recent decisions in *Loving* v. *United States* and *Ridgely* v. *Lew*, where courts held that the IRS lacked the statutory authority to engage in certain forms of enforcement. Also explored is the factor of an agency's expertise in evaluating the scope of its authority.

Chevron Framework

The courts are frequently called on to review a government agency's construction of a statute which is part of the overall statutory construct defining and comprising the agency's jurisdiction. The US Supreme Court has decreed the formulation that courts are to follow in this regard – the *Chevron* principle.[94]

This exercise begins with this framework: "When a court reviews an agency's construction of the statute which it administers, it is confronted with two questions."[95] First, applying the ordinary tools of statutory construction, the court must determine "whether Congress has directly spoken to the precise question at issue."[96] If the "intent of Congress is clear, that is the end of the matter; for the court, as well as the agency, must give effect to the unambiguously expressed intent of Congress."[97] But "if the statute is silent or ambiguous with respect to the specific issue, the question for the court is whether the agency's answer is based on a permissible construction of the statute."[98]

---

[94] Chevron U.S.A., Inc. v. Natural Resources Defense Council, Inc., 467 U.S. 837 (1984). In *City of Arlington*, the Supreme Court referred to the *Chevron* principle as a "now-canonical formulation" (at 1868).

[95] Chevron U.S.A., Inc. v. Natural Resources Defense Council, Inc., 467 U.S. 837, 842 (1984).

[96] *Id.*

[97] *Id.* at 842–843.

[98] *Id.* at 843.

The Court subsequently stated that, under *Chevron* step two, courts may not disturb an agency rule unless it is "arbitrary or capricious in substance, or manifestly contrary to the statute."[99] In ascertaining whether statutory language is ambiguous, a court is to examine the "language [of the statute] itself, the specific context in which that language is used, and the broader context of the statute as a whole."[100] In determining whether a statute is ambiguous and in ultimately determining whether an agency's interpretation is permissible or instead is foreclosed by the statute, a court must employ all the tools of statutory interpretation, including "text, structure, purpose, and legislative history."[101]

Chevron is rooted in a background presumption of congressional intent, namely, that Congress, "when it left ambiguity in a statute" administered by a government agency, "understood that the ambiguity would be resolved, first and foremost, by the agency, and desired the agency (rather than the courts) to possess whatever degree of discretion the ambiguity allows."[102] The Court put this important principle in other terms: "The "power of an administrative agency to administer a congressionally created program necessarily requires the formulation of policy and the making of rules to fill any gap left, implicitly or explicitly, by Congress."[103] As the Court observed: "*Chevron* thus provides a stable background rule against which Congress can legislate: Statutory ambiguities will be resolved, within the bounds of reasonable interpretation, not by the courts but by the administering agency."[104] The Court has noted that Congress "knows to speak in

---

[99] Household Credit Services, Inc. v. Pfennig, 541 U.S. 232, 242 (2004), quoting United States v. Mead Corp., 533 U.S. 218, 227 (2001).

[100] Robinson v. Shell Oil Co., 519 U.S. 337, 341 (1997).

[101] Pharmaceutical Research & Manufacturers of America v. Thompson, 251 F.3d 219, 224 (D.C. Cir. 2001)

[102] Smiley v. Citibank (South Dakota), N.A., 517 U.S. 735, 740–741 (1996).

[103] Chevron U.S.A., Inc. v. Natural Resources Defense Council, Inc., 467 U.S 837, 843 (1984) (internal quotation marks omitted).

[104] City of Arlington, Texas v. Federal Communications Commission, 133 S. Ct. 1863, 1868 (2013), referencing AT&T Corp. v. Iowa Utilities Board, 525 U.S. 366, 397 (1999).

plain terms when it wishes to circumscribe, and in capacious terms when it wishes to enlarge, agency discretion"[105]

Overall, the Court wrote, it has "consistently held that *Chevron* applies to cases in which an agency adopts a construction of a jurisdictional provision of a statute it administers."[106] For example, one of its opinions says that no "exception exists to the normal [deferential] standard of review" for "jurisdictional or legal question[s] concerning the coverage" of an act of Congress.[107] A prime example of deferential review for questions of jurisdiction is a case involving the Commodity Futures Trading Commission's interpretation of a statute, which provides that before the CFTC takes action on a complaint, the complainant must file a bond to cover any reparation award that may be issued by the Commission against the complainant on any counterclaim by the respondent. The CFTC, pursuant to its broad rulemaking authority, interpreted that oblique reference to counterclaims as granting it the power to take jurisdiction over both federal-law and state-law counterclaims. The Court not only deferred under *Chevron* to the Commission's "eminently reasonable ... interpretation of the statute it is entrusted to administer," but also chided the court of appeals for declining to afford deference because of the putatively "statutory interpretation-jurisdictional nature of the question at issue."[108]

The Court afforded *Chevron* deference to the Department of Commerce's determination that its authority to seek antidumping duties extended to uranium imported under contracts for enrichment services.[109] It did the same in connection with the Interstate Commerce Commission's view that courts, not the ICC, possessed "initial jurisdiction with respect to the award of reparations" for unreasonable shipping charges.[110] Likewise, as to the Army Corps of Engineers'

---

[105] City of Arlington, Texas v. Federal Communications Commission, 133 S. Ct. 1863, 1868 (2013).
[106] *Id.* at 1871 (internal quotations omitted).
[107] National Labor Relations Board v. City Disposal Systems, Inc., 465 U.S. 822, 830, note 7 (1984) (internal quotations omitted).
[108] Commodity Futures Trading Commission v. Schor, 478 U.S. 833, 844–845 (1986) (internal quotations omitted).
[109] United States v. Eurodif S.A., 555 U.S. 305 (2009).
[110] Reiter v. Cooper, 507 U.S. 258, 269 (1993).

assertion that is permitting authority over discharges into "waters of the United States" extended to "freshwater wetlands" adjacent to the expressly covered waters.[111] The Court deferred to the Federal Communications Commission's claim that its broad regulatory authority extended to the preemption of conflicting state rules.[112]

The Court's cases hold that *Chevron* applies equally to statutes designed to curtail the scope of agency discretion. For example, the Court considered a statute prohibiting the Environmental Protection Agency from modifying any requirement of a statute as is applies to a pollutant that is on the toxic pollutant list. The EPA construed that statute as not precluding it from granting variances with respect to certain toxic pollutants. Finding no "clear congressional intent to forbid EPA's sensible variance mechanism," the Court deferred to the EPA's construction of this limitation on its regulatory authority.[113]

The *Chevron* framework thus entails a form of judicial deference to an agency's interpretation of a statute the construction of which is within the agency's jurisdiction. One of the fundamental points of *City of Arlington* is that an agency's interpretation of a statutory ambiguity concerning the scope of the agency's regulatory authority (that is, its jurisdiction) can be entitled to deference under *Chevron*.[114] The Court noted that it has "applied *Chevron* where concerns about agency self-aggrandizement are at their apogee: in cases where an agency's expansive construction of the extent of its own power would have wrought a fundamental change in the regulatory scheme."[115] In that *apogee* case, the threshold question was the "appropriate framework" for analyzing the assertion of jurisdiction by the Federal Drug Administration to regulate tobacco products, considered by the Court to pose a question of "vast

---

[111] United States v. Riverside Bayview Homes, Inc., 474 U.S. 121, 123–124 (1985).

[112] City of New York v. Federal Communications Commission, 486 U.S. 691 (1984).

[113] Chemical Manufacturers Association v. Natural Resources Defense Council, Inc., 470 U.S. 116, 125 (1985).

[114] City of Arlington, Texas v. Federal Communications Commission, 133 S. Ct. 1863, 1868 (2013).

[115] *Id.* at 1872, citing as an example Federal Drug Administration v. Brown & Williamson Tobacco Corp., 529 U.S. 120 (2000).

economic and political magnitude."[116] Likewise, the Court applied the *Chevron* framework to the FCC's assertion that the statutory phrase "modify any requirement" gave it authority to eliminate rate-filing requirements, the "essential characteristic of a rate-related industry," for long-distance telephone carriers."[117]

For *Chevron* deference to apply, however, the agency involved "must have received congressional authority to determine the particular matter at issue in the particular manner adopted."[118] In the principal case on this point, the Court denied *Chevron* deference to action, by an agency with rulemaking authority, that was not rulemaking.[119]

Recent court opinions illustrate application of these principles. A federal court of appeals held that, under the Federal Power Act, which unambiguously restricts the Federal Energy Regulatory Commission from regulating the retail market, a rule issued by the FERC that exceeded its authority was an ultra vires act that could be discerned by application of *Chevron* step one.[120]

More on Judicial Deference

The Supreme Court has held that the *Chevron* deference standard is applicable with respect to federal tax regulations.[121] The Court observed that the petitioners in the case did "not advance[] any justification for applying a less deferential standard of review to Treasury Department regulations than we apply to the rules of any

---

[116] Federal Drug Administration v. Brown & Williamson Tobacco Corp., 529 U.S. 120, 133 (2000). The Court held that Congress did not accord the FDA the authority that it sought to exercise. See Chapter 8, text accompanied by notes 49–55.

[117] MCI Telecommunications Corp. v. American Telephone & Telegraph Co., 512 U.S. 218 (1994).

[118] City of Arlington, Texas v. Federal Communications Commission, 133 S. Ct. 1863, 1874 (2013).

[119] United States v. Mead Corp., 533 U.S. 218 (2001).

[120] Electric Power Supply Association v. Federal Energy Regulatory Commission, 753 F.3d 216 (D.C. Cir. 2014).

[121] Mayo Foundation for Medical Education and Research v. United States, 562 U.S. 44 (2011).

other agency."[122] Consequently, the Court continued, it is "not inclined to carve out an approach to administrative review good for tax law only."[123]

As noted, the *Chevron* framework includes the concept of agency rulemaking to fill in any gaps explicitly or implicitly left by Congress in an authorizing statute within the agency's jurisdiction.[124] The Court acknowledged in that case that the formulation of a policy might require "more than ordinary knowledge respecting the matters subjected to agency regulation."[125] Subsequently, the Court stated: "Filling gaps in the Internal Revenue Code plainly requires the Treasury Department to make interpretative choices for statutory implementation at least as complex as the ones other agencies must make in administering their statutes."[126]

Of course, not all agency determinations emerge in the form of regulations.[127] For example, the IRS formulates policy by means of revenue rulings and revenue procedures. The Supreme Court noted that agencies charged with applying a statute "necessarily make all sorts of interpretive choices and ... not all of those choices bind judges to follow them."[128] Even if not binding, these agency choices "certainly may influence courts facing questions the agencies have already answered," and, in this type of instance, the "fair measure of deference to an agency administering its own statute has been understood to vary with circumstances."[129]

The weight accorded an agency's interpretation in this context depends on the "degree of the agency's care, its consistency,

---

[122] *Id.* at 55.
[123] *Id.*
[124] See the text accompanied by *supra* note 103.
[125] Chevron U.S.A., Inc. v. Natural Resources Defense Council, Inc., 467 U.S. 837, 844 (1984) (internal quotation marks omitted).
[126] Mayo Foundation for Medical Education and Research v. United States, 562 U.S. 44, 56 (2011).
[127] In one instance, the Court extended *Chevron* deference to an agency's interpretation of a statute, which was in the form of an amicus brief, stating that "[t]here is simply no reason to suspect that the interpretation does not reflect the agency's fair and considered judgment on the matter in question" (Auer v. Robbins, 519 U.S. 452, 462 (1997).
[128] United States v. Mead Corporation, 533 U.S. 218, 227 (2001).
[129] *Id.*

formality, and relative expertness, and to the persuasiveness of the agency's position."[130] (This is termed *Skidmore* deference.) An IRS revenue ruling is entitled to *Skidmore* (but not *Chevron*) deference.[131] The same is the case with revenue procedures.[132] A US Tax Court decision illustrates circumstances when a revenue ruling or revenue procedure is accorded *Skidmore* deference.[133]

The IRS issues other forms of "public" law in forms such as notices, announcements, delegation orders, instructions that accompany forms, and plain-language publications. (Other agencies have similar pronouncements.) There is not much law on the matter of judicial deference in this context. One court wrote that "[i]t is hornbook law that informal publications all the way up to revenue rulings are simply guides to taxpayers, and a taxpayer relies on them at his peril."[134] Another court held that "authoritative sources of Federal tax law are in the statutes, regulations, and judicial decisions and in ... informal guidance."[135]

Much of the law there is in this area concerns IRS form instructions. Some courts have taken the position that IRS form instructions assist in tax reporting but do not in themselves serve to stipulate tax law consequences.[136] A court cited to IRS form instructions and other publications in support of its conclusions in a tax law case.[137] Another court observed that "general principles of equity dictate that the IRS should not be allowed to issue instructions for completing is forms and later disavow those instructions."[138]

In contrast to these forms of "public" law, the IRS (like other agencies) issues "private" or nonprecedential determinations. These documents principally are private letter rulings, technical memoranda,

---

130 *Id.*, citing Skidmore v. Swift & Co., 323 U.S. 134 (1944).
131 E.g., Omohundro v. United States, 300 F.3d 1065 (9th Cir. 2002).
132 E.g., Tualatin Valley Builders Supply v. United States, 522 F.3d 937 (9th Cir. 2008).
133 Estate of Schaefer v. Commissioner, 145 T.C. 134 (2015).
134 Caterpillar Tractor Co. v. United States, 589 F.2d 1040, 1043 (Ct. Cl. 1978).
135 Zimmerman v. Commissioner, 71 T.C. 367, 371 (1978).
136 E.g., United States v. Josephberg, 562 F.3d 478 (2nd Cir. 2009).
137 Thomas v. United States, 22 Ct. Cl. 749 (1991).
138 Wilkes v. United States, 50 F. Supp. 2d 1281, 1286–1287 (M.D. Fla. 1999), *aff'd*, 201 F.3d 394 (11th Cir. 2000).

and chief counsel advice memoranda. As a matter of statutory law, these determinations may not be cited as legal authority.[139] Thus, a court wrote that IRS private letter rulings "cannot be used or cited as precedent; they cannot be used to advance a particular interpretation of the Internal Revenue Code; and they cannot be used for their substance."[140] The practice of the US Tax Court is to refuse to consider these private determinations.[141]

Nonetheless, these pronouncements can be valuable in understanding IRS thinking on a point of law and, in practice (the statutory prohibition notwithstanding), these documents are cited for the purpose of understanding the IRS positions on issues, such as in court opinions,[142] articles, and books.[143]

Even the IRS occasionally references its references its private letter rulings and the like in its analysis of the federal tax law, including facets of the law of tax-exempt organizations, stating that, while they are "not to be taken as precedent, they are "described" in the agency's writings "for illustrative purposes."[144] In a Tax Court case,[145] the petitioner, in support of one of its arguments, cited an unpublished IRS field service memorandum and an unpublished private letter ruling; the IRS objected to these citations (then distinguished them) but the agency in turn cited two unpublished technical advice memoranda. Congressional committees may cite

---

139 IRC § 6110(k)(3).

140 AmerGen Energy Co., LLC v. United States, 2010–2 U.S.T.C. ¶ 50,600 (U.S. Ct. Fed. Cl. 2010).

141 E.g., National Education Association of the United States v. Commissioner, 137 T.C. 100 (2011); Abdel-Fattah v. Commissioner, 134 T.C. 190 (2010).

142 E.g., Mayo Foundation for Medical Education and Research v. United States, 562 U.S. 44, 59 (2011); Glass v. Commissioner, 471 F.3d 698, 709 (6th Cir. 2006).

143 E.g., it has been written that a "series of similar letter rulings might help the attorney predict for the client the IRS's probable approach in a given situation" (Lederman and Mazza, *Tax Controversies: Practice and Procedure, Third Edition* (San Francisco: LexisNexis, 2009) at 778). There it is observed that private letter rulings constitute authority for avoiding the substantial understatement penalty (IRC § 6662(d)(2)(B)).

144 "Fund Raising," Topic L, 1982 Exempt Organizations Continuing Professional Education Text.

145 National Education Association of the United States v. Commissioner, 137 T.C. 100 (2011).

private letter rulings, as illustrated by an instance where the House Committee on Ways and Means observed, after citing several IRS private letter rulings, that these rulings are "some indication of IRS administrative practice."[146]

Chevron in Federal Tax Law Context

The *Chevron* framework applies, of course, in the federal tax law context. This principle of law was made clear in the *Mayo Foundation* case. Many other recent cases, from the Supreme Court and other courts, have upheld tax regulations. As it happened, however, in two quite recent instances, courts have invalidated Treasury/IRS regulations as reflecting attempts at regulation outside the agency's authority as conferred by Congress: The *Loving* case[147] and the *Ridgely* case.[148]

Mayo Foundation Decision

In *Mayo Foundation*, the US Supreme Court unanimously upheld a Department of the Treasury regulation providing that medical residents must pay employment taxes in accordance with the Federal Insurance Contributions Act because they do not qualify as students and thus are ineligible for the FICA tax student exception.[149]

This case unfolded in classic *Chevron*-model form. First, there was a statute that generally addressed the question involved, namely, the meaning of the word *student* in this context. Congress

---

[146] H. Rep. No. 104-586, 104th Cong., 2nd Sess., at 136, n. 14 (1996). Herein, there are citations to, and in some instances discussion of, over [60] IRS private letter rulings. This is not done in the spirit of citing them as precedent but rather to understand the IRS's "probable approach in a given situation" and as an indication of the IRS's "administrative practice" as to its current role in nonprofit governance.

[147] Loving v. Internal Revenue Service, 742 F.3d 1013 (D.C. Cir. 2014).

[148] Ridgely v. Lew, 55 F. Supp. 3d 89 (D.D.C. 2014). Inexplicably, both of these opinions expressly apply the *Chevron* framework, without any reference to the *Mayo Foundation* opinion.

[149] IRC § 3121(b)(10).

has long exempted certain categories of service and individuals from the FICA requirements. Pertinent to the case was the exclusion from taxation of "service performed in the employ of ... a school, college, or university ... if such service is performed by a student who is enrolled and regularly attending classes at such school, college, or university."[150] For several years, the Treasury Department and the Social Security Administration applied this exception on a case-by-case basis. Then, the federal government decided that a clarifying regulation was needed; one was promulgated, employing the concept that the educational aspect of the relationship between the employer and the employee must be "predominant" in relation to the service (employment) aspect.

The question before the courts was whether the statute was silent or ambiguous on the question whether a medical resident working for a school fulltime is a student and, if so, whether the Treasury Department's regulation is a permissible construction of the statute. The Supreme Court, applying the first step of the *Chevron* parameters, concluded that Congress did not directly address the precise question at issue because the statute does not define the term "student" and does not "otherwise attend to the precise question whether medical residents are subject to FICA."[151] Therefore, because the statute is silent and ambiguous, the Court held that it was necessary to proceed to application of the second step of *Chevron*.

The Court stated that the regulation "easily satisfies" this second step, which asks whether an agency's regulation is a "reasonable interpretation" of the enacted text.[152] The challengers to the regulation conceded the fundamental concept of the rule; they complained only about the time allocations assigned to "workers who study and students who work."[153] The Supreme Court stated: "Focusing on the hours an individual works and the hours he spends

---

[150] *Id.*

[151] Mayo Foundation for Medical Education and Research v. United States, 562 U.S. 44, 52 (2011).

[152] *Id.* at 58.

[153] *Id.* at 59.

in studies is a perfectly sensible way of accomplishing that goal,"[154] the goal being determining who is predominately a student. The rule was also seen as advancing administrative convenience and furthering a purpose of the Social Security Act which is to maximize the breadth of coverage.[155] "Because it is one to which Congress has not directly spoken, and because the Treasury Department's rule is a reasonable construction of what Congress has said,"[156] the Supreme Court validated this regulation as being one promulgated well within the authority of the Department of the Treasury.

Other Supreme Court Tax Regulation Review Decisions

For years, the Supreme Court used two different approaches when analyzing an ambiguous federal tax statute. In 1979, the Court articulated a complex, multifactor analytic scheme for this purpose.[157] In 1984, the Court announced the *Chevron* approach.[158] In 2011, the Court decided, in the *Mayo Foundation* case, that *Chevron* would apply in the federal tax law realm.[159] Using either approach, the Court has had several occasions to review Treasury Department regulations.

Concerning this latter point, the concept of *tax exceptionalism* needs to be considered. Two commentators observed that the tax law, being "complex and its impact pervasive," has evolved to the point that "[n]o other field of law is thought to be so complex or to compel so many to regularly bare their financial souls to the government just to be in compliance with the law."[160] The notion that the tax law is different from other fields of law is given, by them,

---

[154] *Id.*

[155] The Court took that occasion to note that "exemptions from taxation are to be construed narrowly" (Bingler v. Johnson, 394 U.S. 741, 752 (1969)).

[156] Mayo Foundation for Medical Education and Research v. United States, 562 U.S. 44, 60 (2011).

[157] National Muffler Dealers Association, Inc. v. United States, 440 U.S. 472 (1979).

[158] See the text accompanied by *supra* notes 94–126.

[159] See the text accompanied by *supra* notes 149–156.

[160] Abreu and Greenstein, "Tax as Everylaw: Interpretation, Enforcement, and the Legitimacy of the IRS," 69 *Tax Law.* (No. 3) 493, 497 (Spring 2016).

the phrase *tax exceptionalism*. They quoted another commentator as to the idea that "tax law is somehow deeply different from other law, with the result that many of the rules that apply trans-substantively across the rest of the legal landscape do not, or should not, apply to tax" law.[161] They also quoted former Treasury officials on the point: "Federal tax statutes and the legislative process that produces them differ from other legislation in such degree that the difference is tantamount to a difference in kind. The unique nature of the Internal Revenue Code is widely acknowledged."[162]

These two commentators continued: "Nowhere has tax exceptionalism had such profound effects and been subject to greater scrutiny than in the area of administrative law."[163] They added: "For decades Treasury and the IRS had taken the position that unlike regulations in other areas of law, tax regulations were not subject to the notice and comment process provided by the Administrative Procedure Act, and were thought to merit a lesser level of judicial deference than other regulations."[164] The *Mayo Foundation* decision was thought in many quarters to have extinguished the concept of tax exceptionalism. Yet, they conclude, tax exceptionalism "has refused to die."[165]

In one of the classic instances of this genre (Supreme Court review of tax regulations), the Court reviewed a case involving a late-filed federal estate tax return. The law generally requires that an estate tax return be filed within nine months of a decedent's death.[166] Some exceptions to that deadline are available but,

---

[161] Zelenak, "Maybe Just a Little Bit Special, After All?," 63 *Duke L. J.* 1897, 1901 (2014).

[162] Ferguson, Hickman, and Lubick, "Reexamining the Nature and Role of Tax Legislative History in Light of the Changing Realities of the Process," 67 *Taxes* 804, 806 (1989).

[163] Abreu and Greenstein, *supra* note 160, at 498.

[164] *Id.*, at 498–499.

[165] *Id.*, at 499, citing as an example Hickman, "Administering the Tax System We Have," 66 *Duke L.J.* 1717, 1719 (2014). The IRS's incursion into the realm of nonprofit governance, including the way in which the agency has gone about it, is another example of tax exceptionalism clinging to life.

[166] IRC § 6075(a).

overall, to avoid a late-filing penalty,[167] the tax regulations require that the executor exercise "ordinary business care and prudence."[168] The executor in this case retained a lawyer to prepare and file the estate tax return; the lawyer did not timely file the return. After imposition of a penalty, the executor sued for a refund, on the grounds that he was entitled to rely on his lawyer and that to do so was due to "reasonable cause" and "ordinarily business care." The Court disagreed, holding that Congress placed the burden of prompt filing of this return on the executor, not an agent; it is the executor's duty to ascertain and meet the statutory deadline.[169] The Court held that it was an act of "ordinary business care and prudence" to hire the lawyer but that it was not "reasonable" for the executor to assume that the lawyer would comply with the statute. It was held that the IRS's correlation of the statute's reference to "reasonable cause" with the phraseology of "ordinary business care and prudence" in the tax regulations was reasonable as being "consistent with Congress' intent."[170]

Another case involved the tax law consequences of sales by a savings association of participation interests in mortgages to savings and loan associations and simultaneous purchase from them of participation interests in other mortgages. The federal tax law defers the tax consequences of a gain or loss in property until it is realized through the "sale or disposition of [the] property." [171] The tax regulations state that this disposition standard includes a requirement that the properties exchanged be materially different.[172] The Court observed that "[n]either the language nor the history of the [Internal Revenue] Code indicates whether and to what extent property exchanged must differ to count as a 'disposition of property'" for these purposes. [173] The Court deferred to the regulatory interpretation, requiring a material difference, finding that

---

[167] IRC § 6651(a)(1), which excuses the penalty in an instance of "reasonable cause" and lack of "willful neglect."
[168] 26 CFR § 301.6651-1(c)(1).
[169] United States v. Boyle, 469 U.S. 241 (1985).
[170] *Id.* at 246, citing *Chevron* (*id.*, note 4).
[171] IRC § 1001(a).
[172] Reg. § 1.1001-1.
[173] Cottage Savings Association v. Commissioner, 499 U.S. 554, 560 (1991).

interpretation "reasonable."[174] The Court then found the properties involved to be materially different and allowed the claimed losses.[175]

Before enactment of the Tax Reform Act of 1986, the federal tax law accorded property and casualty insurers a full deduction for loss reserves, which are estimated amounts of losses reported but not yet paid, losses incurred but not yet reported, and the administrative costs of resolving claims. In each tax year, not only losses paid, but the full amount of the loss reserves, reduced by the amount of the loss reserves claimed for the prior tax year, were treated as business expenses. The 1986 Act required these insurers, beginning with the 1987 tax year, to discount unpaid losses to present value when claiming them as a deduction. Requiring insurers to subtract undiscounted year-end 1986 reserves from discounted year-end 1987 reserves in computing losses for 1987 would produce artificially low deductions, so the Act included a transitional rule requiring insurers to also discount 1986 reserves. This rule changed the method of accounting for computing taxable income.

To avoid requiring property and casualty insurers to recognize as income the difference between undiscounted and discounted year-end 1986 loss reserves, the Act gave them a "fresh start" in the form of an exclusion from taxable income of the difference between undiscounted and discounted year-end loss reserves.[176] It foreclosed the possibility that they would inflate reserves to manipulate this fresh start by excepting "reserve strengthening" from the exclusion.[177] The Department of the Treasury promulgated a regulation defining reserve strengthening as including any net addition to reserves.[178] The IRS determined that a property and casualty insurer made net additions to its loss reserves in 1986, reduced the fresh start entitlement, and imposed a tax deficiency. This matter of the reasonableness of the tax regulation was litigated, with the Court holding that it represented a reasonable

---

[174] *Id.* at 561, citing National Muffler Dealers Association, Inc. v. United States, 440 U.S. 472, 476–477 (1979).
[175] IRC § 165(a).
[176] IRC § 1023(e)(3)(A).
[177] IRC § 1023(e)(3)(B).
[178] Reg. 1.846-3(c)(3)(ii).

interpretation of the term "reserve strengthening."[179] The Court stated that this regulation "seems to us a reasonable accommodation – and one that the statute very likely intended – of the competing interests of fairness, administrability, and avoidance of abuse."[180]

Under a grievance settlement agreement, a professional baseball company owed eight players back pay for wages due in 1986 and fourteen players for back pay for wages due in 1987. The company paid the back wages in 1994. The question arose as to whether, under the Federal Insurance Contributions Act and the Federal Unemployment Tax Act, the back wages should be taxed by reference to the year they were paid or by reference to the years they should have been paid. Both the tax rates and the amount of wages subject to tax have risen over time. Consequently, allocating the payments in 1994 back to 1986 and 1987 would generate no additional FICA or FUTA tax liability for the company and its former employees, while treating the back wages as taxable in 1994 would subject the company and the employees to significant tax liability. The company paid its share of employment taxes on the back taxes according to the 1994 tax rates and wage bases. The IRS denied its claims for refund; litigation ensued.

When the Court considered the case, it looked at the statutory scheme, coupled with the IRS's regulations interpreting the FICA and FUTA tax provisions.[181] The Court observed that, while the statutes and tax regulations do not specifically address the matter of back pay, the IRS has consistently interpreted the regulations to require taxation of back wages according to the year the wages are actually paid, regardless of when the wages were earned or should have been paid.[182] The Court found that interpretation to be "reasonable," thus "attract[ing] substantial judicial deference."[183]

---

[179] Atlantic Mutual Insurance Co. v. Commissioner, 523 U.S. 382 (1998).

[180] *Id.* at 390–391, citing *Cottage Savings*, which, as noted (*supra* note 174), cited *National Muffler*.

[181] Reg. § 31.3111-2, 3.

[182] United States v. Cleveland Indians Baseball Co., 532 U.S. 200 (2001). The basis for this IRS "interpretation" was two revenue rulings, as to which the Court declined to decide whether to accord them deference, stating that these rulings

Other Court Tax Regulation Review Decisions

In one case, an individual was the sole owner of several limited liability companies, the operation of which resulted in unpaid federal employment taxes. Because this individual was the sole owner of these companies and had not elected to have the businesses treated as corporations (technically, "associations") pursuant to Treasury Department regulations,[184] the LLCs were disregarded for federal tax purposes, that is, they were not regarded as separate taxable entities but rather were treated for federal tax purposes as sole proprietorships.[185] When this individual, as sole proprietor, failed to pay the outstanding employment taxes, the IRS filed notices of determination and, eventually, notified him of its intent to levy on his property to enforce previously filed tax liens.

One of this individual's defenses in court was that the regulations in question (the "check-the-box" regulations) were promulgated in excess of the Treasury Department's authority to issue tax regulations interpreting the Internal Revenue Code. The district court held that these regulations were a reasonable interpretation by the IRS of an ambiguous tax statute,[186] upholding them under *Chevron*.[187] In so doing, the court rejected the argument that the Treasury Department had exceeded its authority in promulgating the entity-classification regulations. This decision was affirmed, with the court of appeals adhering to the "perimeters of [*Chevron*] and its directive to courts to give deference to an agency's interpretation of its statutes that the agency is entrusted to administer and to the rules that govern implementation, as long as they are reasonable, are clear," and are applicable in this case.[188] The appellate court agreed that the statute is ambiguous when applied to emerging hybrid business entities, that the Treasury regulations were developed to fill in the statutory gaps

---

"merely reflect the agency's longstanding interpretation of its own regulations" (United States v. Cleveland Indians Baseball Co., *supra*, at 220).

183 *Id.*

184 Reg. § 301.7701-3(a), (c).

185 Reg. § 301.7701-3(b)(1)(ii).

186 IRC § 7701.

187 Littriello v. United States, 2005-1 U.S.T.C. ¶ 50,385 (W.D. Ky. 2005).

188 Lattriello v. United States, 484 F.3d 372, 377 (6th Cir. 2007), *cert. den.*, 552 U.S. 1186 (2008).

when dealing with these entities, and that overall the check-the-box regulations are "eminently reasonable" as a valid exercise of the agency's authority.[189]

Two recent cases reflect courts' approach in response to the IRS's efforts to expand its regulatory authority. These cases are *Loving* v. *Internal Revenue Service* and *Ridgely* v. *Lew* where, in both instances, regulations promulgated by the IRS were struck down as being ultra vires acts by reason of an incorrect assertion of agency authority. In *Loving*, a federal court of appeals held, in view of the statute involved, that the IRS "may not unilaterally expand its authority through such an expansive, atextual, and ahistorical reading" of the statute.[190] The district court in *Ridgely* essentially followed the appellate court's guidance in *Loving*.

Loving Decision

The *Loving* case presents a typical illustration of application of *Chevron* in the federal tax law setting. Congress enacted a statute that the IRS is obligated to administer; the IRS issued a regulation ostensibly lawfully interpreting the statute. The statute authorizes the IRS to regulate the practice of representatives of persons before the Department of the Treasury.[191] The regulation at issue accorded the IRS the authority to regulate tax-return preparers.[192] The statute was enacted in 1884; the regulation was promulgated in 2011.

Three independent tax-return preparers contended that the IRS's tax-return preparer regulations exceeded the agency authority under the statute. The question before the court was whether the IRS's statutory authority to "regulate the practice of representatives of persons before the Department of the Treasury" encompasses authority to regulate tax-return preparers. The district court ruled against the IRS, relying on the text, history, structure, and context of the statute.[193] The

---

[189] *Id.*, 484 F.3d at 378.
[190] Loving v. Internal Revenue Service, 742 F. 3d 1013, 1022 (D.C. Cir. 2014).
[191] 31 U.S.C. § 330(a)(1).
[192] 31 C.F.R. §§ 10.3-10.6.
[193] Loving v. Internal Revenue Service, 917 F. Supp. 2d 67 (D.D.C. 2013).

court of appeals agreed with the district court that the IRS's statutory authority in this regard "cannot be stretched so broadly" as to encompass authority to regulate tax-return preparers.[194]

The courts found that the IRS's interpretation of the statute failed at step one of the *Chevron* doctrine because it is "foreclosed by the statute," that is, the statute is not ambiguous. Nonetheless, the court of appeals analyzed the IRS's interpretation under step two of the principle, finding failure at that level as well because it is "unreasonable in light of the statute's text, history, structure, and context." [195] The IRS, the appellate court added, "may not unilaterally expand its authority through such an expansive, atextual, and ahistorical reading" of the statute.[196]

The appellate court identified at least six considerations foreclosing the IRS interpretation of the statute under *Chevron* step two. The principal considerations were that tax-return preparers are not "representatives" of taxpayers and these individuals do not "practice" before the Treasury Department. Other factors considered were the history of the statute, the broader statutory framework, the nature and scope of the authority being claimed by the IRS, [197] and the IRS's past approach to the statute involved. Overall, the court said it was following the Supreme Court's admonition that courts should "tak[e] seriously, and apply[] rigorously, in all cases, statutory limits on agencies' authority."[198]

---

[194] Loving v. Internal Revenue Service, 742 F.3d 1013, 1015 (D.C. Cir. 2014).

[195] The appellate court noted that "[i]t might be that allowing the IRS to regulate tax-return preparers more stringently would be wise as a policy matter," but that is a decision for Congress to make (*id.* at 1022). It quoted the Supreme Court as stating the "role of this Court is to apply the statute as it is written –even if we think some other approach might accord with good policy" (Burrage v. United States, 134 S. Ct. 881, 892 (2014)).

[196] Loving v. Internal Revenue Service, 742 F. 3d 1013, 1022 (D.C. Cir. 2014).

[197] This factor is critical to the nonprofit governance analysis, because the Supreme Court has stated that courts should not lightly presume congressional intent to implicitly delegate decisions of major economic or political significance to agencies (Federal Drug Administration v. Brown & Williamson Tobacco Corp., 529 U.S. 120, 160 (2000). See, e.g., Chapter 8, text accompanied by note 21.

[198] City of Arlington, Texas v. Federal Communications Commission, 133 S. Ct. 1863, 1874 (2013)).

Ridgely Decision

To prevent "exploit[ation of] the audit selection process," the IRS prohibited, by issuance of a regulation, a broad range of tax practitioners from charging contingent fees for certain services relating to preparing, filing, or presenting tax returns or refund claims.[199] A practicing certified public accountant sued the Secretary of the Treasury and the Commissioner of Internal Revenue in their official capacities, asserting that the IRS exceeded the scope of its statutory authority in regulating the preparation and filing of "ordinary refund claims."[200] The plaintiff in the case challenged the IRS's proclaimed authority to regulate fee arrangements entered into by CPAs for preparing and filing ordinary refund claims before the commencement of any adversarial proceedings with the IRS or any formal legal representation by the CPA. The district court concluded that the IRS lacks the statutory authority to regulate the preparation and filing of these ordinary refund claims.

The statute applicable in this case is the one that was applicable in *Loving*.[201] The *Ridgely* court, in applying *Chevron* step one, followed the guidance of the court of appeals in *Loving* in stressing the importance of the terms "representative" and "practice" and concluding that the "plain text" of the statute excludes preparers and filers of ordinary refund claims from the ambit of the IRS's regulatory authority. The court also examined the context and history of the statute.

Because the court concluded that the "traditional tools of statutory interpretation unambiguously foreclose the IRS's interpretation – that is, the regulation fails *Chevron* step 1 – the Court need not analyze the regulation under *Chevron* step 2."[202]

---

[199] 31 C.F.R. § 10.27.

[200] "Ordinary refund claims" are refund claims that practitioners file after a taxpayer has filed his or her original tax return but before the IRS has initiated an audit of the return. A taxpayer may adhere to this procedure after filing the return and having determined he or she has overpaid his or her taxes; this must be done prior to filing suit in court for a refund.

[201] 31 U.S.C. 330.

[202] Ridgely v. Lew, 55 F. Supp. 3d 89, 98 (D.D.C. 2014). Another case, challenging the IRS's regulatory jurisdiction, is working its way through the courts.

Factor of Agency Expertise

The *Chevron* (and *Mayo*) approach, at the federal level, is premised on the theory that a statute's ambiguity constitutes an implicit delegation from Congress to the agency to fill in the gaps in the statute.[203] In extraordinary cases, however, there may be reason for a court to hesitate before concluding that Congress has intended this type of an implicit delegation. One reason may be the nature or lack of an agency's expertise in relation to the statute to be administered.

Implicit (but barely) in the courts' analysis in *Loving* and *Ridgely* of the IRS's authority to promulgate a regulation in relation to a statute the agency administers, utilizing the *Chevron* framework,[204] is the factor of an agency's *expertise* in relation to a field it is attempting to regulate. In its principal opinion on the point,[205] the Court stated that it was "confident that Congress could not have intended to delegate a decision of such economic or political significance to agencies."[206] The court in *Loving* construed the Court's admonition in *Brown & Williamson* to mean that "courts should not lightly presume congressional intent to implicitly delegate decisions of major economic or political significance to agencies."[207] Although these passages can be read as courts' emphasis on the nature of a delegation of authority to an agency,

---

This case contests the IRS's jurisdiction to administer a voluntary program allowing previously uncredentialed tax return preparers to be listed in an online directory administered by the agency (American Institute of Certified Public Accountants v. Internal Revenue Service). The US Court of Appeals for the District of Columbia Circuit ruled that the AICPA has standing to bring the lawsuit (804 F.3d 1193 (D.C. Cir. 2015)).

[203] See the text accompanied by *supra* note 103.

[204] The court in *Loving* sifted through all of the elements in its analysis of the scope of the IRS's authority before announcing that the IRS's interpretation contravened both steps of *Chevron* (742 F.3d 1013, 1022 (2014)), so it cannot be determined what factors affected which step. In *Ridgely*, as noted, the court's analysis led it to the conclusion that *Chevron* step one was dispositive of the case (55 F. Supp. 3d 89, 98 (D.D.C. 2014)) and it declined to proceed to step two.

[205] Food and Drug Administration v. Brown & Williamson Tobacco Corp., 529 U.S. 120 (2000).

[206] *Id.* at 160.

[207] Loving v. Internal Revenue Service, 742 F.3d 1013, 1014 (D.C. Cir. 2014)).

rather than on its competence to regulate within the bounds of that authority, the court in *Loving* added that, in light of the text, history, structure, and context of the statute involved, "it becomes apparent that the IRS never before adopted its current interpretation for a reason: It is incorrect."[208]

The court in *Ridgely* assumed a similar stance. In discussing the extent to which the IRS may regulate certified public accountants, the court mocked the IRS's position – which essentially was that the agency can "broadly regulate" the actions of CPAs no matter what they are doing, even if they occasionally practiced before the IRS – finding it "absurd."[209] The court "disagree[d] with the IRS that simply because CPAs may *at times* practice before the IRS, the IRS has authority to regulate their conduct without limit."[210]

This factor came to the surface rather dramatically in connection with the Supreme Court's opinion that the refundable tax credits, created by the Patient Protection and Affordable Care Act,[211] made available to individuals who purchase health insurance on state exchanges are also available if the insurance is acquired from an exchange established by the federal government.[212] The argument advanced by those challenging this conclusion was that the credits are not available in this instance because the statute provides that these subsidies may be offered only in connection with an exchange established by a state. The IRS issued a regulation providing that an individual is eligible for a tax credit if he or she enrolled in an insurance plan through "an Exchange," regardless of whether the exchange is established and operated by a state or the federal government.[213]

The Court ruled in this case that the phrase "an Exchange established by the State" is "ambiguous."[214] This phrase, it was said, "may be limited in its reach" to state exchanges.[215] But, the majority

---

208 *Id.* at 1021.
209 Ridgely v. Lew, 55 F. Supp. 3d 89, 97 (D.D.C. 2014). The court also concluded that the "IRS's regulatory scheme is invalid" (*id.* at 98).
210 *Id.* at 97.
211 IRC § 36B.
212 King v. Burwell, 135 S. Ct. 2480 (2015).
213 45 C.F.R. § 155.20.
214 King v. Burwell, 135 S. Ct. 2480, 2491 (2015).
215 *Id.*

observed, it "could also refer to *all* Exchanges – both State and Federal – for purposes of the tax credits."[216] The rationale for this conclusion was that the "context" of the provision means that the phrase refers to all exchanges.[217] Concluding that confining the availability of these credits to purchases on state exchanges would destabilize the insurance market in states with federal exchanges and could well push states' insurance markets into a "death spiral," the majority observed that it is "implausible" that Congress "meant the Act to operate in this manner."[218]

This case was said by the Court to be the type of case where a court should hesitate before concluding that Congress intended an implicit delegation of authority. The tax credits were characterized by the Court as being one of the Act's "key reforms, involving billions of dollars in spending each year and affecting the price of health insurance for millions of people."[219] The Court stated that "[w]hether these credits are available on Federal Exchanges is thus a question of deep economic and political significance that is central to this statutory scheme; had Congress wished to assign that question to an agency, it surely would have done so expressly."[220] Then the Court said: "It is especially unlikely that Congress would have delegated this decision to the *IRS*, which has no expertise in crafting health insurance policy of this sort."[221]

The Supreme Court concluded: "This is not a case for the IRS."[222]

---

216 *Id*.

217 *Id*.

218 *Id*. at 2494.

219 *Id*. at 2489.

220 *Id*. The reference to "deep economic and political significance" is, of course, to the wordsmithing in *Brown & Williamson* (see Chapter 1, text accompanied by note 100).

221 King v. Burwell, 135 S. Ct. 2480, 2489 (2015).

222 *Id*. While this sentence is somewhat of a mantra for this book, the irony is that the Court, in its overall (majority) decision, validated and upheld the IRS regulation as to accessibility of the Act's tax credits.

Factor of Relevance

A commentator has noted that, "[h]istorically, the IRS has been acutely aware of a limit at some point on its ability to compel information."[223] The extent of this limit has arisen in connection with summons enforcement and incomplete return penalties.

As to summons enforcement, the Department of the Treasury is authorized to examine the books and records as may be "relevant of material" to tax administration. The Supreme Court ruled that an IRS summons must satisfy four requirements to be enforceable: (1) it must be for a legitimate purpose, (2) the information requested under the summons must be relevant to that purpose, (3) the information must not yet be in the possession of the IRS, and (4) the summons must be issued and served under proper procedures.[224] The second of these requirements – relevance – means a showing that the information requested "may be relevant" or "may shed light upon" a potential tax liability,[225] as long as there is a "reasonable expectation rather than an idle hope that something may be discovered."[226] This commentator observed: "While this relevance standard sets a relatively low bar for IRS examiners to meet, it does nevertheless set a bar, and courts have not infrequently refused to enforce summonses on the basis of irrelevance."[227] He added: "That a charity's governance policies and procedures, beyond those specified by the [C]ode, may reflect its institutional attitude toward general tax compliance would not appear to meet the *Powell* requirement of relevancy to a potential tax liability."[228]

As to the matter of incomplete return penalties for tax-exempt organizations, such as whether a return is sufficiently complete to begin running of the statute of limitations, this commentator wrote that the IRS Office of Chief Counsel's views are "contingent on

---

[223] Owens Article at 289.

[224] Lederman and Mazza, *supra* note 143, at 124. The Court's decision is United States v. Powell, 379 U.S. 48, 57–58 (1964).

[225] United States v. Arthur Young & Co., 465 U.S. 805, 814–815 (1984).

[226] United States v. Harrington, 388 F.2d 520, 524 (2nd Cir. 1968).

[227] Owens Article at 289, citing, e.g., United States v. Coopers & Lybrand, 550 F.2d 615 (10th Cir. 1977).

[228] Owens Article at 289.

whether a given return omits information that is "material and thus necessary for the administration of the tax laws."[229] For example, the chief counsel ruled that omission from the 990 series of annual information returns of information that was required and requested, but unsupplied, that was material and necessary for administration of the tax laws, would, in the case of a failure to include the information on a return, without reasonable cause, would subject the filing organization to penalties.[230]

In 1954, a Code provision was enacted that provided that, if an organization determines in good faith that it is a tax-exempt entity and thus files an annual information return (rather than a tax return), and it is ultimately determined that the organization is a taxable entity for a year the filing of the annual information return started the running of the statute of limitations.[231] The Office of Chief Counsel thereafter opined that, as of that year, the Treasury Department "had no authority to require [annual information] returns to include information needed to enforce provisions relating to taxes other than income tax."[232] Subsequently, the statutory language was broadened to accommodate the excise taxes introduced in 1969 that underlie the private foundations limitations and restrictions. Chief counsel also opined that that expansion of the statutory authority could not be used as a basis for eliciting from exempt organizations information relating to the wagering excise tax.[233]

All of this led this commentator to state, as to the revamped Form 990 and its questions as to governance,[234] "[c]learly, an argument can be made that the IRS has exceeded its authority by incorporating questions on governance and other matters that, by its own admission, are not required by the [C]ode."[235] He added: "The executive branch functions – IRS Chief Counsel, the Treasury Department, and the Office of Management and Budget – that would traditionally operate to prevent such overstepping by the tax

---

[229] *Id.* at 289, citing Gen. Couns. Mem. 36372 (Aug. 11, 1975).
[230] Gen. Couns. Mem. 36506 (Dec. 8, 1975).
[231] IRC § 6501(g)(2).
[232] Gen. Couns. Mem. 38382 (May 23, 1980).
[233] *Id.*
[234] See Chapter 5, text accompanied by notes 12–47.
[235] Owens Article at 290.

administrator have not acted, whether merely out of inattention to or perhaps in complicity with the Service's unilateral expansion of its authority."[236] Also: "It is possible that the expansion of the IRS authority might be viewed as a function of congressional oversight," although that surmise was dismissed as "unlikely."[237]

---

236 *Id.*
237 *Id.*

3

Relevant Basic Tax-Exempt Organizations Law

> While a charity's board consisting of related parties "may not necessarily disqualify it for exemption, it provides an obvious opportunity for abuse of the claimed tax-exempt status." These circumstances call for "open and candid disclosure of all facts bearing upon [the entity's] organization, operations, and finances."
>
> *Bubbling Well Church of Universal Love, Inc. v. Commissioner* (*Tax Ct., 1980*)

An understanding of the concept of nonprofit governance and the IRS's involvement in it necessitates some background as to the law of tax-exempt organizations, the law the IRS relies on in connection with its private letter ruling policy, and the little federal tax law there is on the subject of nonprofit governance.

Organization of IRS

The IRS is fundamentally organized with four operating divisions, one of which is the Tax Exempt/Governmental Entities (TE/GE) Division. Within this Division is the Exempt Organizations Division, which develops policy concerning and administers the law of tax-exempt organizations. The Director of the Exempt Organizations Division, who reports to the Commissioner of the TE/GE Division, is responsible for planning, managing, and executing nationwide IRS activities in the realm of exempt organizations. This director supervises and is responsible for various functions within the Division, including Rulings and Agreement and Examinations.

The IRS, late in 2014, addressed the transfer of certain technical responsibility for issues involving tax-exempt organizations to the

Office of Chief Counsel that occurred with a realignment of the Tax Exempt and Government Entities Division (TE/GE).[1] The technical responsibility for preparing revenue rulings, revenue procedures, and certain other forms of published guidance, and issuance of technical advice memoranda and certain letter rulings shifted from TE/GE to the office of Associate Chief Counsel (Tax Exempt and Government Entities) (TE/GE Counsel). The Exempt Organizations office of TE/GE (Exempt Organizations) retained the authority to issue determination letters, essentially determination letters denying recognition of the exempt status of organizations (from the TE/GE office in Cincinnati) and revocations of exemption (from TE/GE Examinations in Dallas).

General Federal Tax Law Rules

Overview

A nonprofit organization that is tax-exempt[2] because it is a charitable, educational, religious, scientific, or similar entity[3] is required to be organized and operated exclusively for one or more exempt purposes. This requirement thus entails compliance with an *organizational test* and an *operational test*. If an organization fails to meet either of these tests, it cannot be tax-exempt.[4] There are, either expressly or impliedly, comparable tests in connection with other categories of tax-exempt organizations.

An organization is regarded as operated *exclusively* for one or more exempt purposes only if it engages primarily in activities that

---

[1] Ann. 2014-34, 2014-51 I.R.B. 949. The transfer was more formally recognized on March 2, 2015, when the IRS issued Delegation Order 30-7.

[2] That is, exempt from federal income taxation by reason of IRC § 501(a).

[3] That is, an organization that is described in IRC § 501(c)(3). These organizations are referenced throughout as "charitable" organizations. They are entities that are eligible to receive deductible charitable contributions for federal income tax purposes (e.g., IRC § 170). Almost all of the IRS private letter rulings concerning nonprofit governance involve entities seeking to be recognized as tax-exempt charitable organizations (see Chapter 6).

[4] Reg. § 1.501(c)(3)-1(a)(1).

accomplish one or more exempt charitable purposes. An organization will not be so regarded if more than an insubstantial part of its activities is not in furtherance of an exempt purpose.[5] This is known as the *primary purpose rule*.[6]

An organization of this nature must engage in one or more charitable purposes.[7] To be exempt, however, an organization must do more than engage in exempt purposes. It must be in compliance with several statutory restrictions, including the private inurement doctrine,[8] prohibition on substantial legislative activities,[9] and the prohibition on political campaign activities.[10]

As an overlay to this statutory regime, the Supreme Court has imposed the *public policy doctrine*, which must be adhered to if an organization is to be tax-exempt. This doctrine, inherent in the law of charity, amply predates the federal tax law of exempt organizations (initially enacted in 1913). Thus, over five decades earlier, the Court stated that "courts of chancery will sustain and protect ... a gift ... to public charitable uses, provided the same is consistent with local laws and public policy."[11] Thereafter, the Court observed that a "charitable use, where neither law nor public policy forbids, may be applied to almost any thing that tends to promote the well-doing and well-being of social man."[12] In the modern application of this doctrine, where the Court held that racial

---

[5] Reg. § 1.501(c)(3)-1(c)(1).

[6] Thus, in this context, the word *exclusively* is a term of art that means *primarily*.

[7] The tax regulations include some of the definitions of the word *charitable* (Reg. § 1.501(c)(3)-1(d)(1)(i)(b)).

[8] IRC § 501(c)(3) (see *supra* note 3) includes the requirement that, to be tax-exempt, "no part of the net earnings of [the organization] may inure[] to the benefit of any private shareholder or individual." See *infra* text accompanied by notes 42–53.

[9] IRC § 501(c)(3) includes the requirement that, to be tax-exempt, "no substantial part of the activities [of the charitable organization may be] "carrying on propaganda, or otherwise attempting to influence legislation." If this rule is transgressed, the charitable organization involved may lose or be denied exempt status.

[10] IRC § 501(c)(3) includes the requirement that, to be tax-exempt, a charitable organization may "not participate in, or intervene in (including the publishing or distributing of statements), any political campaign on behalf of (or in opposition to) any candidate for public office." If this rule is violated, the charitable organization involved may lose or be denied exempt status.

[11] Perin v. Carey, 24 How. 465, 501 (1861).

[12] Ould v. Washington Hospital for Foundlings, 95 U.S. 303, 311 (1878).

discrimination in education is contrary to public policy, the Court wrote that "[c]haritable exemptions are justified on the basis that the exempt entity confers a public benefit – a benefit which the society or the community may not itself choose or be able to provide, or which supplements and advances the work of public institutions already supported by tax revenues."[13] The Court added: "History buttresses logic to make clear that to warrant exemption under § 501(c)(3), an institution must fall within a category specified in that section and must demonstrably serve and be in harmony with the public interest."[14]

At the federal level, there are 76 separate categories of tax-exempt organizations. Each of these categories has been, of course, the subject of congressional legislation. Thus, it is Congress that determines which types of nonprofit organizations are eligible for tax-exempt status. Put another way, the IRS does not *grant* tax-exempt status. The role of the IRS in this regard is to *recognize* tax-exempt status; the exempt status itself (assuming it exists) is already in being.

Nearly all categories of charitable (including educational, scientific, and religious) organizations, are required, to be tax-exempt, to file an application for recognition of exemption with the IRS.[15] This process, of course, gives the agency the opportunity to review the organization's purposes, programs, overall operations, and relationships with other persons to ascertain whether there is an impediment to exemption. If the IRS determines that the organization qualifies for exemption, it will issue a favorable ruling (generally known as a "determination letter"). Otherwise, there are a host of administrative appeal and litigation rights available to an organization that is of the view it was wrongly denied a favorable ruling.

Nearly all nonprofit, tax-exempt organizations are required to file an annual information return with the IRS.[16] The particular form to be filed depends on the size and/or type of the organization. The principal return in this regard – the one that has played a major role

---

[13] Bob Jones University v. United States, 461 U.S. 574, 591 (1983).
[14] *Id.* at 591–592.
[15] IRC § 508(a).
[16] IRC § 6033.

in the IRS's assumption of regulatory authority over the governance of nonprofit organizations [17] – is the Form 990. Smaller organizations that are not required to file annual information returns must submit annual notices to the IRS about their existence and status. [18] An exempt organization that does not file an annual information return and/or submit an annual notice will lose its tax-exempt status by operation of law.[19]

Public Charities and Private Foundations

The federal tax law differentiates between two categories of exempt charitable organizations, those that are *public* and those that are *private*.[20] Public charities are of several varieties. One set of public charities are generally well-known institutions, such as churches, universities, colleges, other types of schools, hospitals, medical research organizations, and agricultural research organizations.[21]

As to churches, the law has changed dramatically in recent years. For some time, the IRS relied on a 14-point test for determining whether a religious organization could qualify as a church. At that time, if an organization could meet a majority of these criteria, it was determined to be a church. Then, around 2012, the IRS shifted position on the point; now, the IRS stated, an organization had to meet certain basic criteria to qualify as a church, namely, it had to have a place of worship and regular worship services. [22] This change of view came in the immediate aftermath of a major court decision holding that another critical requirement for a church was a regular congregation; this standard

---

[17] Form 990. See Chapter 5, text accompanied by notes 12–47.
[18] IRC § 6033(i).
[19] IRC § 6033(j).
[20] IRC § 509.
[21] IRC § 170(b)(1)(A)(i)–(v), (ix), cross-referenced into IRC § 509(a)(1).
[22] E.g., Priv. Ltr. Ruls. 201235022 (June 8, 2012), 201242014 (July 24, 2012), and 201251018 (September 26, 2012).

was termed the *associational test.*[23] Consequently, today, the IRS's position is that, to be a church under the federal tax law, a religious organization must have regular worship services conducted at a regular location with a regular congregation.[24] At no time has the IRS 14-point inventory of church criteria, the associational test rule, or the IRS's current ruling policy included any requirement that there be public "oversight" or "control" of a church

Another set of public charities, of which there are several varieties, are known as publicly supported charities.[25] Two other types of public charity are supporting organizations [26] and organizations that test for public safety.[27]

An exempt charitable entity that cannot qualify as a public charity is a private foundation, which usually is a charity that is funded from one source (such as an individual, a family, or a for-profit business) and governed by a board of related individuals, often members of the same family, which is often relatively small in number.

Private Benefit Doctrine

Still another rule that exempt charitable organizations (both public and private) must adhere to is the *private benefit doctrine*. This doctrine is predicated on a sentence in the tax regulations that states that an organization is not organized and operated exclusively for one or more charitable purposes "unless it serves a public rather than a private interest."[28] The regulations add that "it is necessary for an organization to establish that it is not organized and operated for the benefit of private interests such as designated individuals, the

---

[23] Foundation of Human Understanding v. United States, 2009-2 U.S.T.C. ¶ 50,519 (U.S. Ct. Fed. Cl. 2009), *aff'd*, 614 F.3d 1383 (Fed. Cir. 2010), *cert. den.*, 562 U.S. 1286 (2011).

[24] E.g., Priv. Ltr. Rul. 201609006 (April 9, 2015).

[25] E.g., IRC §§ 170(b)(1)(A)(vi), 509(a)(2).

[26] IRC § 509(a)(3).

[27] IRC § 509(a)(4).

[28] Reg. § 1.501(c)(3)-1(d)(1)(ii).

creator or his family, shareholders of the organization, or persons controlled, directly or indirectly, by such private interests."[29]

Despite these absolute statements, the IRS has repeatedly ruled that the private benefit prohibition is not to be utilized where the private benefit is merely *incidental*. According to the IRS, the word *incidental* has qualitative and quantitative connotations.[30]

One of the principal private benefit cases was decided by the US Tax Court in 1989. On that occasion, the court held that an organization that, as its primary activity, operated a school to train individuals for careers as political campaign professionals was not operated exclusively for exempt charitable purposes because the school's activities conferred impermissible private benefit in that all of its graduates went on to serve candidates of the Republican Party.[31] The court defined *private benefit* as being "nonincidental benefits conferred on disinterested persons that serve private interests."[32]

Another significant private benefit case was decided by the Tax Court in 1979. In the facts of that case, several for-profit est organizations were held to exert considerable indirect control over a nonprofit entity, that was seeking recognition of exemption as a charitable entity, by means of contractual arrangements. The court concluded that the for-profit organizations were using the nonprofit entity as an "instrument" to further their for-profit purposes.[33] Neither the fact that the for-profit entities lacked structural control over the organization nor the fact that amounts paid to these entities pursuant to the contracts were reasonable affected the court's decision. Consequently, the private benefit doctrine precluded the nonprofit entity from qualifying as an exempt charitable organization.

---

[29] *Id.*

[30] As to the former, e.g., Rev. Rul. 70-186, 1970-1 C.B. 128. As to the latter, e.g., Rev. Rul. 76-152, 1976-1 C.B. 151.

[31] American Campaign Academy v. Commissioner, 92 T.C. 1053 (1989).

[32] *Id.* at 1069. The reference to *disinterested persons* is used to distinguish those who are *insiders* with respect to a tax-exempt organization; when insiders are involved, the private inurement doctrine (see *supra* note 7) applies.

[33] est of Hawaii v. Commissioner, 71 T.C. 1067 (1979), *aff'd* (unpublished opinion), 647 F.2d 170 (9th Cir. 1981).

Also, the case law shows that impermissible private benefit is not confined to economic benefits. Prohibited private benefit may also consist of non-economic or intangible benefits.[34]

The sanction for violation of the private benefit doctrine is denial of recognition of, or revocation of, tax exemption. The private benefit doctrine is supposed to be applied only in instances where a private benefit transaction or arrangement has occurred. The IRS, however, often will invoke the private benefit doctrine sanction where it merely speculates that private benefit may arise. For example, the IRS denied recognition of tax exemption in an instance where it concluded that the "structure" of the organization "indicates that it *can* be used to benefit private individuals."[35] Similarly, the IRS refused to recognize exemption because it concluded that the "potential for private benefit clouds every aspect of [the] organization's operations.[36] Likewise, another organization failed to secure recognition of tax exemption because a governing board of three individuals was said by the IRS to provide a "window of opportunity for private benefit."[37] As a third illustration of this point, recognition of exemption was denied an organization because it had "not demonstrated that there are sufficient safeguards in place to prevent … [it] from operating for [the] private benefit" of its two-individual board.[38]

The private benefit doctrine has little bearing on the matter of nonprofit governance. Only one court opinion – in the *Bubbling Well Church* case – discusses the point.[39] As will be discussed, the IRS relies

---

[34] E.g., Manning Association v. Commissioner, 93 T.C. 596 (1989); Benjamin Price Genealogical Association v. United States, 79-1 U.S.T.C. ¶ 9361 (D.D.C. 1979); Callaway Family Association v. Commissioner, 71 T.C. 340 (1978) (nonprofit genealogical associations were held to be operating for the private interests of their members, with any educational benefits considered incidental).

[35] Priv. Ltr. Rul. 200830028 (April 28, 2008) (emphasis added).

[36] Priv. Ltr. Rul. 201221022 (March 1, 2012).

[37] Priv. Ltr. Rul. 201242014 (July 24, 2012).

[38] Priv. Ltr. Rul. 201332013 (May 17, 2013). The federal tax law does not mandate any such "safeguards."

[39] See the text accompanied by *infra* notes 94–102. The point is also referenced in Church of Ethereal Joy v. Commissioner, 83. T.C. 20 (1984), although *Church of Ethereal Joy* is essentially a repeat of *Bubbling Well Church*. See the text accompanied by *infra* notes 103–108.

heavily on the private benefit doctrine as justification for its ruling policy as to nonprofit governance.[40] One of the principal themes of this book is that the IRS, in its rulings as to nonprofit governance, almost always misconstrues the private benefit doctrine.[41]

Private Inurement Doctrine

The doctrine of private inurement is one of the most important sets of rules constituting the law of tax-exempt organizations. It is the fundamental defining principle of law distinguishing nonprofit organizations from for-profit organizations. This doctrine also is a statutory criterion for federal income tax exemption for nearly all categories of exempt organizations.

The oddly phrased and thoroughly antiquated language of the private inurement doctrine requires that the tax-exempt organization be organized and operated so that "no part of ... [its] net earnings ... inures to the benefit of any private shareholder or individual."[42] The contemporary meaning of this statutory language is barely reflected in its literal form and transcends the over-100-year formulation. What the doctrine means today is that none of the income or assets of an exempt organization subject to the doctrine may be permitted to directly or indirectly unduly benefit an individual or other person (including an entity) who has a close relationship with the organization, where he, she, or it is in a position to, or actually does, exercise a significant degree of control over the organization.

The case law teaches that the private inurement doctrine is broad and wide-ranging.[43] The rules concerning excess benefit transactions[44] have brought some exactitude to the doctrine.

---

[40] See Chapter 6.

[41] The private benefit doctrine is discussed in greater detail in Hopkins, *The Law of Tax-Exempt Organizations, Eleventh Edition* (John Wiley & Sons: Hoboken 2015) § 20.12.

[42] E.g., IRC § 501(c)(3).

[43] E.g., Variety Club Tent No. 6 Charities, Inc. v. Commissioner, 74 T.C.M. 1485, 1494 (1997).

[44] IRC § 4958.

Further, the rules as to self-dealing involving private foundations[45] continue to bring examples of private inurement transactions.

The doctrine of private inurement does not prohibit transactions or arrangements between a tax-exempt organization subject to the doctrine and those who have a close relationship with it. Thus, as is the case with the excess benefit transactions rules and generally the doctrine of private benefit,[46] the private inurement doctrine requires that these transactions be tested against a standard of reasonableness. This standard calls for an approximately equal exchange of benefits between the parties.

A potential private inurement transaction or arrangement is one that is between a tax-exempt organization that is subject to the doctrine and a person (or persons) who has a special, close relationship with the organization. To put a name to the latter, the federal tax law appropriated the term *insider* from the federal securities laws.[47] Generally, an *insider* is an individual who has a unique relationship with the exempt organization involved, by which that individual can cause application of the organization's funds or assets for the private benefit of the individual by reason of the individual's exercise of control or influence over, or being in a position to exercise that control or influence over, the organization.[48] Insiders include an organization's trustees, directors, officers, key employees, members of the family of these individuals, and entities controlled by them.[49]

The concept of the private inurement transaction has many manifestations. The most common instance of private inurement is excessive (or unreasonable) compensation. Whether an amount of compensation is reasonable is a question of fact. The basic standard, which has long been in the federal tax law, is that reasonable compensation is that amount as would ordinarily be paid for like

---

[45] IRC § 4941.

[46] See the text accompanied by *supra* notes 28–41.

[47] Sound Health Association v. Commissioner, 71 T.C. 158, 185 (1978).

[48] E.g., American Campaign Academy v. Commissioner, 92 T.C. 1053 (1989).

[49] In some contexts, these persons are termed *disqualified persons*.

services by like enterprises under like circumstances.[50] A multifactor test is usually used to determine reasonable compensation.[51]

The other principal forms of private inurement involve rental arrangements, lending arrangements, sales of assets, capital improvements, equity distributions, assumptions of liability, provision of employee benefits, a variety of tax avoidance schemes, the rendering of services, and business referral operations. Again, transactions and arrangements in these contexts are tested against the standard of reasonableness.

The IRS remains of the view that there is no such thing as incidental private inurement. The agency, however, may elect to apply the intermediate sanctions penalties against the insider rather than revoke tax-exempt status.[52] In that sense – private inurement that does not lead to loss of exemption – there can be incidental private inurement.

The sanction for violation of the private inurement doctrine is denial of recognition of, or revocation of, tax-exempt status. As is the case with the private benefit doctrine, this sanction is supposed to be invoked only when an act of private inurement occurs. But, just as it does with the private benefit doctrine, the IRS on occasion applies the private inurement doctrine in situations where there is merely a potential for private inurement. For example, the IRS ruled, in finding an organization ineligible for exemption, that it had "not demonstrated that there are sufficient safeguards in place to prevent [the organization's] net earnings from inuring to the benefit of" its two directors (insiders).[53]

Application Recognition Process

The IRS, generally supported by the courts, usually will refuse to recognize an organization as a tax-exempt entity unless the

---

[50] E.g., Reg.§ 1.162-7(b)(3).
[51] E.g., Miller & Son Drywall, Inc. v. Commissioner, 89 T.C. 1279 (2005)
[52] The criteria by which the IRS makes that determination are the subject of Reg. § 1.501(c)(3)-1(f).
[53] Priv. Ltr. Rul. 201332013 (May 17, 2013). See *supra* note 38.

organization tenders sufficient information regarding its operations and finances. For example, an organization submitted an application for recognition of exemption, stating its "long-range plan" to form a school; it was unable to substantively respond to any of the requests from the IRS for additional information. The IRS declined to recognize the organization as an exempt entity; a court agreed, holding that the entity "failed to supply such information as would enable a conclusion that when operational, if ever, ... [the organization] will conduct all of its activities in a manner which will accomplish its exempt purposes."[54] The court chided the entity for having only "vague generalizations" of its ostensibly planned activities and strongly suggested that the organization had "no plan to operate a school in the foreseeable future."[55]

Likewise, a court concluded that an organization failed to meet its burden of proof as to its eligibility for tax exemption because it did not provide a "meaningful explanation" of its activities to the IRS.[56] In another instance, a court concluded that an organization's failure to respond "completely or candidly" to many of the inquiries of the IRS precluded it from receiving a determination as to its exempt status. [57] In another case, exemption was said to be precluded because the organization involved "provided only generalizations and conclusory statements in response to repeated requests ... for more detail regarding its proposed activities."[58]

The IRS refuses to grant recognition of tax exemption when the application, in the agency's view, provides "only general information," lacks "sufficient detail," does not "fully describe" the organization's programs and other activities, and otherwise is "vague." [59] Matters can further decline when the information submitted to the IRS in response to follow-up queries is "contradictory."[60] In one instance, the IRS did not recognize exempt

---

[54] Pius XII Academy, Inc. v. Commissioner, 43 T.C.M. 634, 636 (1982).
[55] *Id.*
[56] Public Industries, Inc. v. Commissioner, 61 T.C.M 1626, 1629 (1991).
[57] National Association of American Churches v. Commissioner, 82 T.C. 18, 32 (1984).
[58] Ohio Disability Association v. Commissioner, 98 T.C.M. 462, 465 (2009).
[59] Priv. Ltr. Rul. 200536021 (November 15, 2004).
[60] E.g., Priv. Ltr. Rul. 200851033 (June 9, 2005).

status in connection with an organization that did not provide acceptable financial information; indeed, the agency asserted that the organization's budget estimates "do not appear to be grounded in reality."[61]

An organization is considered by the IRS to have made the requisite "threshold showing," however, where it describes its activities in "sufficient detail" to permit a conclusion that the entity will meet the pertinent requirements for exemption,[62] particularly where the organization answered all of the questions propounded by the IRS.[63] In another instance, a court observed that, although the law "requires that the organization establish reasonable standards and criteria for its operation as an exempt organization," that requirement does not entail "some sort of metaphysical proof of future events."[64]

Nonprofit Governance

Federal tax and other federal law is generally silent on the subject of nonprofit governance and its relationship to tax-exempt status.[65] There is no federal tax (or other) statute on the point, nor is there any tax regulation or revenue ruling addressing the topic.

Nonprofit governance has traditionally been the subject of state law, enforced principally by states' attorneys general and secondarily by states' secretaries of state. The statutory basis for much of this regulatory and enforcement authority is state charitable trust, limited liability company, and nonprofit corporation laws. The latter body of law usually addresses many nonprofit law governance issues, such as governing board size, board member terms, term limits, role of the board, officer positions and terms, indemnification, and dissolution.

---

[61] Priv. Ltr. Rul. 200535029 (September 25, 2008).

[62] Rev. Proc. 2017-5, 2017-1 I.R.B. 230.

[63] E.g., The Church of the Visible Intelligence That Governs the Universe v. United States, 83-2 U.S.T.C. ¶ 9726 (Ct. Cl. 1983).

[64] American Science Foundation v. Commissioner, 52 T.C.M. 1049, 1051 (1986).

[65] The six exceptions are summarized *infra* text accompanied by notes 66–83.

Other state statutes that may apply to nonprofit organizations include securities and antitrust laws, insurance laws (such as the regulation of charitable gift annuities), and investment standards (most likely, a state's version of the Uniform Prudent Management of Institutional Funds Act). Still other laws that will pertain to nonprofit organizations' practices include the state charitable solicitation acts, which regulate fundraising by charitable and similar organizations. These acts usually will require fundraising organizations to register in the jurisdiction before undertaking fundraising activities and file reports, impose similar requirements on professional fundraisers and professional solicitors, state terms that must be in fundraising contracts, entail a list of prohibited transactions, require disclosures to potential donors, and impose sanctions for failure to comply with these statutes.

Federal Tax Law as to Nonprofit Board Composition

The federal tax statutory and regulatory law has little to say about the composition and/or structure of the governing boards of tax-exempt organizations. However (as evidence that Congress, the Department of the Treasury, and the IRS know how to write formal rules concerning nonprofit governance), there are six instances where the tax law addresses the matter of these types of boards.

Federal Tax Statutory Law

The most detailed of these federal tax rules is a body of statutory law pertaining to the membership of nonprofit boards in circumstances where the organization is seeking to qualify as a tax-exempt credit counseling organization.[66] This type of entity must have, at all times, a governing board (1) that is controlled by

---

[66] IRC § 501(q). These entities may be tax-exempt by reason of IRC § 501(c)(3) or 501(c)(4).

individuals who represent the broad interests of the public, such as public officials acting in their capacities as such, individuals having special knowledge or expertise in credit or financial education, and community leaders; (2) not more than 20 percent of the voting power of which is vested in individuals who are employed by the organization or who will benefit financially, directly or indirectly, from the organization's activities (other than through the receipt of reasonable directors' fees or the repayment of consumer debt to creditors other than the credit counseling organization or its affiliates); and (3) not more than 49 percent of the voting power of which is vested in individuals who are employed by the organization or who will benefit financially, directly or indirectly, from the organization's activities (other than through the receipt of reasonable directors' fees).[67]

The second of these federal tax board composition laws provides that supporting organizations[68] may not be controlled, directly or indirectly, by one or more disqualified persons (other than its managers and supported organization(s)).[69] For this purpose, *disqualified persons* principally are substantial contributors to the organization,[70] owners of more than 20 percent of a business entity which is a substantial contributor, members of the family of an individual[71] in the foregoing categories, and business entities in which persons described in the foregoing categories own more than 35 percent of the combined voting power or profits or beneficial interest.[72]

Federal Tax Regulatory Law

As to federal tax regulatory law concerning nonprofit governance, one way for an organization to qualify as a donative-

---

[67] IRC § 501(q)(1)(D).
[68] That is, charitable organizations (IRC § 501(c)(3) entities) that have their public charity status based on IRC § 509(a)(3). See the text accompanied by *supra* note 26.
[69] IRC § 509(a)(3)(C).
[70] IRC § 507(d)(2).
[71] IRC § 4946(d).
[72] IRC § 4946(a)(1)

type publicly supported charity [73] is to satisfy a facts-and-circumstances test, [74] one of the elements of which is that the organization have a representative governing body (that is, a board that represents the broad interests of the public).[75]

Publicly supported charitable organizations [76] are required to receive, over a multiyear period, at least one-third of their financial support from various sources of "public" funding. The nature of qualifying support depends on the type of publicly supported organizations involved; the donative publicly supported charity or the service provider publicly supported charity. In either case, however, certain contributions and grants may be excluded from the computation of the public support ratio where the inclusion of them would cause loss of public charity status. These amounts are termed *unusual grants;* a grant or contribution is considered unusual if it is an unexpected and substantial gift attracted by the public nature of the organization and received from a disinterested party.[77] Whether a grant or contribution can be excluded depends on a variety of factors, one of which is whether the organization has a "representative governing body."[78] This type of governing body is one that is comprised of public officials or individuals chosen by public officials acting in their capacity as such; individuals having special knowledge in the particular field or discipline in which the organization is operating; community leaders, such as elected officials, members of the clergy, and educators; or, in the case of a membership organization, individuals elected pursuant to the organization's governing instrument or bylaws by a broadly based membership.[79] This characteristic does not exist if the membership of the organization's governing body is such as to indicate that it

---

[73] That is, an organization described in IRC § 170(b)(1)(A)(vi) and thus one of the ways to be described in IRC § 509(a)(1).

[74] Reg. § 1.170A-9(e)(3).

[75] Reg. § 1.170A-9(e)(3)(v).

[76] See the text accompanied by *supra* note 25.

[77] Reg. §§ 1.170A-9(f)(6)(ii)(A), 1.509(a)-3(c)(3).

[78] Reg. §§ 1.170A-9(f)(6)(iii), 1.509(a)-3(c)(4)(viii).

[79] Reg. § 1.509(a)-3(d)(3)(i).

represents the personal or private interests of disqualified persons,[80] rather than the interests of the community or the public.[81]

Tax-exempt health care institutions must meet a community benefit standard, which includes a requirement that they have governing boards that are representative of their communities.[82]

The sixth of these elements of law applies in the context of public interest law firms which, under certain circumstances, can qualify as tax-exempt charitable entities.[83] One of the requirements is that the firm has a governing board that is representative of the public and not controlled by the organization's employees.

The IRS has not published any revenue rulings that address the overall substance of nonprofit governance. The agency has, however, cited five revenue rulings in its private letter rulings it has been issuing on the subject of nonprofit governance.

IRS Revenue Rulings

The IRS ruled that an organization will not be "precluded from establishing an exempt status ... [under the federal tax law] merely because the creator of the organization (if a trust) is either the sole or controlling trustee or merely because the organization is controlled by one individual."[84]

One of these revenue rulings concerned the issue as to whether an association composed of professional private duty nurses and practical nurses, where the organization's primary activity was operation of a nurses' registry to afford greater employment opportunities for its members, was eligible for tax-exempt status as a charitable entity. The IRS ruled that the organization was precluded from exemption by reason of the private benefit doctrine, in that it was providing personal employment services principally for the

---

[80] See the text accompanied by *supra* note 49.
[81] Reg. § 1.509(a)-3(d)(3)(i).
[82] Rev. Rul. 69-545, 1969-2 C.B. 117.
[83] Rev. Proc. 92-59, 1992-2 C.B. 411.
[84] Rev. Rul. 66-219, 1966-2 C.B. 208.

benefit of its members.[85] The IRS stated: "Public participation in the management and support of [this] organization is negligible. This is shown by the fact that it draws its support primarily from members and is controlled by a board of trustees composed of professional nurses, without public participation of any kind."

The IRS contrasted this "professional society" with a "community nursing bureau," which maintained a register of qualified nursing personnel for the benefit of hospitals, health agencies, and physicians. It was primarily financially supported by grants from various community organizations and contributions from the public. It was controlled by a board of directors drawn principally from public health and welfare organizations and the public at large. Following a survey of this entity's programs, the IRS stated that "it is apparent that the purposes and activities of [this] organization are directed to the relief of conditions relating to the health of the community, which is a matter of public concern." This organization was recognized as a tax-exempt charitable entity.[86]

The IRS ruled that a nonprofit organization formed to help reduce personal bankruptcy by informing the public on personal money management and aiding low-income individuals and families with financial problems is tax-exempt as a charitable and educational entity.[87] This organization's program of providing counseling without charge and a means for the orderly discharge of indebtedness to be charitable because it was relieving the poor and distressed. Also, by providing the public with information on budgeting, buying practices, and the sound use of consumer credit, the organization was said to be instructing the public on subjects useful to the individual and beneficial to the community. In the facts of this ruling, it was stated that the entity's board of directors was comprised of "representatives from religious organizations, civic groups, labor unions, business groups, and educational institutions."

The IRS ruled that a tax-exempt public charity that enters into a joint venture (such as by means of a limited liability company) with a for-profit company, under circumstances by which the charity cedes

---

[85] Rev. Rul. 61-170, 1961-2 C.B. 112.
[86] Rev. Rul. 55-656, 1955-2 C.B. 262.
[87] Rev. Rul. 69-441, 1969-2 C.B. 115.

control of its operations to the company (such as by being in a minority position on the venture's board of directors), the charity will lose its exempt status by application of the private benefit doctrine.[88]

Commentary on Revenue Rulings

The IRS stated in one of its revenue rulings, as noted, that an organization will not be precluded from tax exemption "merely because the organization is controlled by one individual." This statement, however, is inconsistent with the agency's private letter ruling position[89] and its litigating position.[90] This revenue ruling is never cited in either of these contexts.

The revenue ruling concerning denial of tax exemption in the case of a professional association operating a nurses' registry is surely correct as to its conclusion. These associations are typically business leagues and are usually tax-exempt.[91] The ruling makes much of the fact that the association "draws support primarily from its members" and is "controlled by a board of trustees composed of professional nurses." But those are inherent characteristics of tax-exempt business leagues.[92] The ruling states that "[p]ublic participation in the management and support off the organization is negligible." But this is true of exempt business leagues in general; there is no requirement in the federal tax law that there be "public participation" in their governance.[93] The same is true for public charities; that statement is in the ruling as an element of fact concerning the particular organization involved – it is not a general requirement for exemption as a charitable entity.

The same is true for the revenue ruling that observed that the organization involved is "controlled by a board of directors drawn

---

[88] Rev. Rul. 98-15, 1998-1 C.B. 718.
[89] See Chapter 6, text accompanied by notes 38–44.
[90] See the text accompanied by *infra* notes 109–111.
[91] IRC § 501(a) as organizations described in IRC § 501(c)(6).
[92] Indeed, current IRS ruling policy is to deny recognition of exemption to business leagues where significant membership involvement and support is lacking (e.g., Priv. Ltr. Rul. 201349021 (July 2, 2013)).
[93] See Chapter 7, note 129.

principally from public health and welfare organizations and the public at large." That is merely a fact statement pertaining to the particular organization involved. It is not a requirement for tax exemption.

Federal Tax Case Law on Governance

Merely four federal tax cases concern matters of nonprofit governance, all initially litigated in the US Tax Court.

Bubbling Well Church Opinion

In the principal case on point, a nonprofit corporation sought recognition by the IRS of tax exemption and classification as a church. [94] The entity's governing instruments stated that the corporation has two classes of members. The first of these classes were the voting members, which consisted of the members of the entity's board of directors. The second class (of non-voting members), termed associate members, were individuals who made contributions to the organization. The members of the board of directors consisted of three individuals, all members of the same family. As the trial court stated the matter, this family "thus completely controlled [the organization's] operations and were in a position, as the only voting members, to perpetuate that control."[95]

This organization was not forthcoming in providing factual information as to its eligibility for tax exemption to the IRS, which ultimately ruled that the entity was organized and operated for private benefit, and thus was not exempt. Because of the organization's lack of candor, the court construed most of the facts

---

[94] Bubbling Well Church of Universal Love, Inc. v. Commissioner, 74 T.C. 531 (1980), *aff'd*, 670 F.2d 104 (9th Cir. 1981). Despite its age, *Bubbling Well* Church derives much of its potency from the fact that it is the most-frequently cited opinion by the IRS in support of its position as to application of the private benefit doctrine in the nonprofit governance context. See Chapter 6.

[95] Bubbling Well Church of Universal Love, Inc. v. Commissioner, 74 T.C. 531, 532 (1980).

against it, applying the rule that a failure to disclose gives rise to a logical inference that the facts, if disclosed, would show that the organization did not meet the requirements for exemption. The court held that the entity failed to show that it "was not operated for the private benefit of the ... family."[96]

The court wrote that this family "was not subject to any outside interference or influence in the control of [its] affairs," so that the family, "without challenge, could dictate [the organization's] program and operation, prepare its budget, and spend its funds, and could continue to do so indefinitely."[97]

The court also stated that, "[w]hile this domination of [the entity] by the three [family members], alone may not necessarily disqualify it for exemption, it provides an obvious opportunity for abuse of the claimed tax-exempt status."[98] The court added: These circumstances call for "open and candid disclosure of all facts bearing upon [the entity's] organization, operations, and finances so that the Court, should it uphold the claimed exemption, can be assured that it is not sanctioning an abuse of the revenue laws."[99]

The trial court held that this organization "has not shown that no part of its net earnings inure[s] to the benefit of [this] family or that [the organization] was not operated for the private benefit of" the family.[100]

A court of appeals essentially reiterated this lower court's findings. The appellate court stated that the organization "failed to show that no part of its net income inured to the benefit of private individuals."[101] The court of appeals added that it "agree[d] with the [lower court] that the potential for abuse created by the [family's]

---

[96] *Id.* at 539.

[97] *Id.* at 535

[98] *Id.*

[99] *Id.* This "open and candid disclosure" rule is repeated in the *Ohio Disability Association* opinion (discussed in the text accompanied by *infra* notes 306–308; 98 T.C.M. at 466). It is also recited, without amplification, in Basic Unit Ministry of Alma Karl Schurig v. Commissioner, 511 F. Supp. 166, 168 (D.D.C. 1981), *aff'd*, 670 F.2d 120 (D.C. Cir. 1982).

[100] Bubbling Well Church of Universal Love, Inc. v. Commissioner, 74 T.C. 531, 539 (1980).

[101] Bubbling Well Church of Universal Love, Inc. v. Commissioner, 670 F.2d 104, 105 (9th Cir. 1981).

control of the church required open and candid disclosure of facts bearing on the exemption application."[102]

Church of Ethereal Joy Opinion

Another nonprofit organization sought recognition by the IRS of tax exemption and classification as a church.[103] As with the *Bubbling Well Church* case, the emphasis by the court was on the nonprofit organization's inability to meet its burden of proof that it is organized and operated for exempt (here, religious) purposes and that it is not operating for private interests. The court agreed with the IRS that this burden was not met, with the court writing that the entity "has written many words to the Internal Revenue Service in its efforts to obtain tax-exempt status but, as far as we can tell from those words, [the organization] has done little, if anything, else."[104]

This organization had a three-individual board of directors. The court observed that they "have complete control of all of [this organization's] operations, whatever those operations may turn out to be."[105] It added: "They are a small self-perpetuating group who could, without challenge, dictate [the entity's] programs and operations, prepare its budget, and spend its funds. And they could continue to do so indefinitely."[106]

The court stated that, "[a]though control by such a small group may not necessarily disqualify it for exemption," it cited *Bubbling Well Church* for the point that "it [this board structure] provides an obvious opportunity for abuse of the claimed tax-exempt status."[107] Ruling that this organization did not qualify for tax exemption, the court was "not convinced that [the entity] would not abuse its exempt status if such were granted."[108]

---

[102] *Id.*
[103] Church of Ethereal Joy v. Commissioner, 83 T.C. 20 (1984).
[104] *Id.* at 22.
[105] *Id.* at 23.
[106] *Id.*
[107] *Id.* (internal quotes omitted).
[108] *Id.*

Ohio Disability Association Opinion

Another relevant court opinion involved a nonprofit corporation with one individual who was the sole director (permitted under applicable state law), the only officer, and its single corporate member; in this instance, the IRS denied recognition of exemption principally by reason of application of the doctrine of private inurement.[109]

The court held that this organization did not sufficiently describe its proposed activities to the IRS, and that the record did not permit the court to conclude that the organization will operate exclusively for exempt purposes and that there will not be private inurement. It noted that the IRS asked the organization to "modify the board of directors to include unrelated individuals selected from the community the corporation will serve";[110] this request was refused. The court wrote that the sole director was "vested with all of the decision-making power within [the] organization," "there are no procedures or personnel in place to ensure that either the [organization's conflict-of-interest] policy will be followed or private inurement will not occur," and the "record does not demonstrate that there is oversight to prevent the organization from being operated to benefit" the sole director.[111]

Council for Education Opinion

In the fourth of these cases, the court held that a nonprofit corporation formed to "investigate academic fraud" was ineligible for tax-exempt status because of failure to prove that it is engaging in charitable activities and because of operations that further its founder's private interests.[112]

The founder of this organization, and also its president, secretary, and sole director and employee, was a student at the University of California at Santa Barbara. He became a vocal critic

---

[109] Ohio Disability Association v. Commissioner, 98 T.C.M. 462 (2009).
[110] *Id.* at 464.
[111] *Id.* at 466–467.
[112] The Council for Education v. Commissioner, 106 T.C.M. 669 (2013).

of the university system and UCSB specifically. Over a nine-year period, he filed a large number of administrative complaints and lawsuits charging academic fraud, civil rights violations, extortion, violations of the Racketeer Influenced and Corrupt Organizations Act, and more. None of these efforts were successful; he was declared by a court to be a "vexatious litigant."[113] This nonprofit organization was formed in the aftermath of these activities. One of its first activities was initiation of a lawsuit similar to one filed by its founder personally. The IRS repeatedly sought information during the processing of the application for recognition of exemption; the organization was not forthcoming in its answers. The IRS eventually denied recognition of exemption in the case.

The court reviewed the organization's proposed activities, which include investigation of state-administered student loan programs and commissioning a report on institutional misconduct. The court stated that "we cannot say on the basis of this record that [the organization] has been or will be operated in a manner that will further a charitable purpose." [114] It also observed that the organization was "less than open and candid"[115] in responding to the IRS and that "[w]e also would be hard pressed to say that [the organization's] operations do not more than incidentally further [the founder's] private interests."[116]

The court was critical of the organization's governance structure. It initially correctly stated the applicable standard: "[W]here an individual creates and controls the affairs of an organization seeking tax-exempt status, there is an obvious opportunity for abuse, which necessitates an open and candid disclosure of all facts bearing upon the organization and its operations and finances so that the Court can be assured that by granting the claimed exemption it is not sanctioning an abuse of the revenue laws."[117] As noted, the court found that this organization failed the *open-and-candid* test.

---

[113] *Id.* at 675.
[114] *Id.* at 676.
[115] *Id.* at 675.
[116] *Id.* at 676.
[117] *Id.* at 675. See the text accompanied by *supra* note 99.

The court wrote that the organization "has not adopted an operating structure or procedures necessary to ensure that its activities are properly focused to further its alleged charitable purpose."[118] It added that "prominent" among these "shortcomings" are the "lack of a formal business plan and an independent board of directors to provide operational guidance and oversight."[119] Moreover, the court concluded that it is "not persuaded that [the founder, who is not a lawyer] has demonstrated the legal skills or business acumen needed to conduct [the organization's] operations to achieve its charitable purpose or to further the public good."[120]

The other cases cited by the IRS in support of its position are either instances where private benefit transactions occurred[121] (none involving board composition), private inurement transactions took place,[122] or the commerciality doctrine was applied (which is not relevant to the subject of nonprofit governance).[123]

Although the holding of the court is outside the scope of the subject of nonprofit governance, the facts stated in two court opinions reflect the practice of some IRS agents to demand (and obtain) changes in the board composition of nonprofit organizations and/or adoption of one or more governance policies or procedures as a condition of obtaining recognition of tax exemption.[124]

---

[118] The Council for Education v. Commissioner, 106 T.C.M. 675 (2013).

[119] *Id.*

[120] *Id.*

[121] E.g., Miss Georgia Scholarship Fund, Inc. v. Commissioner, 72 T.C. 267 (1979).

[122] E.g., Founding Church of Scientology v. United States, 412 F.2d 1197 (Ct. Cl. 1969), *cert. den.*, 397 U.S. 1009 (1970).

[123] E.g., Living Faith, Inc. v. Commissioner, 950 F.2d 365 (7th Cir. 1991), *aff'g*, 60 T.C.M. 710 (1990).

[124] George v. Commissioner, 110 T.C.M. 190 (2015); Exploratory Research, Inc. v. Commissioner, 95 T.C.M. 1347 (2008).

Commentary on Case Law

Clearly, the *Bubbling Well Church* decision is the most important federal nonprofit governance case in the tax law context.[125] The organization failed to achieve recognition of tax exemption because it was unable to convince the Tax Court and the Ninth Circuit that it was not operated for the private benefit of one family. Thus, this is a burden-of-proof case, with the applicant organization unable to meet the requisite evidentiary standard.

The import of this decision, however, is that domination of a public charity by a family does not necessarily disqualify it from tax exemption. Rather, this type of fact situation calls for a higher level of scrutiny, requiring an organization to be "open and candid," to be certain there is no abuse of the federal tax laws. This decision is by no means authority for the proposition that the existence of a small board and/or a related board of a charitable organization is automatically an indicator of private inurement or private benefit. This decision is marred, nonetheless, for its observation that this family was "not subject to any outside interference or influence in the control of [the organization's] affairs."[126] This "outside interference or influence" element is not part of the federal tax law; it never has been.

The *Church of Ethereal Joy* case essentially is a repeat of the elements in the *Bubbling Well Church* case. This time around, however, the court was unduly critical of the structure. Three-individual board are common; they are authorized by the nonprofit corporation laws in most of the states. The court was critical of such a board, writing that the board had "complete control of all of [the organization's] operations."[127] But that is almost always true. The court was also critical of the fact that the board was self-

---

[125] Overall, the most significant federal nonprofit governance case is California Independent System Operator Corporation v. Federal Energy Regulatory Commission, 372 F.3d 395 (D.C. Cir. 2004), discussed in Chapter 7, text accompanied by notes 39–95.

[126] Bubbling Well Church of Universal Love, Inc. v. Commissioner, 74 T.C. 531, 535 (1980). The court did not provide any authority for this position.

[127] Church of Ethereal Joy v. Commissioner, 83 T.C. 20, 23 (1984).

perpetuating; this too is commonplace. It stated that this board could "dictate [the entity's] program ms and operations, prepare its budget, and spend its funds."[128] Yet this is what boards of charities and other tax-exempt organizations are supposed to do.[129] The court went a bit further in this case than it did in *Bubbling Well Church*, stating that it was "not convinced that [the organization] would not abuse its exempt status if such were granted."[130] The assessment by the court was colored by its finding that the organization had a relationship with the Universal Life Church, which caused the courts to "have been presented with numerous cases in which the Internal Revenue Service has disallowed purported charitable deductions by individuals to the local organizations spawned by the mail-order activities" of the ULC.[131]

The organization in the *Ohio Disability Association* case was unsuccessful in securing recognition of exemption largely because it insufficiently described its activities to the IRS and the disclosures it made demonstrated it was not being operated for charitable purposes. The Tax Court was incorrect in again writing that there must be outside "oversight" of the operations of an exempt charitable organization.[132] The court was obviously troubled by the fact that this organization has only one director, even though that is permissible under state law. The IRS and the Tax Court lack the authority to preempt state law in this regard.

The court was uncomfortable with the fact that this individual "is vested with all of the decision-making power within [the] organization."[133] But that is usually the case, irrespective of the size of the governing board. The court emphasized that "there are no procedures or personnel in place to ensure that the stated [conflict-of-interest] policy will be followed or private inurement will not occur."[134] However, as a matter of law, a conflict-of-interest policy is

---

[128] *Id.*
[129] See the various statements of board responsibilities and duties in Chapter 4.
[130] Church of Ethereal Joy v. Commissioner, 83 T.C. 20, 23 (1984).
[131] *Id.* at 26.
[132] Ohio Disability Association v. Commissioner, 98 T.C.M. 462, 467 (2009). Again, no authority was cited in support of this assertion.
[133] *Id.* at 466–467.
[134] *Id.* at 467.

not required to begin with, let alone any procedures to ensure that the policy will be followed. Likewise, there is no requirement for procedures to ensure that private inurement will not occur. Indeed, there is no legal requirement for any "personnel." Other than citing to the *Bubbling Well Church* standard for "open and candid disclosure," there is no authority referenced for any of these propositions. This, unfortunately, is a situation where the special trial judge simply invented governance requirements that cannot be buttressed by any statutory or administrative law.

The IRS, of course, is quite fond of the *Ohio Disability Association* opinion. In private letter rulings, the agency makes much of the fact that, in this case, one individual served as the organization's "sole director, officer, employee, and member."[135] Thus, the IRS intones, this individual "was vested with all of the organization's decision making power." The IRS states that "there were no procedures in place to enforce the [organization's] conflict of interest policy, and there were no personnel in place to ensure that private inurement would not occur."[136] The IRS quotes the court when it wrote that the "record d[id] not demonstrate that there [was] oversight to prevent the organization from being operated to benefit" its sole member.[137] The IRS concludes its analysis of the case by solemnly declaring that the agency "denied [recognition of] exemption to the organization based on these factors,"[138] as well as the organization's failure to adequately respond to requests by the agency for additional information.[139]

The *Council for Education* case also largely involved an organization that did not adequately describe its program and other activities to the IRS, and engaged in noncharitable activities. This opinion is the most distressing of these three Tax Court opinions, in

---

[135] In this context, there is no mention of the revenue ruling discussed in the text accompanied by *supra* note 84.

[136] The IRS does not mention that there is no requirement in law for such "procedures" or "personnel"; presumably, the agency's top officials know this, although they can now cite this case for authority for these "requirements."

[137] Ohio Disability Association v. Commissioner, 98 T.C.M. 462, 467 (2009).

[138] These quotes by the IRS are taken from Priv. Ltr. Rul. 201332013 (May 17, 2013).

[139] As to this basis for denial of recognition of exemption, see the text accompanied by *supra* notes 54–64.

terms of inaccuracy and lack of support in the law. The court found two "shortcomings" in the organization's "operating structure or procedures": lack of an "independent board of directors to provide operational guidance and oversight" and lack of a "formal business plan."[140] The "requirement" of an "independent" board of directors and a "business plan" is not part of the federal tax law and it never has been.[141] Also, there is no precedent or authority enabling the IRS or a court to pass judgment on the competence of an individual to be a director of a public charity, once state law requirements as to qualification for the position are satisfied.

Consequently, the federal tax case law concerning nonprofit governance is rather skimpy and troublesome. The *Bubbling Well Church* opinion is often misunderstood and too frequently misconstrued by the IRS. It states a correct principle of law but has been distorted by the IRS to mean nearly the opposite of what the court stated. The *Ohio Disability Association* and *Council for Education* opinions, while they admittedly presented the Tax Court with legitimate concerns, are filled with governance "requirements" that have been conjured by the judges from (apparently) their personal beliefs as to what the law ought to be and that in fact have no basis in statutory or regulatory law.

---

[140] *Id.*

[141] The only authority cited by the special trial judge for these ostensible "shortcomings" is P.L.L. Scholarship Fund v. Commissioner, 82 T.C. 196 (1984), which it was said, "discuss[es] the importance of an independent board of directors" (*Council for Education* at 675). In fact, that opinion does no such thing; there is not even a reference to an "independent" board in the opinion or to the "importance" of one. All that was found in *Scholarship Fund* was, in one sentence (rather than a "discussion"), that the *activities* of a nonprofit corporation and a for-profit company "were so interrelated as to be functionally inseparable" (at 200).

4

Nonprofit Organizations' Governance Standards

> The number of standards-setting watchdog agencies has "proliferated" and each of them has its "own approach and mission."
>
> *George Wilhelm*

Regulators, lawmakers, and other policymakers at the federal and state level are intensely focusing on the subject of the principles of governance of nonprofit, tax-exempt organizations, with an emphasis on public charities.

Governance Philosophy in General

In some quarters, the philosophy underlying the concept of governance of nonprofit organizations is changing. The traditional roles of the nonprofit board have been oversight of the organization's operations and policy determination; historically, the implementation of policy and management have been, the responsibilities of the officers and key employees. An emerging view, sometimes referred to as best practices, imposes on the members of nonprofit boards greater responsibilities and functions (and thus potentially greater liability), intended to immerse the board more deeply in management. This new view is nicely reflected in the characterization of the nonprofit board in the American National Red Cross Governance Modernization Act: the "governance and strategic oversight board."[1]

---

[1] See the text accompanied by *infra* notes 18, 19.

The origins of this shift of view regarding the appropriate role of the governing board of a nonprofit organization are difficult to find. There has been the occasional scandal in the nonprofit management context, such as that involving the United Way of America;[2] these scandals in the nonprofit realm have increased somewhat in recent years, due in large part to greater focus by the media on charitable organizations and the various investigations conducted by the staff of the Senate Finance Committee.[3] These incidents alone, however, do not account for the contemporary magnitude of interest in nonprofit organization governance. Certainly, a major factor contributing to this phenomenon is the raft of recent scandals in the for-profit sector and the resulting enactment of the Sarbanes-Oxley Act, which has had an enormous impact on the evolution, over the past few years, of nonprofit organization governance principles and practices.

Sarbanes-Oxley Act

Historic federal accounting reform and for-profit corporate responsibility legislation – the Sarbanes-Oxley Act – was signed into law in 2002.[4] This measure is focused on publicly traded companies and large accounting firms. The emergence of this law; however; raises a number of questions for nonprofit organizations as to the applicability of the Act's principles to them; the leadership of these organizations often voluntarily adopts many of its precepts.

This body of law does not apply to nonprofit organizations (other than protection of whistleblowers and the criminal law rule concerning destruction of evidence). Nonetheless, Sarbanes-Oxley standards for corporate governance parallel in many ways the fiduciary principles

---

[2] E.g., Glaser, *The United Way Scandal: An Insider's Account of What Went Wrong and Why* (New York: John Wiley & Sons, 1994).

[3] Entities that have been and are the subject of these inquiries include the American National Red Cross, American University, the Nature Conservancy, the Smithsonian Institution, and the Statue of Liberty Foundation, along with, in general, tax-exempt hospitals, colleges, and universities (particularly as to student athletics and use of endowment funds) and evangelical church ministries.

[4] Public Law No. 107-204, 116 Stat. 745 (2002).

applicable to exempt organizations. The Act has had much to do with the nonprofit organizations' focus on matters such as audit committees and various policies, particularly conflict-of-interest, document retention and destruction, and whistleblower policies.

Watchdog Agencies' Standards

Charitable organizations, particularly those that are engaged in fundraising, often become subject to standards set and enforced by one or more watchdog agencies. These agencies, while not promulgators of law, can have a powerful impact on the public perception of a charitable organization and its ability to successfully generate gifts and grants. Indeed, watchdog agencies have long been in the forefront of standards setting for nonprofit organizations.

What follows is an inventory of the principle sets of good governance standards designed particularly for public charities and other types of tax-exempt organizations.

Philanthropic Advisory Service Standards

The Philanthropic Advisory Service was the division of the Council of Better Business Bureaus that monitored and reported on charitable organizations that solicit nationwide, contributions, and grants. The primary goal of the division, which began substantive operations in 1971, was to promote ethical standards of business practices and protect consumers through self-regulation and monitoring activities. The PAS standards, which have been superseded by the Wise Giving Affiance standards (summarized below), are recounted here because of their historical significance as being the first of the efforts to disseminate and enforce a set of nonprofit governance principles.

The PAS evaluated charitable organizations according to the "CBBB Standards for Charitable Solicitations." These standards covered five basic areas: public accountability, use of funds, solicitations and informational materials, fundraising practices, and governance.

Public Accountability

The PAS required that a charity provide, on request, an annual report that included various items of information about the charity's purposes, current activities, governance, and finances. Additionally, a charity was required to provide on request a complete annual financial statement, including an accounting of all income and fundraising costs of controlled or affiliated entities.

A charity also was required to "present adequate information [in financial statements] to serve as a basis for informed decisions." According to the PAS, information needed as a basis for informed decisions included items such as significant categories of contributions or other income, expenses reported in categories corresponding to major programs and activities, a detailed description of expenses by "natural classification" (e.g., salaries, employee benefits, and postage), accurate presentation of fundraising and administrative costs, the total cost of multipurpose activities, and the method used for allocating costs among the activities.

Organizations that receive a substantial portion of their income as the result of fundraising activities of controlled or affiliated entities were required to provide, on request, an accounting of all income received by and fundraising costs incurred by these entities.

Use of Funds

The PAS required that a charity spend a "reasonable percentage" of total income on programs, as well as a "reasonable percentage" of contributions on activities that are in accordance with donor expectations. In this context, PAS defined a "reasonable percentage" to mean "at least" 50 percent. Charities were also expected to ensure that their fundraising costs were "reasonable." In this context, fundraising costs were reasonable if those costs did "not exceed" 35 percent of related contributions. In the area of total fundraising and administrative costs, the PAS standards also provided that these costs be "reasonable." In this latter context, these costs were reasonable if they did "not exceed" 50 percent of total income. A charity was expected to establish and exercise "adequate controls" over its disbursements.

Soliciting organizations were to substantiate, on request, their application of funds, in accordance with donor expectations, to the programs and other activities described in solicitations.

Solicitations and Informational Materials

The PAS standards required that the solicitation and informational materials be "accurate, truthful and not misleading, both in whole or in part." These terms were not defined. Solicitation materials also were required to include a "clear description" of the program and other activities for which funds were requested. Solicitations that described an issue, problem, need, or event but did not clearly describe the programs or other activities for which funds were requested did not meet the standard for accuracy and truthfulness.

Direct contact solicitations (including telephone appeals) were required to identify the solicitor and his or her relationship to the benefiting organization, the benefiting organization or cause, and the programs or other activities for which funds were requested. Solicitations in conjunction with the sale of goods, services, or admissions had to identify, among other things, the "actual or anticipated portion" of the sales or admission price that would benefit the charitable organization or cause.

Fundraising Practices

The PAS standards for fundraising practices provided that soliciting organizations must "establish and exercise controls" over fundraising activities by their officers, employees, volunteers, consultants, and contractors, including the use of written contracts and agreements. Organizations were required to establish and exercise "adequate controls' over the contributions they received. Donor requests for confidentiality were to be honored, including requests that a donor's name not be exchanged, rented, or sold. Fundraising was to be conducted "without excessive pressure";

examples of this type of pressure included solicitations in the guise of invoices, harassment, intimidation, coercion, threats of public disclosure or economic retaliation, and "strongly emotional appeals which distort the organization's activities or beneficiaries."

Governance

The PAS standards required three elements of governance. First, an "adequate governing structure" was required. This meant that the governing instruments must set forth the organization's goals and purposes, define the organization's structure, and identify the body having authority over policies and programs (including the authority to amend the governing instruments). A governing structure was considered inadequate if any policymaking decisions of the governing body or executive committee were made by "fewer than three persons."

Second, there had to be an "active governing body." To meet this standard, the governing body was required, among other things, to meet formally "at least three times annually, with meetings evenly spaced over the course of the year, and with a majority of the members in attendance (in person or by proxy) on average." If the full board met only once annually, there had to be at least two additional, evenly spaced executive committee meetings during the year.

Third, adequate governance required that there be an "independent governing body." Organizations did not meet this standard if "directly and/or indirectly compensated board members constitute more than one-fifth (20%) of the total voting membership of the board or of the executive committee." (The ordained clergy of a "publicly soliciting church," however, were excepted from this 20 percent limitation.) Organizations failed to meet this third standard if board members had material conflicting interests resulting from any relationship or business affiliation.

Better Business Bureau Wise Giving Alliance Standards

The BBB (Better Business Bureau) Wise Giving Alliance was formed in 2001, the product of the merger of the National Charities Information Bureau (another early watchdog agency) into the CBBB Foundation and the PAS. The Alliance is affiliated with the CBBB.

According to its website, the Alliance "collects and distributes information on hundreds of nonprofit organizations that solicit [contributions] nationally or have national or international program services." It "routinely asks such organizations for information about their programs, governance, fund raising practices, and finances when the charities have been the subject of inquiries." The Alliance "selects charities for evaluation based on the volume of donor inquiries about individual organizations." The organization serves "donors' information needs" and helps donors "make their own decisions regarding charitable giving."

The Alliance developed its "Standards for Charity Accountability" to "assist donors in making sound giving decisions and to foster public confidence in charitable organizations." One of the purposes of these standards is to "promote ethical conduct" by charitable organizations. The BBB states that these standards are "voluntary."

Governance and Oversight

These standards state that the governing board "has the ultimate oversight authority for any charitable organization." The standards seek to ensure that the "volunteer board is active, independent and free of self-dealing." A board must provide "adequate oversight of the charity's operations and staff." This type of oversight is indicated by factors such as "regularly scheduled appraisals of the CEO's performance, evidence of disbursement controls such as board approval of the budget, fund raising practices, establishment of a conflict of interest policy, and establishment of accounting procedures sufficient to safeguard charity finances."

A board is to be comprised of a "minimum of five voting members." There is to be a "minimum of three evenly spaced meetings per year of the full governing body with a majority in attendance, with face-to-face participation," although this standard is immediately somewhat tempered with the observation that a "conference call of the full board can substitute for one of the[se] three meetings."

The standards provide that no more than one or 10 percent (whichever is greater) "directly or indirectly compensated person(s) [may] serv[e] as voting member(s) of the board." Further, "[c]ompensated members shall not serve as the board's chair or treasurer." The standards forbid "transaction(s) in which any board or staff members have material conflicting interests with the charity resulting from any relationship or business affiliation." Factors that are considered in determining whether a transaction entails a conflict of interest and if so whether the conflict is material include "any arm's length procedures established by the charity; the size of the transaction relative to like expenses of the charity; whether the interested party participated in the board vote on the transaction; if competitive bids were sought[;] and whether the transaction is onetime, recurring or ongoing."

Measuring Effectiveness

The standards provide that an organization "should regularly assess its effectiveness in achieving its mission." An organization should have "defined, measurable goals and objectives in place and a defined process in place to evaluate the success and impact of its program(s) in fulfilling the goals and objectives of the organization" and a process that "identifies ways to address any deficiencies."

An organization should "[h]ave a board policy of assessing, no less than every two years, the organization's performance and effectiveness and of determining future actions required to achieve the mission." There should be a submission to the board, "for its approval, a written report that outlines the results of the aforementioned performance and effectiveness assessment and recommendations for future actions."

Finances

These standards require that an organization "[s]pend at least 65% of its total expenses on program activities," "[s]pend no more than 35% of related contributions on fund raising," avoid unwarranted accumulation of funds, disclose the organization's annual financial statements, and have a board-approved annual, budget.

Fundraising and Informational Materials

The Alliance standards require that an organization's solicitation and other informational materials be "accurate, truthful, and not misleading"; that an organization prepare an annual report that is available to the public; that an organization post its annual information returns on its website; that the charity disclose how it benefits from a cause-related marketing campaign; and that an organization promptly respond to an inquiry from the BBB.[5]

Evangelical Council for Financial Accountability Standards

Religious organizations have established watchdog agencies that focus only on religious entities. Among them is the Evangelical Council for Financial Accountability, which states that it is an "accreditation agency dedicated to helping Christian ministries earn the public's trust through adherence to seven Standards of Responsible Stewardship." The ECFA states that these standards, "drawn from Scripture, are fundamental to operating with integrity." In addition to these standards, the ECFA developed a series of best practices that are intended to "encourage [its] members to strive for the highest levels of excellence." Founded in 1979, the ECFA states that its constituency comprises more than 2,000 evangelical Christian

---

[5] Of all the watchdog agency standards, the Alliance's standards are the only ones that make failure to comply with an agency inquiry itself a violation of the standards.

organizations. An organization that cannot comply with one or more of the standards is ineligible for membership in the ECFA.[6]

Use of Resources

Every member of the ECFA must "exercise the management and financial controls necessary to provide reasonable assurance that all resources are used (nationally and internationally) in conformity with applicable federal and state laws and regulations to accomplish the exempt purposes for which they are intended." According to one of the best practices, a member organization should ensure, "by collaborating with the board and the CEO, Executive Director, or President (or similar position), that the organization has a clear financial plan that is aligned with strategic, operating, and development plans."

Board of Directors

A "responsible" board must, according to the ECFA standards, govern member organizations. These boards must have at least five individuals, a majority of whom must be "independent."[7] The board must meet at least semiannually to "establish policy and review its accomplishments." The board, or a committee consisting of a majority of independent members, must "review the annual financial statements and maintain direct communication between the board and the independent certified public accountants."

The ECFA best practices guidelines as to board members include the following:

---

[6] This information about the ECFA is based on material on its website. These standards are titled "Standards and Best Practices."

[7] The ECFA standards do not define the word *independent*; in its best practices, "independent-minded" board members are referenced as "those with the ability to place the organization's interests first, apart from the interests of the staff and other board members."

- Board members should "annually pledge to carry out in a trustworthy and diligent manner their duties and obligations as a board member."
- The board "should understand the organization's financial health."
- In "linking budgeting to strategic planning," the board "should approve the annual budget and key financial transactions, such as major asset acquisitions, that can be realistically financed with existing or attainable resources."
- Board time "should be spent on governance, not on management issues."
- The board should "utilize a committee, whose members have financial expertise, totally comprised of independent members to annually review the financial statements."
- This committee should "[c]onduct at least a portion of the committee meeting to review the financial statements with the accounting firm in the absence of staff"; if the board "handles the financial review function, staff should be recused from a portion of the meeting with the representative(s) from the accounting firm."
- The board should "[r]equest the periodic rotation of the lead or review partners, if this is feasible for the accounting firm."
- The board should obtain "competitive fee quotes every few years." If, however, the accountants are "independent, providing quality service at competitive fees, it is generally wise to continue with the current accounting firm."
- The board should "[a]pprove and document annually and in advance the compensation and fringe benefits of the CEO, Executive Director, or President (or similar position) unless there is a multi-year contract in force and there is no change in the compensation and fringe benefits except for an inflation or cost-of-living adjustment."
- The board should "[a]nnually and formally evaluate the CEO, Executive Director, or President (or similar position)."
- The board should "[r]outinely compare board actions and corporate bylaws."
- The board should "[p]eriodically review organizational and governing documents."

- If the organization files an annual information return (usually Form 990),[8] a "board committee should annually review the form." If the full board "handles the financial statement review responsibilities, Form 990 should be reviewed by the full board or an appropriate board committee."
- There should be "adequate communication to board members between board meetings."
- The board should "[d]etermine and adjust the optimal board size by assessing organizational needs."
- The board should "[s]tructure board membership and the board's voting with more than a mere majority of independent board members."
- The board meetings should be conducted "with *more* than a *mere* majority of independent board members in attendance."
- There should be an annual monitoring of "individual board performance against the board members' service commitments."
- The board should develop an "effective process to plan ahead for recruiting new board members."
- There should be a process for "[p]roperly orient[ing] new board members for their board service and provid[ing] ongoing education to ensure that the board carries out its oversight functions and that individual members are aware of their legal and ethical responsibilities."
- An organization should establish "clear policies and procedures on the length of terms and on the removal of board members."
- Board member participation should be evaluated "before extending terms"; board, member evaluation and/or term limits should be used to "ensure that the organization is only served by effective members."
- Board members "should generally serve without compensation for board service other than reimbursement for expenses incurred to fulfill their board duties." If

---

[8] See Chapter 5, text accompanied by notes 12–47.

compensation is paid to board members, however, "information on the compensation should be provided by the charity, upon request, to allow an evaluation of the reasonableness of the compensation."

- Board members "should understand clearly if they are expected to participate in stewardship activities and individual giving."
- The board should use "routine and periodic board self-evaluations to improve meetings, restructure committees, and address individual board member performance."
- The board should "[f]ind opportunities to keep valuable individuals connected with the organization after their board terms expire."

Financial Statements

Every organization that is an accredited member of the ECFA must obtain an annual audit performed by an independent certified public accounting firm, including a financial statement prepared in accordance with generally accepted accounting principles. The ECFA may provide for an alternative category of membership that does not require audited financial statements, in which case the organization must have financial statements that are compiled or reviewed by an independent certified public accounting firm.

An ECFA best practice has the organization ensuring that "all material related-party transactions are disclosed in the financial statements."

Financial Disclosure

Every ECFA member must provide a copy of its current financial statements (including audited financial statements if required) on written request and provide other disclosures "as the law may require." A member "must provide a report, on written request, including financial information, on any specific project for which it is soliciting gifts."

One of the ECFA best practices recommendations is that the organization post its most recent annual financial statement and annual information return (Form 990) (if the organization files such a return) on its website.

Conflicts of Interest

ECFA member organizations are to "avoid conflicts of interest." Nonetheless, members may engage in transactions with related parties if (1) a material transaction is fully disclosed in the audited financial statements of the organization, (2) the related party is excluded from the discussion and approval of the transaction, (3) a competitive bid or comparable valuation exists, and (4) the organization's board has demonstrated that the transaction is in the best interest of the entity.

The ECFA best practices include the following:

- "A conflict-of-interest policy relating to the governing board and key executives should be adopted."
- "The governing board and key executives should document annually any potential related-party transactions."
- "All significant related-party transactions should be initially approved and, if continuing, reapproved annually by the governing board."

Policies and Procedures

According to the ECFA best practices, the following should be done:

- The organization should "[p]roperly document the proceedings of all board and board, committee meetings in order to protect the organization." Board minutes "should identify all voting board members as present or absent to clearly document a quorum."

- The organization should develop a mission statement, "putting into words why the organization exists and what it hopes to accomplish." This statement should be "[r]egularly reference[d]" to ensure that it is being "faithfully followed." The organization should "[h]ave the courage to refocus the mission statement, if appropriate."
- The organization should adopt a "stewardship philosophy statement."
- The organization should adopt an "executive compensation philosophy statement."
- The organization should adopt "appropriate policies," such as policies with respect to conflicts of interest (including annual approval of all significant related-party transactions), whistleblowing, accountable expense reimbursements, record retention, board confidentiality, donor confidentiality, and ownership of intellectual property.
- Board policies should be regularly reviewed to determine whether revisions are needed.
- The organization's compliance with board policies should be monitored.
- All Board policies should be maintained in a policy manual.
- The organization should develop a "vision statement communicating a compelling and inspirational hope for the future of the organization."

Fundraising

The ECFA has several requirements in the area of fundraising. Representations of fact, description of the organization's financial condition, or narrative about events must be "current, complete, and accurate"; "material omissions or exaggerations of fact" are not permitted. Member organizations "must not create unrealistic donor expectations of what a donor's gift will actually accomplish within the limits of the organization's ministry." Organizations are asked to make every effort to "avoid accepting a gift from or entering into a contract with a prospective donor which would knowingly place a hardship on the donor, or place the donor's future wellbeing in jeopardy." When dealing with donors regarding commitments on "major estate assets," organizations must "seek to guide and advise donors so they have adequately considered the broad interests of the family and the various ministries they are currently supporting before they make final decisions."

These standards state that compensation of outside fundraising consultants or a member's employees, based directly or indirectly on a percentage of charitable contributions raised, is prohibited. The ECFA standards also state that officers and directors may not receive any royalties for any product that is used for fundraising or promotional purposes by the organization. The ECFA member must honor all statements it made in its fundraising appeals about the use of the gift.

The ECFA best practices state that an organization should "[g]enerate compensation arrangements for development personnel (internal and external) based on merit." These practices add: "Pay-for-performance plans may be structured if it [sic] avoids compensation based on [a] percentage of gift amounts."

Other Practices

The ECFA's best practices state that an organization should spend a "reasonable percentage" of its annual expenditures "on programs in pursuance of the organization's mission." An organization should "[p]rovide sufficient resources for effective administration and, if the organization solicits contributions, for appropriate fundraising activities."

An organization should "[e]stablish and implement policies that provide clear guidance for paying or reimbursing expenses incurred when conducting business or traveling on behalf of the organization, including listing the types of expenses that can be paid for or reimbursed and the documentation required." An organization should "[a]void loans or the equivalent to executives or board members."

Standards for Excellence Institute Standards

The Standards for Excellence Institute is a membership organization of charitable entities that claims, in its marketing material, to uphold standards that are higher "than the minimal requirements imposed by local, state and federal laws and regulations." This program was launched to "strengthen nonprofit governance and management, while also enhancing the public's trust in the nonprofit sector." This organization "promotes widespread application of a comprehensive system of self-regulation in the nonprofit sector." These standards are based on "fundamental values" such as "honesty, integrity, fairness, respect, trust, compassion, responsibility and accountability," and provide guidelines for how nonprofit organizations should act to be "ethical and accountable in their programs operations, governance, human resources, financial management and fundraising."[9]

Mission and Program

The Institute's standards provide that an organization's "purpose, as defined and approved by the board of directors, should be formally and specifically stated." The organization's "activities should be consistent with its stated purpose."

A nonprofit organization "should periodically revisit its mission (e.g., every 3 to 5 years) to determine if the need for its programs continues to exist." An organization "should evaluate whether the mission needs to be modified to reflect societal changes, its current programs should be revised or discontinued, or new programs need to be developed."

A nonprofit organization "should have defined, cost-effective procedures for evaluating, both qualitatively and quantitatively, its programs and projects in relation to its mission." These procedures "should address programmatic efficiency and effectiveness, the

---

[9] These standards are titled "An Ethics and Accountability Code for the Nonprofit Sector."

relationship of these impacts to the cost of achieving them, and the outcomes for program participants." Evaluations, which "should include input from program participants," should be "candid, be used to strengthen the effectiveness of the organization and, when necessary, be used to make programmatic changes."

Board Responsibilities and Conduct

The board of an organization "should engage in short-term and long-term planning activities as necessary to determine the mission of the organization, to define specific goals and objectives related to the mission, and to evaluate the success of the organization's programs toward achieving the mission." The board "should establish policies for the effective management of the organization, including financial and, where applicable, personnel policies."

The board "annually should approve the organization's budget and periodically should assess the organization's financial performance in relation to the budget." As part of this annual budget process, the board "should review the percentages of the organization's resources spent on program, administration, and fundraising." The full board "should also approve the findings of the organization's annual audit and management letter and plan to implement the recommendations of" that letter.

The board or a board committee "should hire the executive director, set the executive's compensation, and evaluate the director's performance at least annually." Where a committee performs this role, details should be reported to the board. The board "should periodically review the appropriateness of the overall compensation structure of the organization." The board should approve written personnel policies and procedures "governing the work and actions of all employees and volunteers of the organization."

The board "is responsible for its own operations, including the education, training and development of board members, periodic (i.e., at least every two years) evaluation of its own performance, and[,] where appropriate, the selection of new board members." The board "should establish stated expectations for board members, including expectations for participation in fundraising activities, committee service, and program activities." The board "'should meet as frequently as is needed to fully and adequately conduct the business of the organization"; the board should, at a minimum, meet four times a year.

The organization "should have written policies that address attendance and participation of board members at board meetings." These policies "should include a process to address noncompliance." Written meeting minutes "reflecting the actions of the board, including reports of board committees when acting in the place of the board, should be maintained and distributed to board and committee members."

Board Composition

The Institute's standards state that the governing board of an organization "should be composed of individuals who are personally committed to the mission of the organization and possess the specific skills needed to accomplish the mission."

An organization's governing board should, under these standards, have at least five unrelated directors; seven or more directors are preferable. Where an employee of the organization is a voting member of the board, there must be assurance that that individual will "not be in a position to exercise undue influence."

There should be term limits for the service of board members. Board membership should reflect the "diversity of the communities" served by the organization. Board members should serve without compensation for their service as board members; they "may only be reimbursed for expenses directly related to carrying out their board service."

Conflict of Interest

The Institute's standards state that a nonprofit organization should have a written conflict-of-interest policy. This policy "should be applicable to all board members and staff, and to volunteers who have significant independent decision making authority regarding the resources of the organization." The policy "should identify the types of conduct or transactions that raise conflict of interest concerns, should set forth procedures for disclosure of actual or potential conflicts, and should provide for review of individual transactions by the uninvolved members of the board of directors."

A nonprofit organization "should provide board members, staff, and volunteers with a conflict of interest statement that summarizes the key elements of the organization's conflict of interest policy." This statement "should provide space for the board member, employee or volunteer to disclose any known interest that the individual, or a member of the individual's immediate family, has in any business entity which transacts business with the organization." The statement should be provided to and signed by board members, staff, and volunteers, "both at the time of the individual's initial affiliation with the organization and at least annually thereafter."

Financial Accountability

The Institute's standards require that an organization "operate in accordance with an annual budget that has been approved by the board of directors." Accurate financial reports should be maintained on a timely basis. Internal financial statements "should be prepared no less frequently than quarterly, should be provided to the board of directors and should identify and explain any material variation between actual and budgeted revenues and expenses." The accuracy of the financial reports of an organization with annual revenue in excess of $300,000 should be audited by a certified public accountant.

Organizations "should provide employees a confidential means to report suspected financial impropriety or misuse of organization resources and should have in place a policy prohibiting retaliation against persons reporting improprieties." They "should have written financial policies adequate for the size and complexity of their organization governing: (a) investment of the assets of the organization [,] (b) internal control procedures, (c) purchasing practices, and (d) unrestricted current net assets."

Legal Compliance and Accountability

Organizations must be "aware of and comply with all applicable Federal, state, and local laws." These laws include those pertaining to fundraising, licensing, financial accountability, document retention and destruction, human resources, lobbying and political advocacy, and taxation.

Organizations "should periodically assess the need for insurance coverage in light of the nature and extent of the organization's activities and its financial capacity." A decision to forego general liability or directors' and officers' liability insurance coverage "shall only be made by the board of directors and shall be reflected in" the appropriate board minutes. An organization "should periodically conduct an internal review" of its compliance with "legal, regulatory and financial reporting requirements"; a summary of the results of this review should be provided to the organization's governing board.

Openness

The Institute's standards require an organization to "prepare, and make available annually to the public, information about the organization's mission, program activities, and basic audited (if applicable) financial data." This report should also "identify the names of the organization's board of directors and management staff."

An organization "should provide members of the public who express an interest in the affairs of the organization with a meaningful opportunity to communicate with an appropriate representative of the organization." An organization "should have at least one staff member who is responsible to assure that the organization is complying with both the letter and the spirit of Federal and state laws that require disclosure of information to members of the public."

Public Education and Advocacy

The Institute's standards state that a nonprofit organization "should assure that any educational information provided to the media or distributed to the public is factually accurate and provides sufficient contextual information to be understood." An organization "should have a written policy on advocacy defining the process by which the organization determines positions on specific issues." The standards add that nonprofit organizations "engaged in promoting public participation in community affairs shall be diligent in assuring that the activities of the organization are strictly nonpartisan."

Fundraising

The Institute's standards as to fundraising state that an organization's fundraising costs "should be reasonable over time." That is, on average, over a five-year period, a charity should realize revenue from development activities that is "at least three times the amount spent on conducting them." Organizations with a fundraising ratio of less than 3:1 "should demonstrate that they are making steady progress toward achieving this goal, or should be able to justify why a 3:1 ratio is not appropriate for the individual organization."

Solicitation and program materials "should be accurate and truthful and should correctly identify the organization, its mission, and the intended use of the solicited funds." All statements made by a charitable organization in its fundraising appeals "about the use of a contribution should be honored." A charitable organization "must honor the known intentions of a donor regarding the use of donated funds."

Charitable organizations should respect the privacy of donors and "safeguard the confidentiality of information that a donor reasonably would expect to be private." Charities should provide donors with an opportunity to make anonymous gifts. They should provide donors the opportunity to have their names removed from any mailing lists that are sold, rented, or exchanged. Charities should honor requests by a donor to curtail repeated mailings or telephone solicitations from in-house lists. Solicitations should be "free from undue influence or excessive pressure," and be "respectful of the needs and interests of the donor or potential donor."

A charitable organization should have policies governing the acceptance and disposition of charitable gifts, including procedures to determine any limits on individuals or entities from which the organization will accept a gift, the purposes for which donations will be accepted, the type of property that will be accepted, and whether an "unusual or unanticipated" gift will be accepted in view of the organization's "mission and organizational capacity."

Fundraising personnel, whether employees or consultants, should not be compensated on the basis of a "percentage of the amount raised or other commission formula." When using the services of a paid professional fundraising counsel or professional solicitor, a charitable organization should only contract with those persons who are "properly registered with applicable regulatory authorities." Organizations should exercise control over any staff, volunteers, consultants, other contractors, businesses, or other organizations that solicit contributions on their behalf.

American Institute of Philanthropy Standards

The American Institute of Philanthropy is, according to its website, a "nationally prominent charity watchdog service whose purpose is to help donors make informed giving decisions." It provides ratings of charities, using letter grades A–F.

Fundraising Expenses

Like all of the watchdog agencies, AIP believes fundraising costs should be reasonable. In this organization's view, this means that a charity should expend at least 60 percent of its outlays for charitable purposes. The balance, of course, is to be allocated to fundraising and administration. Fundraising expenses should not exceed 35 percent. These percentages are based on related contributions, not total income (thereby usually making the fundraising cost ratio higher). AIP sometimes takes it on itself to adjust an organization's fundraising expense ratio, such as where it is allocating a portion of its expenses to program in the context of direct mail fundraising.

Asset Reserves

In the view of AIP, a reserve of assets to enable an organization to function without fundraising for less than three years is reasonable. Organizations with "years of available assets" of more than five years are considered the "least needy." (This fact earns an organization the grade of "F" irrespective of other considerations.)

Other Watchdog Agencies

Other charity watchdog organizations have come into being. One observer concluded that the number of them has "proliferated" and that each of them has its "own approach and mission."[10] These recent entrants into the field include Charity Navigator and Ministry Watch. Another organization, the Philanthropy Group, provides customized research about charitable organizations for a fee.[11]

These groups do not focus on governance issues; their emphasis is on program and fundraising. For example, Charity Navigator rates public charities on the basis of their organizational efficiency and organizational capacity. As to organizational efficiency, this rating process analyzes four categories of performance: program expenses, administrative expenses, fundraising expenses, and fundraising efficiency. (A charity that spends less than one-third of its annual revenue on program is automatically given an organizational efficiency score of zero.) Organizational capacity is rated on the basis of primary revenue growth, program expenses growth, and working capital ratio. Charities that are rated by

---

[10] Wilhelm, "Charity Under Scrutiny," XV *Chron. of Phil.* (No. 4) 22 (Nov. 28, 2002).
[11] *Id.* at 22–26.

Charity Navigator receive zero (exceptionally poor) to four (exceptional) stars.

California's Nonprofit Integrity Act

The state of California has the most extensive set of rules concerning governance of nonprofit organizations; these provisions were enacted in 2004 in the form of the Nonprofit Integrity Act.[12] This legislation contains laws concerning governance of and fundraising by charitable organizations doing business in the state.

Financial Audits

Charitable corporations that have gross revenues of at least $2 million and are required to register and file reports with the state's attorney general must have annual financial statements prepared, audited by an independent certified public accountant. The CPA must, in this regard, follow generally accepted auditing standards; the statements must be prepared in accordance with generally accepted accounting principles. If the accounting firm and CPA performing the audit also provide non-audit services to the charitable organization, they must follow independence standards promulgated by the US Comptroller General. The audited financial statements must be made available for inspection by the attorney general and the public no later than nine months after the close of the fiscal year covered by the financial statement.

---

[12] California Nonprofit Integrity Act of 2004, Senate Bill 1262, amending Section 17510.5 of the California Business and Professional Code, and amending Sections 12581–12586, 12599, and 12599.1 of, and adding Sections 12599.3, 12599.6, and 12599.7 to, the California Government Code.

Audit Committees

Charitable corporations with gross revenues of at least $2 million, and that are required to register and file reports with the state's attorney general must establish and maintain an audit committee. This audit committee, which must be appointed by the organization's governing board, may include individuals who are not board members. The committee, however, cannot include members of the organization's staff or the organization's president, chief executive officer, treasurer, or chief financial officer. If the organization has a finance committee, members of that committee may serve on the audit committee, although those individuals cannot comprise more than one-half of the members of the audit committee.

The audit committee, under the supervision of the organization's board, is responsible for making recommendations to the board as to the hiring and dismissal of independent certified public accountants. The audit committee can negotiate the CPA firm's compensation, on behalf of the board. This committee must confer with the auditor to satisfy committee members that the financial affairs of the charitable organization are in order, review the audit and decide whether to accept it, approve non-audit services by the CPA firm, and ensure that the non-audit services conform to the standards issued by the US Comptroller General.

Executive Compensation

Charitable organizations, including trusts, must have their governing board, or a designated committee of the board, review and approve the compensation of the organization's president, chief executive officer, chief financial officer, and treasurer. There must be a determination that this compensation, including benefits, is "just and reasonable." This review and approval must occur at the time of initial hiring, when a term is renewed or extended, and when the compensation is modified.

Fundraising Regulation

A fundraising counsel and a commercial fundraiser must notify the California attorney general before starting a solicitation campaign for a charitable organization and must have a written contract with the charity. This law dictates the elements to be included in these contracts. Charitable organizations and commercial fundraisers are prohibited from engaging in misrepresentation and certain other acts when soliciting contributions. Commercial fundraisers must retain records of solicitation campaigns for at least 10 years.[13]

Senate Finance Committee Staff Paper

The Senate Committee on Finance, in 2004, held a hearing on a range of subjects pertaining to nonprofit, tax-exempt organizations.[14] In connection with that hearing, the staff of the committee prepared a paper as a discussion draft that contained a variety of proposals, including a section on "strong governance and best practices" for exempt organizations.

Board Duties

This paper stipulated that a charitable organization must be "managed" by its board of directors or trustees. The paper stated that, in performing board duties, a board member "has to perform his or her duties in good faith; with the care an ordinarily prudent person in a like position would exercise under similar circumstances; and in a manner the director reasonably believes to be in the best

---

[13] In general, Silk & Fei, "California's Nonprofit Integrity Act of 2004," 7 *Int'l J. of Not-for-Profit Law* (no. 2) 66 (Feb. 2005).

[14] "Charity Oversight and Reform: Keeping Bad Things from Happening to Good Charities," Hearing before the Senate Committee on Finance, US Senate, June 24, 2004 [Senate Hearing 108-603], 108th Cong., 2nd Sess. (2004).

interests of the mission, goals, and purposes of the corporation." The paper added that an individual who has "special skills or expertise has a duty to use such skills or expertise" in his or her board service. Federal law liability for breach of these duties was recommended.

The paper stated that any compensation consultant providing services to a charitable organization must be hired by and report to the board; the consultant must be independent. Compensation for all management positions would have to be approved by the board in advance and annually (unless there is no change in compensation other than an inflation adjustment). Compensation arrangements would have to be "explained and justified and publicly disclosed (with such explanation) in a manner that can be understood by an individual with a basic business background."

This paper asserted that the governing board of a charitable organization must:

- "[E]stablish basic organizational and management policies and procedures of organization and review any proposed deviations."
- "[E]stablish, review, and approve program objectives and performance measures and review and approve significant transactions."
- "[R]eview and approve the auditing and accounting principles and practices used in preparing the organization's financial statements and must retain and replace the organization's independent auditor." An independent auditor would have to be hired by the board; each auditor could be retained for no more than five years.
- "[R]eview and approve the organization's budget and financial objectives as well as significant investments, joint ventures, and business transactions."
- "[O]versee the conduct of the corporation's business and evaluate whether the business is being properly managed."
- "[E]stablish a conflicts-of-interest policy which would be required to be disclosed/with the [Form] 990, and require a summary of conflicts determinations made during the 990 reporting year."

- "[E]stablish and oversee a compliance program to address regulatory and liability concerns."
- "[E]stablish procedures to address complaints and prevent retaliation against whistleblowers."

In general, all of these requirements would have to be "confirmed" on the organization's annual information return (Form 990).

Board Composition

Boards of charitable organizations would have to be comprised of at least three members, with a maximum of 15 members. No more than one board member could be directly or indirectly compensated by the organization. A compensated board member could not serve as the chair of the board or treasurer of the organization. In the case of public charities, at least one board member or one-fifth of the board would have to be independent; a "higher number of independent board members might be required in limited cases." An independent board member would be defined as an individual who is "free of any relationship with the corporation or its management that may impair or appear to impair the director's ability to make independent judgments."

Board/Officer Removal

In this paper, the Committee staff proposed that an individual who is not permitted to serve on the board of a publicly traded company, because of a law violation, be barred from serving on the board of a tax-exempt organization. A criminal conviction would preclude an individual from serving as director or officer of an exempt organization for a five-year period following the conviction. An individual who has been convicted of a crime under a law enforced by the Federal Trade Commission, US Postal Service, or state attorney general for actions related to service as an officer or director of an exempt organization (or where the crime arose from an organization that falsely presented itself as an exempt organization) could not serve as an officer or director of an exempt organization for five years. An organization, or its officers or members, that knowingly retained an individual who is not permitted to serve the organization, pursuant to one or more of these rules, would be subject to a penalty.

A proposal would accord the IRS the authority to require the removal of a board member, officer, or employee of a tax-exempt organization who violated self-dealing rules, conflict-of-interest standards, excess benefit transaction rules, private inurement rules, or charitable solicitation laws. The IRS would be able to require that such an individual not serve on any other exempt organization's board for a period of years. An organization that knowingly retained an individual who is not permitted to serve, pursuant to one or more of these rules, would have its exempt status revoked or be subject to a penalty.

US Treasury Department's Voluntary Best Practices

The Treasury Anti-Terrorist Financing Guidelines[15] provide that a charitable organization's governing instruments should (1) delineate the organization's basic goal(s) and purpose(s); (2) define the structure of the charity, including the composition of the board, how the board is selected and replaced, and the authority and responsibilities of the board; (3) set forth requirements concerning financial reporting, accountability, and practices for the solicitation and distribution of funds; and (4) state that the charity shall comply with all applicable federal, state, and local law.

These guidelines state that the board of directors of a charitable organization is responsible for the organization's compliance with relevant laws, and should (1) be an "active governing body"; (2) oversee implementation of the governance practices to be followed by the organization; (3) exercise "effective and independent"

---

[15] U.S. Department of the Treasury Anti-Terrorist Financing Guidelines: Voluntary Best Practices for U.S. Based Charities (2006).

oversight of the charity's operations; (4) establish a conflict-of-interest policy for board members and employees; (5) establish procedures to be followed if a board member or employee has a conflict, or perceived conflict, of interest; and (6) maintain records of all decisions made, with these records available for inspection by the appropriate regulatory and law enforcement authorities.

The guidelines contain other governance practices, including (1) an annual budget approved and overseen by the board; (2) a board-appointed financial/accounting officer who is responsible for day-to-day management of the charity's assets; (3) an audit of the finances of the organization, when annual gross income is in excess of $250,000, by an independent certified public accounting firm, with the audited financial statement available for public inspection; (4) accounting for all funds received and disbursed in accordance with generally accepted accounting principles, including the name of each recipient of funds, the amount disbursed, and the date of the disbursement; (5) the prompt, deposit of all funds into an account maintained by the charity at a financial institution; and (6) the making of disbursements by check or wire transfer, rather than in currency, whenever that is reasonably feasible.

Pursuant to these guidelines, charities, should (1) maintain and make publicly available a current list of their board members and the salaries they are paid; (2) maintain records (while fully respecting individual privacy rights) containing additional identifying information about their board members, such as home addresses, Social Security numbers, and citizenship; and (3) maintain records (while respecting individual privacy rights) identifying information about the board members of any subsidiaries or affiliates receiving funds from them. As to key employees, charities should (1) maintain and make publicly available a current list of their five highest paid or most influential employees and the salaries and/or other direct or indirect benefits they are provided; (2) maintain records (while respecting privacy rights) containing identifying information about their key, non-US employees working abroad; and (3) maintain records (while respecting individual privacy rights) identifying information about the key employees of any subsidiaries or affiliates receiving funds from them.

Moreover, pursuant to these guidelines, charitable organizations should (1) maintain and make publicly available a current list of any branches, subsidiaries, and/or affiliates that receive resources and services from them; (2) make publicly available or provide to any member of the public, on request, an annual report, which describes the charity's purposes, programs, activities, tax-exempt status, structure and responsibility of the governing body, and financial information; and (3) make publicly available or provide to any member of the public, on request, complete annual financial statements, including a summary of the results of the most recent audit, which present the overall financial condition of the organization and its financial activities in accordance with generally accepted accounting principles and reporting practices.

Committee for Purchase Proposed Best Practices

The Committee for Purchase from People Who Are Blind or Severely Disabled proposed various criteria and tests that it believes are "widely considered as benchmarks of good nonprofit agency governance practices." [16] Pursuant to these proposed "best practices," (1) a nonprofit organization's board of directors should be composed of individuals who are "personally committed to the mission of the organization and possess the specific skills needed to accomplish the mission"; (2) where an employee of the organization is a voting member of the board, the "circumstances must [e]nsure that the employee will not be in a position to exercise 'undue influence"'; (3) the board should have at least five unrelated directors; (4) the chair of the board should not simultaneously be serving as the entity's chief executive officer /president; (5) there should be term limits for board members; (6) board membership should reflect the "diversity of the communities" served by the organization; (7) board members should serve without compensation; (8) the board or a designated committee of it should

[16] 70 *Fed. Reg.* (No. 241) 74722–74723 (Dec. 16, 2005).

hire the executive director, establish the executive's compensation, and evaluate the director's performance at least annually; (9) the board should periodically review the "appropriateness of the overall compensation structure" of the organization; (19) the board should have at least one "financial expert" among its membership; (11) the board should approve the findings of the organization's annual audit and management letter; and (12) the board should approve a plan to implement the recommendations of the management letter.

According to these best practices, nonprofit organizations should (1) have a written conflict-of-interest policy that identifies the types of conflict or transactions that raise conflict-of-interest concerns, sets forth procedures for disclosure of actual or potential conflicts, and provides for review of individual transactions by the "uninvolved" members of the board of directors; (2) subject the accuracy of the organization's financial reports to audit by a certified public accountant; (3) periodically conduct an internal review of the organization's compliance with existing statutory, regulatory, and financial reporting requirements, and should provide a summary of the results of the review to the board; (4) prepare and make available annually to the public information about the organization's mission, program activities, and basic audit (if applicable) financial data; (5) require the board of directors to monitor compensation paid to the chief executive officer/president and "highly compensated individuals"; and (6) require the board to approve all compensation packages for the chief executive officer/president and all highly compensated employees through a rebuttable presumption process to determine the reasonableness of the compensation.

Panel on Nonprofit Sector Recommendations

The Panel on the Nonprofit Sector convened by Independent Sector prepared a report to Congress and the nonprofit sector.[17] In

---

[17] Panel on the Nonprofit Sector, "Strengthening Transparency Governance Accountability of Charitable Organizations" (June 2005).

this report, the Panel recommended that the federal tax regulations be amended to generally require that tax-exempt charitable organizations have a minimum of three members on their governing boards. Generally, at least one-third of the members of the board of a public charity would have to be independent. Independent board members would be individuals (1) who have not been compensated as an employee or independent contractor by the organization within the past 12 months, except for reasonable compensation for board service; (2) whose compensation, except for board service, is not determined by individuals who are compensated by the organization; (3) who do not receive, directly or indirectly, material financial benefits from the organization, except as a member of the charitable class served by the organization; and (4) who are not related to any of the foregoing individuals.

Another recommendation of the Panel was to prohibit individuals who, are barred from service on boards of publicly traded companies or convicted of crimes directly related to breaches of fiduciary duty in their service as an employee or board member of a charitable organization from serving on the board of a charitable organization for five years following their removal or conviction.

The Panel observed that experts in the realm of nonprofit organization board governance "are not of one mind as to the ideal maximum size of nonprofit boards." It was noted that board size "may depend upon such factors as the age of the organization, the nature and geographic scope of its mission and activities, and its funding needs." Some experts believe that a "larger board may be necessary to ensure the range of perspectives and expertise required for some organizations or to share in fundraising responsibilities." Others argue that "effective governance is best achieved by a smaller board, which then demands more active participation from each board member." The Panel concludes that each charitable organization must determine the most appropriate size for its board and the appropriate number and responsibilities of board committees to ensure that the board is able to fulfill its fiduciary and other governance duties responsibly and effectively."

As to the recommendation concerning independent board members of public charities, the Panel wrote that "it is important that at least one-third of their board members be free of the conflicts of interest that can arise when they have a personal interest in the financial transactions of the charity." It concluded that the "effort to find independent members is important to the long-term success and accountability of the organization and should be a legal requirement for public charities that are eligible to receive tax-deductible contributions on the most favorable terms."

In its report, the Panel discourages board compensation by charitable organizations and strongly "encourages charitable organizations to support the long-standing tradition of asking boards of directors to serve on a voluntary basis." The Panel also states that "[a]ll boards should establish strong and effective mechanisms to ensure that the board carries out its oversight functions and that the board members are aware of their legal and ethical responsibilities in ensuring that the organization is governed properly."

American National Red Cross Governance Modernization Act Principles

The American National Red Cross Governance Modernization Act of 2007 was signed into law on May 11, 2007.[18] This legislation amended the congressional charter of the Red Cross to modernize its structure and otherwise strengthen its governance. Changes include a substantial reduction in the size of the organization's board, delegation to management of the day-to-day operations of the organization, elimination of distinctions as to how board members are elected, and transition of some board members into an advisory council.

The essence of the legislation is unique to the National Red Cross entity. Yet, there are elements of the act with larger significance. For example, the legislation refers to the governing board as a "governance and strategic oversight board."[19] It outlines the board's responsibilities (a checklist for boards in general):

---

[18] Pub. L. No. 110-26,110th Cong., 1st Sess. (2007); 36 U.S.C. § 300101.
[19] *Id.* § 2(a)(5).

- Review and approve the organization's mission statement.
- Approve and oversee the organization's strategic plan and maintain strategic oversight of operational matters.
- Select, evaluate, and determine the level of compensation of the organization's chief executive officer.
- Evaluate the performance and establish the compensation of the senior leadership team and provide for management succession.
- Oversee the financial reporting and audit process, internal controls, and legal compliance.
- Ensure that the chapters of the organization are geographically and regionally diverse.
- Hold management accountable for performance.
- Provide oversight of the financial stability of the organization.
- Ensure the inclusiveness and diversity of the organization.
- Provide oversight of the protection of the brand of the organization.
- Assist with fundraising on behalf of the organization.

This legislation contains the following "sense of Congress" that (1) "charitable organizations are an indispensable part of American society, but these organizations can only fulfill their important roles by maintaining the trust of the American public," (2) "trust is fostered by effective governance and transparency," and (3) "Federal and State action play an important role in ensuring effective governance and transparency by setting standards, rooting out violations, and informing the public."

Panel on Nonprofit Sector Good Governance Principles

The Panel on the Nonprofit Sector, convened by Independent Sector, issued, on October 18, 2007, its "Principles for Good Governance and Ethical Practice" for public and private charitable organizations." The principles are predicated on the need for a "careful balance between the two essential forms of regulation –that is, between prudent legal mandates to ensure that organizations do not abuse the privilege of their exempt status, and, for all other aspects of sound operations, well-informed self-governance and mutual awareness among nonprofit organizations." These principles, somewhat revised in 2015, organized under four categories, are as follows.

Legal Compliance and Public Disclosure

The Panel's first principle is that an organization "must comply with all applicable federal laws and regulations, as well as applicable laws and regulations of the states and the local jurisdictions in which it is formed or operates." If the organization conducts programs outside the US, it must abide by applicable international laws and conventions that are legally binding on the US. The Panel observed that an organization's governing board is "ultimately responsible for overseeing and ensuring that the organization complies with all its legal obligations and for detecting and remedying wrongdoing by management." The Panel added that, "[w]hile board members are not required to have specialized legal knowledge, they should be familiar with the basic rules and requirements with which their organization must comply and should secure the necessary legal advice and assistance to structure appropriate monitoring and oversight mechanisms."

The Panel stated that an organization should have a "formally adopted, written code of ethics with which all of its directors or trustees, staff and volunteers are familiar and to which they adhere." This principle is predicated on the thought that "[a]dherence to the law provides a minimum standard for an organization's behavior." The adoption of a code of ethics "helps demonstrate the organization's commitment to carry out its responsibilities ethically and effectively." The code should be "built on the values that the organization embraces, and should highlight expectations of how those who work with the organization will conduct themselves in a number of areas, such as the confidentiality and respect that should be accorded to clients, consumers, donors, and fellow volunteers and board and staff members."

An organization should "adopt and implement policies and procedures to ensure that all conflicts of interest (real and potential), or the appearance thereof, within the organization and the governing board are appropriately managed though disclosure, recusal, or other means." A conflict-of-interest policy "must be consistent with the laws of the state in which the nonprofit is organized and should be tailored to specific organizational needs and characteristics." This policy "should require full disclosure of all potential conflicts of interest within the organization" and "should apply to every person who has the ability to influence decisions of the organization, including board and staff members and parties related to them."

An organization "should establish and implement policies and procedures that enable individuals to come forward with information on illegal practices or violations of organizational policies." This whistleblower policy "should specify that the organization will not retaliate against, and will protect the confidentiality of, individuals who make good-faith reports." The Panel recommended that "information on these policies ... be widely distributed to staff, volunteers[,] and clients, and should be incorporated both in new employee orientations and ongoing training programs for employees and volunteers." These policies "can help boards and senior managers become aware of and address problems before serious harm is done to the organization" and "can also assist in complying with legal provisions that protect individuals working in charitable organizations from retaliation for engaging in certain whistle-blowing activities."

An organization should "establish and implement policies and procedures to protect and preserve the organization's important documents and business records." The Panel observed that a document-retention policy "is essential for protecting the organization's records of its governance and administration, as well as business records that are required to demonstrate legal compliance." This type of policy "also helps to protect against allegations of wrongdoing by the organization or its directors and managers."

An organization's board "should ensure that the organization has adequate plans to protect its assets – its property, documents and data, financial and human resources, programmatic content and material, and its integrity and reputation – against damage or loss." The board "should review regularly the organization's need for general liability and directors' and officers' liability insurance, as well as take other actions necessary to mitigate risks." The Panel noted that the board is "responsible for understanding the major risks to which the organization is exposed, reviewing those risks on a periodic basis, and ensuring that systems have been established to manage them." It was observed that the "level of risk to which the organization is exposed and the extent of the review and risk management process will vary considerably based on the size, programmatic focus, geographic location, and complexity of the organization's operations."

The Panel wrote that an organization "should make information about its operations, including its governance, finances, programs[,] and activities, widely available to the public." Charitable organizations "also should consider making information available on the methods they use to evaluate the outcomes of their work and sharing the results of those evaluations." The theme underlying this principle is that charities should "demonstrate their commitment to accountability and transparency" by offering additional information about their finances and operations to the public, such as by means of annual reports and websites, with the latter containing mission statements, codes of ethics, conflict-of-interest policies, whistleblower policies, and the like.

Effective Governance

An organization must have a governing body that is "responsible for reviewing and approving the organization's mission and strategic direction, annual budget and key financial transactions, compensation practices, and fiscal and governance policies." The board "bears the primary responsibility for ensuring that a charitable organization fulfills its obligations to the law, its donors, its staff and volunteers, its clients, and the public at large." The board "must protect the assets of the organization and provide oversight to ensure that its financial, human[,] and material resources are used appropriately to further the organization's mission." The board "also sets the vision and mission for the organization and establishes the broad policies and strategic direction that enable the organization to fulfill its charitable purpose."

The board of an organization "should meet regularly enough to conduct its business and fulfill its duties." Regular board meetings provide the "chief venue for board members to review the organization's financial situation and program activities, establish and monitor compliance with key organizational policies and procedures, and address issues that affect the organization's ability to fulfill its charitable mission." The Panel observed: "While many charitable organizations find it prudent to meet at least three times a year to fulfill basic governance and oversight responsibilities, some with strong committee structures, including organizations with widely dispersed board membership, hold only one or two meetings of the full board each year."

The board of an organization "should establish its own size and structure, and review these periodically." The board "should have enough members to allow for full deliberation and diversity of thinking on governance and other organizational matters." Except for small organizations, "this generally means that the board should have at least five members." Nonetheless, the Panel noted that the "ideal size of a board depends on many factors, such as the age of the organization, the nature and geographic scope of its mission and activities, and its funding needs."

The board of an organization should include members with the "diverse background (including, but not limited to, ethnic, racial and gender perspectives), experience, and organizational and financial skills necessary to advance the organization's mission." Boards of charitable organizations, "generally strive to include members with expertise in budget and financial management, investments, personnel, fundraising, public relations and marketing, governance, advocacy, and leadership, as well as some members who are knowledgeable about the charitable organization's area of expertise or programs, or who have a special connection to its constituency." Some organizations "seek to maintain a board that respects the culture of and reflects the community served by the organization." An organization should "make every effort" to ensure that at least one member of the board has "financial literacy."

A "substantial majority of the board of a public charity, usually meaning at least two-thirds of the members, should be independent." "Independent" members are those who are not compensated by the organization, do not have their compensation determined by individuals who are compensated by the organization, do not receive material financial benefits from the organization (except as a member of the charitable class served by the organization), or are not related to or residing with any of the foregoing persons. An individual who is not independent is, in the view of the Panel, potentially in violation of the directors' duty of loyalty, which requires the directors to "put the interests of the organization above their personal interests and to make decisions they believe are in the best interest of the nonprofit." The Panel declared that it is "important to the long-term success and accountability of the organization that a sizeable majority of the individuals on the board be free of financial conflicts of interest."

The board should "hire, oversee, and annually evaluate the performance of the chief executive officer of the organization, and should conduct such an evaluation prior to any change in that officer's compensation," unless a multiyear contract is in force or the change consists solely of routine adjustments for inflation or the cost of living. The Panel stated that "[o]ne of the most important responsibilities of the board ... is to select, supervise, and determine a compensation package that will attract and retain a qualified chief executive." The organization's governing documents should require the full board to evaluate the executive's performance and approve his or her compensation.

The board of an organization that has paid staff "should ensure that the positions of chief staff officer, board chair, and board treasurer are held by separate individuals." Organizations without paid staff should ensure that the positions of board chair and treasurer are separately held. The Panel was of the view that "[c]oncentrating authority for the organization's governance and management practices in one or two people removes valuable checks and balances that help ensure that conflicts of interest and other personal concerns do not take precedence over the best interests of the organization."

The board "should establish an effective, systematic process for educating and communicating with board members to ensure that they are aware of their legal and ethical responsibilities, are knowledgeable about the programs and [other] activities of the organization, and can carry out their oversight functions effectively." The Panel observed that all board members "should receive oral and written instruction regarding the organization's governing documents, finances, program activities, and governing policies and practices." Encompassed by this principle is the thought that board members should receive agendas and background materials well in advance of board meetings.

Board members "should evaluate their performance as a group and as individuals no less frequently than every three years, and should have clear procedures for removing board members who are unable to fulfill their responsibilities." The Panel noted that a "regular process of evaluating the board's performance can help to identify strengths and weaknesses of its processes and procedures and to provide insights for strengthening orientation and educational programs, the conduct of board and committee meetings, and interactions with board and staff leadership." The board "should establish clear guidelines for the duties and responsibilities of each member, including meeting attendance, preparation[,] and participation; committee assignments; and the kinds of expertise board members are expected to have or develop in order to provide effective governance."

The board "should establish clear policies and procedures setting the length of terms and the number of consecutive terms a board member may serve." The matter of term limits continues to be controversial. The Panel stated the view in favor of term limits as follows: "Some organizations have found that such limits help in bringing fresh energy, ideas[,] and expertise to the board through new members." The contrary view: "Others have concluded that term limits may deprive the organization of valuable experience, continuity[,] and, in some cases, needed support provided by board members."

The board should review the "organizational and governing instruments no less frequently than every five years." This process will "help boards ensure that the organization is abiding by the rules it has set for itself and determine whether changes need to be made to those instruments." The board may elect to delegate some of this deliberation to a committee; if so, the "full board should consider and act upon the committee's recommendations."

The board "should establish and review regularly the organization's mission and goals and should evaluate, no less frequently than every five years, the organization's programs, goals and [other] activities to be sure they advance its mission and make prudent use of its resources." Every board should "set strategic goals and review them annually." The Panel noted that, "[b]ecause organizations and their purposes differ, it is incumbent on each organization to develop its own process for evaluating effectiveness." At a minimum, "interim benchmarks can be identified to assess whether the work is moving in the right direction."

Board members are "generally expected to serve without compensation, other than reimbursement for expenses incurred to fulfill their board duties." An organization that provides compensation to its board members should use "appropriate comparability data" to determine the amount to be paid, document the decision, and provide full disclosure to anyone, on request, of the amount of and rationale for the compensation. Board members of charitable organizations are responsible for "ascertaining that any compensation they receive does not exceed to a significant degree the compensation provided for positions in comparable organizations with similar responsibilities and qualifications." It is the view of the Panel that board members "of public charities often donate both time and funds to the organization, a practice that supports the sector's spirit of giving and volunteering."

Strong Financial Oversight

An organization "must keep complete, current, and accurate financial records." Its board "should receive and review timely reports of the organization's financial activities and should have a qualified, independent financial expert audit or review these statements annually in a manner appropriate to the organization's size and scale of operations." Each organization "must ensure that it has its annual financial statements audited or reviewed as required by law in the states in which it operates or raises funds or as required by government or private funders." The Panel observed that a charitable organization "that has its financial statements independently audited; whether or not it is legally required to do so, should consider establishing an audit committee composed of independent board members with appropriate financial expertise.

The board of an organization "must institute policies and procedures to ensure that the organization (and, if applicable, its subsidiaries) manages and invests its funds responsibly, in accordance with all legal requirements." The full board "should review and approve the organization's annual budget and should monitor actual performance against the budget." The Panel observed that "[s]ound financial management is among the most important responsibilities of the board of directors," which "should establish clear policies to protect the organization's financial assets and ensure that no one person bears the sole responsibility for receiving, depositing, and spending its funds."

An organization "should not provide loans (or the equivalent, such as loan guarantees, purchasing or transferring ownership of a residence or office, or relieving a debt or lease obligation) to directors, officers, or trustees." These practices have "created both real and perceived problems for public charities." (The Panel noted that the federal tax law has prohibitions in this regard in the case of private foundations, supporting organizations, and donor-advised funds.)

An organization "should spend a significant percentage of its annual budget on programs that pursue its mission." The budget "should also provide sufficient resources for effective administration of the organization, and, if it solicits contributions, for appropriate fundraising activities." The Panel, noting that some watchdog groups assert that public charities should (or must) spend at least 65 percent of their funds on program activities, found that standard to be "reasonable for most organizations," yet also noted that "there can be extenuating circumstances that require an organization to devote more resources to administrative and fundraising activities."

An organization "should establish clear, written policies for paying or reimbursing expenses incurred by anyone conducting business or traveling on behalf of the organization, including the types of expenses that can be paid for or reimbursed and the documentation required." These policies "should require that travel on behalf of the organization is to be undertaken in a cost-effective manner." The Panel advised that decisions as to travel expenditures "should be based on how best to further the organization's charitable purposes, rather than on the title or position of the person traveling," noting that "lavish, extravagant or excessive" expenditures are to be avoided.

An organization "should neither pay for nor reimburse travel expenditures for spouses, dependents[,] or others who are accompanying someone conducting business for the organization unless they, too, are conducting such business." Nonetheless, the Panel added that, if an organization "deems it proper to cover expenses for a spouse, dependent, or other person accompanying someone on business travel, the payment generally must, by law, be treated as compensation to the individual traveling on behalf of the organization."

Responsible Fundraising

Solicitation materials and other communications addressed to prospective donors and the public "must clearly identify the organization and be accurate and truthful." The Panel stated that a prospective donor "has the right to know the name of anyone soliciting contributions, the name and location of the organization that will receive the contribution, a dear description of its activities, the intended use of the funds to be raised, a contact for obtaining additional information, and whether the individual requesting the contribution is acting as a volunteer, employee of the organization, or hired solicitor."[20]

Contributions "must be used for purposes consistent with the donor's intent, whether as described in the relevant solicitation materials or as specifically directed by the donor." The Panel stated that solicitations should "indicate whether the funds they generate will be used to further the general programs and operations of the organization or to support specific programs or

---

[20] The source of this ostensible right is not identified.

types of programs." The Panel advised charitable organizations to "carefully review the terms of any contract or grant agreement before accepting a donation."

An organization "must provide donors with specific acknowledgments of charitable contributions, in accordance with [federal tax law] requirements, as well as information to facilitate the donor's compliance with tax law requirements." The Panel noted that not only is this type of acknowledgment generally required by law, "it also helps in building donors' confidence in and support for the activities they help to fund."

An organization should adopt "clear policies, based on its specific exempt purpose, to determine whether accepting a gift would compromise its ethics, financial circumstances, program focus[,] or other interests." The Panel warned that "[s]ome charitable contributions have the potential to create significant problems for an organization or a donor," noting that funds may be disbursed for "illegal or unethical" purposes, may subject the donee organization to legal liability (e.g., under environmental protection laws), or result in unrelated business income.

An organization "should provide appropriate training and supervision of the people soliciting funds on its behalf to ensure that they understand their responsibilities and applicable federal, state[,] and local laws, and do not employ techniques that are coercive, intimidating, or intended to harass potential donors." The Panel amplified this principle by recommending that a charitable organization should ensure that its fundraisers "are respectful of a donor's concerns and do not use coercive or abusive language or strategies to secure contributions, misuse personal information about potential donors, pursue personal relationships that are subject to misinterpretation by potential donors, or mislead potential donors in other ways."

An organization "should not compensate internal or external fundraisers based on a commission or a percentage of the amount raised." Compensation on this basis "can encourage fundraisers to put their own interests ahead of those of the organization or the donor and may lead to inappropriate techniques that jeopardize the organization's values and reputation and the donor's trust in the organization," and can lead to or be perceived as "excessive compensation."

An organization "should respect the privacy of individual donors and, except where disclosure is required by law, should not sell or otherwise make available the names and contact information of its donors without providing them an opportunity at least once a year to opt out of the use of their names." The Panel observed that "[p]reserving the trust and support of donors requires that donor information be handled with respect and confidentiality to the maximum extent permitted by law."

Perspective

According to the foregoing principles, the governing board of a public charity or perhaps other type of tax-exempt organization should consist of at least three individuals (PAS, Nonprofit Sector Panel), or five (Alliance, ECFA, Institute, Nonprofit Sector Panel Principles), or whatever number is most suitable for the particular organization. The PAS regarded boards of fewer than three persons as an "inadequate governing structure," even if state law permitted it. Despite its five-member rule, the ECFA standards also state that the board should determine its "optimal size." Its three-member minimum notwithstanding, the Nonprofit Sector Panel's recommendations included a discussion concluding that there is no agreement as to the "appropriate size" of nonprofit boards. The Nonprofit Sector Principles add that the board of an organization should established "its own size and structure." The Institute and Committee for Purchase believe that the five (plus) board members should be "unrelated." In one instance, the board should number no more than 15 (Senate Finance Committee paper). Boards often should be independent or perhaps independent-minded (ECFA). In some instances, boards should be "active" (PAS), have a diverse background (Nonprofit Sector Panel Principles), "possess the specific skills needed to accomplish the [organization's] mission" (Committee for Purchase), and/or "be familiar with the basic rules and requirements with which their organization must comply" (Nonprofit Sector Panel Principles).

Should there be term limits on board service? The answer is yes (ECFA, Institute, Committee for Purchase). The ECFA, however, hedges on that one, also stating that opportunities should be found to keep "valuable individuals" connected with the organization after expiration of board terms. The Nonprofit Sector Panel Principles avoid a position on the matter, providing instead arguments for and against these limits, stating they are "controversial."

How frequently should board meet? Generally, it is three times annually (PAS), semiannually (ECFA), "as frequently as is needed to fully and adequately conduct the business of the organization" (Institute), and "regularly enough to conduct its business and fulfill its duties" (Nonprofit Sector Panel Principles).

As to conflicts of interest, they should be avoided (PAS), or avoided if they are material (Alliance). The ECFA agrees that conflicts are to be avoided, then sketches circumstances when they are permissible. The Nonprofit Sector Panel Principles proclaim that a "sizeable majority of the individuals on the board be free of financial conflicts of interest."

Should board members be compensated? Some standards say no. Others, like the Nonprofit Sector Panel Principles, say generally no, then go on to state the procedures to be followed when board members are compensated. In general, as always, this compensation must be reasonable (which is difficult to ascertain in the absence of adequate data as to comparability).

How much should charities spend on program? That depends on what set of standards are used. The PAS requirement was a "reasonable percentage," which was defined as at least 50 percent of total income. The AIP goes with 60 percent. The Alliance states that these outlays should be at least 65 percent of total expenditures. The ECFA states that these amounts must be "reasonable." Charity Navigator automatically accords an organization an "organizational efficiency score" of zero where program outlays are less than one-third of annual revenue. The Nonprofit Sector Panel Principles state that an organization "should spend a significant percentage of its annual budget on programs."

What about fundraising expenses? The PAS said those also must be "reasonable," although there the applicable percentage was 35 percent. The Alliance agrees with that 35 percent standard. The AIP also uses a 35-percent standard, although it reserves the right to "adjust" an organization's fundraising expense ratio (usually to make it higher). The ECFA standards are silent on this point. The Institute states that fundraising outlays should not exceed one-third of total expenditures, measured over a five-year period; they also provide standards for entities the fundraising ratios of which do not meet the one-third requirement. The Nonprofit Sector Panel Principles tilt the other way, encouraging organizations to "devote sufficient resources" for "appropriate fundraising activities."

The Red Cross list of board member responsibilities includes protection of the organization's brand; no other set of standards addresses that point. Only the Institute's standards and Nonprofit Sector Principles speak to the matter of insurance coverage. The AIP is the only standards-setting agency to consider the matter of organization's reserves. The Institute requires charities to comply with all applicable federal and state laws, then bans percentage-based fundraising compensation, which is an antitrust law violation. The Nonprofit Sector Principles mandate a code of ethics for board members, staff, and volunteers.

There is some near-unanimity on certain points, such as the adoption of various policies (although the ones specifically identified often differ), truth in fundraising, and compliance with the law. The descriptions of board member duties and responsibilities, however, vary widely.

One of the principal points of this chapter is to highlight the array of good governance principles that have been designed and are being applied in the realm of nonprofit governance. Another principal point is to highlight the absence of homogeneity in this context. The IRS likes to make reference to "commonly accepted standards of good governance."[21] They do not exist.

---

[21] See Chapter 5, text accompanied by note 6.

5

Evolution of IRS Policy as to Nonprofit Governance

> For the IRS to propound and enforce good governance principles, the agency would have to go "beyond its traditional spheres of activity."
>
> *Steven Miller, April 26, 2007*

The initial federal tax statutory law concerning tax exemption for nonprofit charitable organizations was enacted in 1913. Ninety-four years after this statutory law was created, the IRS decided to invoke regulatory jurisdiction over the governance of nonprofit, tax-exempt organizations, principally public charities.[1]

This change in policy did not come about by reason of a statute, regulation, revenue ruling, court opinion, or the like. There was no directive from Congress of any type to the IRS requiring it to leap into the nonprofit governance regulation fray. To use language from the Supreme Court, there is "not a word" in the legislative history of any statute giving the IRS authority of any nature remotely suggesting it undertake regulation of nonprofit organizations' governance.[2]

The IRS's decision was announced as part of a speech.

---

[1] This is not, however, the IRS's record on the topic. The tax-return preparer regulations, that were found by two courts to be outside the range of the IRS's jurisdiction, were promulgated in 2011; the underlying statute was enacted in 1884 (see Chapter 2, text following note 192).

[2] Community Television of Southern California v. Gottfried, 459 U.S. 498, 509–510 (1983).

IRS Officials' Speeches

The policy of the IRS concerning tax-exempt organizations (particularly public charities) and regulation of the governance of them began to unfold in 2007. The best evidence of the contours of the evolution of this policy is the content of three speeches delivered by Steven Miller, during 2007–2008, in his capacity as the Tax Exempt/Government Entities (TE/GE) Commissioner.

As related at the outset of Chapter 1, one of the most dramatic and consequential events in the development of contemporary nonprofit law occurred on April 26, 2007. On that occasion, Mr. Miller gave the first of his speeches on the subject of nonprofit governance.[3]

When the TE/GE Commissioner began talking about the IRS's role in nonprofit governance, on this occasion, he conceded that for the IRS to propound and enforce good governance principles, the agency would have to go "beyond its traditional spheres of activity." Mr. Miller said that a "well-governed organization is more likely to be compliant [with the tax law], while poor governance can easily lead an exempt organization into trouble." He spoke, for example, of an "engaged, informed, and independent board of directors accountable to the community [that the tax-exempt organization] serves."

By the time the TE/GE Commissioner returned to this subject in a speech a few months later in 2007, his attitude and tone had dramatically changed.[4] No more pondering, musing, and speculating. Rather, the Commissioner stated that "[w]hile a few continue to argue that governance is outside our jurisdiction, most now support an active IRS that is engaged in this area."[5] He expressed his view that the IRS "contributes to a compliant, healthy charitable sector by expecting the tax-exempt community to adhere to commonly accepted standards of good governance." He said that IRS involvement in this area is "not new"; the agency has been

---

[3] The formal text of this speech is available at Bureau of National Affairs (BNA), *Daily Tax Report* (no. 81) TaxCore (April 27, 2007).

[4] The formal text of this speech is available at BNA, *Daily Tax Report* (no. 222) TaxCore (Nov. 19, 2007).

[5] No evidence was provided then or since then in support of that observation.

"quietly but steadily promoting good governance for a long time."[6] He noted that "[o]ur determination agents ask governance-related questions" and "our agents assess an organization's internal controls as the agents decide how to pursue an examination." He continued: "We are comfortable that we are well within our authority to act in these areas." And: "To more clearly put our weight behind good governance may represent a small step beyond our traditional sphere of influence, but we believe the subject is well within our core responsibilities."

When the annual Georgetown University Law School conference on nonprofit law took place in 2008, the TE/GE Commissioner was at the podium. He had once again significantly evolved in his thinking on these points. In two speeches he made his views clear: (1) the IRS has a "robust role" to play in the realm of charitable organizations' governance, (2) the IRS does not even entertain the thought that involvement in nonprofit governance matters is beyond the sphere of the agency's jurisdiction, and (3) he cannot be convinced that, "outside of very, very small organizations and perhaps family foundations, the gold standard should be to have an active, independent and engaged board of directors overseeing the organization."[7] Thus, he stated, the "question is no longer whether the IRS has a role to play in this area, but rather, what that role will be."

In the aftermath of these speeches, the then-Director of the Exempt Organizations Division stated that the IRS is stepping back from recommending best practices as to governance of nonprofit organizations and is focusing instead on education as to good governance.[8] On that occasion, she conceded that "not all IRS agents have gotten this message."[9]

---

[6] No evidence was provided in support of this declaration either. Lawyers practicing in the nonprofit field on a fulltime basis for many years were wholly unaware of this promotional effort. I have not found any instance of IRS involvement in nonprofit governance before Mr. Miller's announcement on April 26, 2007 (see *supra* note 3).

[7] The formal text of these speeches is available at BNA, *Daily Tax Report*, TaxCore (April 30, 2008).

[8] A summary of this speech (by Lois Lerner) is available at BNA, *Daily Tax Report*, TaxCore (June 20, 2008).

[9] Apparently, many of the revenue agents in the exempt organizations context have not, to this day, "gotten this message."

The then-Commissioner of Internal Revenue made his first public comments about nonprofit governance in 2008.[10] After expressing his admiration for the nonprofit sector, and its "diversity, its creativity, and its risk taking," he stated that the IRS "shouldn't supplant the business judgment of organizational leaders, and certainly shouldn't determine how a nonprofit fulfills its individual mission." He said that he "clearly see[s] our role as working with you and others to promote good governance, beginning with the proposition that an active, engaged, and independent board of directors helps assure that an organization is carrying out a tax-exempt purpose and acts as its best defense against abuse." The Commissioner concluded his remarks by saying that "[w]e want to arm you with information and guidance you need to help you comply."

A new TE/GE Commissioner took office in 2009. In her first public address on nonprofit governance, she said: The IRS "has a clear, unambiguous role to play in governance [of tax-exempt organizations]. Some have argued that we do not need to be involved, because we can count on the states to do their job and the sector to stay on the path of self-regulation. While both state regulation and sector self-regulation are important, and I welcome and respect them, they do not get the IRS off the hook. Congress gave us a job to do, and we cannot delegate to others our obligation to enforce the conditions of federal tax exemption. The federal tax law must be applied consistently across the country, and we will use both our education and outreach programs and a meaningful enforcement presence to accomplish this."[11]

Today, for many public charities and their lawyers, IRS review of governance of their organizations is taken for granted; this oversight and, in some cases regulation, is seen as commonplace. But, until Commissioner Miller's famous speech in the spring of 2007, and

---

[10] The formal text of this speech (by Douglas Shulman) is available at BNA, *Daily Tax Report*, p. G-1, TaxCore (Nov. 12, 2008).

[11] The formal text of this speech (by Sarah Hall Ingram) is available at BNA, *Daily Tax Report*, p. G-6, TaxCore (June 24, 2009). Her remark that "Congress gave us a job to do" has never been explained. Ms. Ingram no longer holds this position; subsequent Commissioners of Internal Revenue, TE/GE Commissioners, and Directors of the Exempt Organizations Division have been publicly silent on the subject of nonprofit governance.

his subsequent presentations, no one (outside of the IRS) thought of the agency as an overseer of public charities' and other exempt organizations' board composition and other governance functions.

Revamped Annual Information Return

As noted, nearly every tax-exempt organization is required to file, with the IRS, an annual information return.[12] There are variations of this document; the principal form of it is IRS Form 990. In one of the most dramatic developments in the history of the law of tax-exempt organizations, the IRS completely overhauled the Form 990, launching the new version for tax year 2008. The revamped Form 990 became much longer and much more complicated. But its influence is greater than that: By reason of the mammoth revised annual information return and its accompanying detailed instructions, it became one of the few government forms to create new law. It is not an understatement to say that the form and its instructions are the equivalent of a major regulation project. The principal area of law that was created in this fashion was the federal law of nonprofit governance.

The concept underlying the revised return was to provide a "core form," that all tax-exempt organizations prepare and file, accompanied by a battery of schedules, covering topics where the IRS wanted additional information on particular types of organizations, activities, and/or transactions. The core form consists of 12 pages; there are 16 schedules.[13]

The core form has twelve parts.[14] Part III enables the filing organization to report on its programs and their results; these are known as "program service accomplishments." Part IV of the Form

---

[12] See Chapter 3, text accompanied by notes 16–19.

[13] This core form (Form 990) is filed by the larger tax-exempt organizations (of which there are about 350,000). Medium-sized exempt organizations (those with gross receipts of no more than $200,000 or total assets valued at no more than $500,000) generally file Form 990-EZ; these filers may have to file one or more of the schedules. Organizations with gross receipts of less than $50,000 may file Form 990-N. Private foundations (of any size) file Form 990-PF.

[14] This analysis of the Form 990 is based on the version for filing year 2015.

990 is a checklist of required schedules; it is designed to assist the filing organization in determining which schedules it is required to file. Part V of the form enables the organization to ascertain whether other federal forms must be filed. Part VI of the revised return focuses on nonprofit governance.

It is worth recalling that, with six minor exceptions,[15] there is no statute or regulation that ties eligibility for tax-exempt status to compliance with nonprofit governance principles. Yet an important portion of the annual information return asks many questions about the extent of that type of compliance. Thus, Part VI of the Form 990 and the IRS's private letter ruling policy[16] form the basis for the agency's regulation of nonprofit governance.

IRS officials are fond of calling Part VI of the revised annual information return the "crown jewel" of the revamped Form 990. This designation is meant to convey the importance of Part VI as the IRS's standards for regulating the governance of public charities and other tax-exempt organizations. Part VI of the Form 990 (and its accompanying instructions) is the closest document there is to an IRS regulation pertaining to nonprofit governance.

Part VI is comprised of three sections. Section A pertains to the governing body and management. A chief focus of this section is on the size and composition of the filing organization's governing body. The IRS wants to know the number of voting members of the board,[17] the number of voting members that are "independent" (that is, not compensated or related),[18] and any instances of family relationship or business relationship among the directors (and officers and key employees).[19] The form asks if the board has delegated any of its duties to a management company,[20] whether the organization made any significant changes to its governing documents since the prior

---

[15] See Chapter 3, text accompanied by notes 66–83.

[16] See Chapter 6.

[17] Form 990, Part VI, Section A, question 1a.

[18] *Id.*, question 1b.

[19] *Id.*, question 2.

[20] *Id.*, question 3.

filing,[21] and whether the organization became aware during the year of a significant diversion of its assets.[22]

A question inquires as to whether the filing organization has members or stockholders. [23] Another question asks if the organization has members, stockholders, or other persons who may elect one or more members of the filing organization's governing body. [24] A similar question asks whether any decisions of the governing body are subject to approval by members, stockholders, or other persons.[25] Still another question is whether the organization contemporaneously documented the meetings held or written action undertaken during the year by the governing body or a committee with authority to act on behalf of the governing body.[26]

Section B of Part VI of the revamped Form 990 focuses on various policies. The IRS wants to know if the organization has local chapters, branches, or affiliates.[27] This leads to the first of many IRS-driven policies; the form inquires as to whether the organization has written policies and procedures governing the activities of the chapters, branches, and affiliates to ensure their operations are consistent with the exempt purposes of the organization.[28]

Also, the IRS inquires as to whether a complete copy of the Form 990 was provided to all of the members of the organization's governing body before it was filed.[29] Organizations are required to describe the process, if any, the organization uses to obtain review of the Form 990.[30]

The next question is whether the filing organization has a written conflict-of-interest policy.[31] If the answer is yes, the IRS wants to know whether trustees, directors, officers, and key employees are

---

[21] *Id.*, question 4.
[22] *Id.*, question 5
[23] *Id.*, question 6.
[24] *Id.*, question 7a.
[25] *Id.*, question 7b.
[26] *Id.*, question 8.
[27] Form 990, Part VI, Section B, question 10a.
[28] *Id.*, question 10b.
[29] *Id.*, question 11a.
[30] *Id.*, question 11b.
[31] *Id.*, question 12a.

required to annually disclose interests that could give rise to conflicts.[32] The organization is asked whether it regularly and consistently monitors and enforces compliance with the policy. If yes, the organization is asked to describe how this is done.[33] Other policies that are the subject of questions in Part B pertain to written whistleblower policies[34] and written document retention and destruction policies.[35]

The IRS also wants to know whether the organization has a process for determination of the compensation, including a review and approval by independent persons, comparability data, and contemporaneous substantiation of the deliberation and decision, of the organization's chief executive officer, executive director, or top management official.[36] The same question is posed in connection with other officers or key employees of the organization.[37]

The IRS asks whether the organization invested in, contributed assets to, or participated in a joint venture or similar arrangement with a taxable entity during the year.[38] If the answer to this question is yes, the IRS asks whether it follows a written policy or procedure requiring the organization to evaluate its participation in these joint venture arrangements under the federal tax law and has taken steps to safeguard the organization's exempt status with respect to the arrangements.[39]

Despite its title, Section B is not the only place on the Form 990 and its schedules calling for policies. Indeed, overall, the form and its schedules inquire about 30 policies, including an investment policy,[40]

---

[32] *Id.*, question 12b.
[33] *Id.*, question 12c.
[34] *Id.*, question 13.
[35] *Id.*, question 14.
[36] *Id.*, question 15a.
[37] *Id.*, question 15b.
[38] *Id.*, question 16a.
[39] *Id.*, question 16b.
[40] Form 990,

an expense reimbursement policy,[41] a gift acceptance policy,[42] and a policy concerning compliance with tax-exempt bond laws.[43]

Section C of Part VI is devoted to matters of disclosure. By statute, an exempt organization is required to make its application for recognition of exemption, annual information return, and (in the case of charitable organizations) annual unrelated business income tax return available to the public.[44] The Form 990 asks how the organization adheres to this disclosure requirement; options include posting of the return on the organization's website, posting it on another website, or providing a copy of the return in response to a request.[45] The filing organization is also required to describe whether and, if so, how its makes its governing documents, conflict-of-interest policy, and financial statements available to the public.[46] The IRS also asks the filing organization to list the states with which a copy of the Form 990 is filed.[47]

An oddity about this is that generally none of this information is required by law. It certainly is not mandated by any law pertaining to eligibility for tax-exempt status. Yet the IRS, admitting this dichotomy, asks for the information anyway. Thus, the Form 990 instructions state that "[a]lthough federal tax law generally does not mandate particular management structures, operational policies, or administrative practices, every organization is required [by the IRS] to answer each question in Part VI."[48] And: "Even though the information on policies and procedures request in Section B generally is not required under the Internal Revenue Code, the IRS

---

[41] Form 990,

[42] Form 990,

[43] Form 990,

[44] IRC § 6104.

[45] Form 990, Part VI, Section C, question 18. If the organization provides its annual information return to the public in any other manner, it is asked to explain it in Schedule O.

[46] Form 990, Part VI, Section C, question 19. The latter two categories of documents are not required, as a matter of federal law, to be disclosed to the public.

[47] Form 990, Part VI, Section C, question 17.

[48] IRS Specific Instruction for Form 990 (2015), Part VI.

considers such policies and procedures to generally improve tax [law] compliance."[49]

Thus, although the Form 990 has nonprofit governance considerations scattered throughout, the core portion of the annual information return is, from a governance perspective, Part VI.

Exempt Organizations Division 2009 Annual Report

The IRS announced in late 2008 that it was continuing its work in the tax-exempt organizations governance area by (1) development of a checklist to be used by revenue agents in examinations of exempt organizations to determine whether the organizations' governance practices "impacted the tax compliance issues identified in the examination and to educate organizations about possible governance considerations"; (2) commencement of a training program to educate its employees about exempt organizations governance implications in the determinations, rulings and agreements, and education and outreach areas; and (3) identification of annual information return (Form 990) governance questions that could be used in conjunction with other annual return information in possible compliance initiatives, such as those involving executive compensation, transactions with interested persons, solicitation of noncash contributions, or diversion or misuse of exempt organizations' assets.[50]

Draft IRS Good Governance Principles

Over the years, many nonprofit organizations have devised and published statements of nonprofit good governance principles.[51] When the IRS decided to commence regulation in this area, it

---

[49] *Id.*

[50] IRS Exempt Organizations 2008 Annual Report at 20.

[51] See Chapter 4.

likewise published a set of these principles. On February 7, 2007, the IRS unveiled its draft of the agency's "Good Governance Practices" for public charitable organizations.

The IRS, as part of these principles, stated that it is of the view that governing boards of tax-exempt public charitable organizations should be composed of individuals who are informed and active in overseeing the organization's operations and finances. If a governing board tolerates a climate of secrecy or neglect, the IRS stated, charitable assets are more likely to be used to advance an impermissible private interest. Successful governing boards, according to the agency's principles, include individuals who are not only knowledgeable and passionate about the organization's programs but also have expertise in "critical areas" involving accounting, finance, compensation, and ethics.

The IRS opined that charitable organizations with very small or very large governing boards may be problematic: small boards generally do not represent a public interest; large boards may be less attentive to oversight duties. The IRS suggested that, if a public charity's governing board is very large, it may want to establish an executive committee with delegated responsibilities or establish advisory committees.

The IRS recommended that public charitable organizations review and consider a variety of practices to help ensure that directors understand their roles and responsibilities and actively promote good governance practices. While adopting a particular practice is not a requirement for tax exemption, the agency believes that a charitable organization that adopts some or all of these practices is more likely to be successful in pursuing its exempt purposes and earning public support.

The IRS advocated a clearly articulated mission statement that is adopted by a charitable organization's board of directors because it will explain and popularize the charity's purposes and serve as a guide to the organization's work. A well-written mission statement, the IRS wrote, shows why the charity exists, what it hopes to accomplish, and what activities it will undertake, where, and for whom.

The IRS said that the public expects a public charity to abide by ethical standards that promote the public good. The board of directors bears the ultimate responsibility for setting ethical standards and ensuring that they permeate the organization and inform its practices. To that end, the IRS stated, the board should consider adopting and regularly evaluating a code of ethics that describes behavior it wants to encourage and behavior it wants to discourage. The code of ethics should be a principal means of communicating to all personnel a strong culture of compliance with the law and ethical integrity.

The board of directors of a public charity should, the IRS opined, adopt an effective policy for handling employee complaints and establish procedures for employees to report in confidence suspected financial impropriety or misuse of the charity's resources.

The directors of a public charity must, the IRS declared, exercise due diligence consistent with a duty of care that requires a director to act in good faith, with the care an ordinarily prudent individual in a like position would exercise under similar circumstances, and in a manner the director reasonable believe to be in the charity's best interests. Directors should see to it that policies and procedures are in place to help them meet their duty of care, such as by (1) being familiar with the charity's activities and knowing whether the activities promote the charity's mission and achieve its goals, (2) being fully informed about the charity's financial status, and (3) having full and accurate information to make informed decisions.

The directors of a public charity owe it a duty of loyalty. This duty requires a director to act in the interest of the charity rather than in the personal interest of the director or some other individual or organization. In particular, the duty of loyalty requires a director to avoid conflicts of interest that are detrimental to the charity. To that end, the board of directors should adopt and regularly evaluate an effective conflict-of-interest policy that (1) requires directors and staff to act solely in the interests of the charity, without regard for personal interests; (2) includes written procedures for determining whether a relationship, financial interest, or business affiliation results in a conflict of interest; and (3) prescribes a certain course of action in the event a conflict of interest is identified. Directors and staff should be required to disclose annually in writing any known financial interest that the individual, or a member of the individual's family, has in any business entity that transacts business with the charity.

By making full and accurate information about its mission, activities, and finances publicly available, a public charity, the IRS said, demonstrates transparency. The board of directors should adopt and monitor procedures to ensure that the charity's Form 990, annual reports, and financial statements are complete and accurate, are posted on the organization's website, and are made available to the public on request.

The IRS observed that charitable fundraising is an important source of financial support for many public charities. Success at fundraising requires care and honesty. The board of directors should adopt and monitor policies to ensure that fundraising solicitations meet federal and state law requirements and solicitation materials are accurate, truthful, and candid. Charities should keep their fundraising costs reasonable. In selecting paid fundraisers, a charity should use those that are registered with the state and that can provide good references. Performance of professional fundraisers should be continuously monitored.

Directors must, the IRS determined, be good stewards of a public charity's financial resources. A charity should operate in accordance with an annual budget approved by the board of directors. The board should ensure that financial resources are used to further charitable purposes by regularly receiving and reading up-to-date financial statements, including Form 990, auditor's letters, and finance and audit committee reports. If the charity has substantial assets or annual revenue, the board of directors should ensure that an independent auditor conduct an annual audit. The board can establish an independent audit committee to select and oversee the independent auditor. The auditing firm should be changed periodically (e.g., every five years) to ensure a fresh look at the financial statements. For a charity with lesser assets or annual revenue, the board should ensure that an independent certified public accountant conduct an annual audit. Substitute practices for very small organizations would include volunteers who would review financial information and practices. Trading volunteers between similarly situated organizations who would perform these tasks would also help maintain financial integrity without being too costly.

A successful public charity, the IRS said, pays no more than reasonable compensation for services rendered. Charities should generally not compensate persons for service on the board of directors, except to reimburse direct expenses of such service. Director compensation should be allowed only when determined to be appropriate by a committee composed of persons who are not compensated by the charity and have no financial interest in the determination. Charities may pay reasonable compensation for services provided by officers and staff.

An effective public charity will, according to the IRS, adopt a written policy establishing standards for document integrity, retention, and destruction. The document retention policy should include guidelines for handling electronic files. The policy should cover backup procedures, archiving of documents, and regular check-ups of the reliability of the system.

These proposed good governance principles did not last long. They were jettisoned in early 2008, with the IRS asserting that its positions on nonprofit governance were better reflected and advanced in the revamped Form 990 that the agency developed in that year.[52]

IRS Agents' Training Materials

The IRS, in mid-2014, released the materials that it had been using for the training of its agents in the field of nonprofit governance, for their edification in reviewing applications for recognition of exemption and annual information returns, and during examinations.[53] For the most part, these materials did not contain anything new in relation to what the IRS had been saying over recent years about its positions on governance issues pertaining to public charities and other categories of tax-exempt organizations.

---

[52] See the text accompanied by *supra* notes 12–47. A commentary on these principles is in Chapter 7, text accompanied by notes 148–152.

[53] This training consisted of a two-hour presentation as part of a 3½-day continuing professional education conference for all exempt organizations examination agents and managers.

Restated was the ultimate rationale the IRS invokes in justifying its involvement in nonprofit governance matters. The agency "believes that a well-governed charity is more likely to obey the tax laws, safeguard charitable assets, and serve charitable interests than one with poor or lax governance." The IRS stated that a charity that has "clearly articulated purposes that describes its mission, a knowledgeable and committed governing body and management team, and sound management practices is more likely to operate effectively and consistent with tax law requirements." It added, however, that the federal tax law "generally does not mandate particular management structures, operational policies, or administrative practices."

As to a charitable organization's governing body, the training materials state that the IRS "encourages an active and engaged board [,] believing that it is important to the success of a charity and to its compliance with applicable tax law requirements." Concerning board size, the materials stated that "[a]ttention should also be paid to the size of the board [,] ensuring that it is the appropriate size to effectively make sure that the organization obeys tax laws, safeguards its charitable assets, and furthers its charitable purposes."

The IRS wrote that the Internal Revenue Code "does not require charities to have governance and management policies." It nonetheless added: The IRS "will review an organization's application for [recognition of] exemption and annual information returns to determine whether the organization has implemented policies relating to executive compensation, conflicts of interest, investments, fundraising, documenting governance decisions, document retention and destruction, and whistleblower claims."

The IRS stated that a governing board "should include independent members and should not be dominated by employees or others who are not, by their very nature, independent individuals because of family or business relationships." (Elsewhere the materials state that this is a suggestion and the IRS will not treat this standard as a requirement.) The agency stated that the "nominating process" for members of the governing body "should reach out for candidates, actively recruiting individuals whose commitment, skills, life experience, background, perspective, and other characteristics will serve the public charity and its needs." The IRS also proclaimed that "[a]ttention should also be paid to the size of the board ensuring that it is the appropriate size," governing boards "should be composed of persons who are informed and active in overseeing a charity's operations and finances," and "[t]erm limits for board members are an effective way to ensure board vitality."[54]

IRS Agents' Governance Check Sheet

The IRS, on December 10, 2009, made public the Governance Check Sheet that its examination agents have been using to gather data about the governance practices of public charities, [55] accompanied by a set of instructions.

This check sheet asks whether the organization has a written mission statement that articulates its tax-exempt purposes. There is a question as to whether the organization's bylaws set forth information about its governing body, such as payment of compensation, duties, qualifications, and voting rights. The IRS asks about the extent to which copies of the organization's articles of organization and bylaws have been distributed (e.g., to the board and/or the public. A question inquires about the frequency of meetings of voting board members with a quorum present.

The check sheet asks whether compensation arrangements for all trustees, directors, officers, and key employees are approved in advance by an authorized body of the organization, composed of individuals with no conflict of interest with respect to the arrangement. Questions are asked as to whether this body relies on comparability data in making compensation determinations and whether the basis for compensation determinations is contemporaneously documented.

The check sheet requires the examining agent to ask whether any of the organization's voting board members have a family relationship and/or outside business relationship with any other voting or nonvoting trustee, director, officer, or key employee.

---

[54] A commentary on these training materials is in Chapter 7, text accompanied by note 153.

[55] IRS Form 14114.

Another question is whether effective control of the organization rests with a single individual or a select few individuals.

The check sheet includes a question as to whether the organization has a written conflict-of-interest policy and, if so, whether it addresses recusals and requires annual disclosures of conflicts. The agent is to note, if any actual or potential conflicts of interest were disclosed, whether the organization's policy was followed.

The check sheet inquires as to whether there are systems or procedures in place intended to ensure that the organization's assets are properly used, consistent with the entity's mission. A question inquires as to the frequency with which the organization provided its board members with written reports on its financial activities. The check sheet includes a question asking whether, prior to its filing, the organization's annual information return was reviewed by the full board and/or a committee. A question asks whether an independent accountant's report was prepared and, if so, whether it was considered by the board and/or a committee. The portion of the check sheet concludes with a question as to whether an independent accountant prepared a management letter and, if so, whether this letter was reviewed by the board and/or a committee and whether the organization adopted any of the recommendations in the letter.

The check sheet asks whether the organization has a written policy for document retention and destruction, and, if so, whether the entity adheres to this policy. A question inquires as to whether the board contemporaneously documents its meetings and retains this documentation.[56]

Data as to Correlation

As noted, the IRS has from the outset rationalized its claimed obligation to regulate nonprofit governance one the basis of an ostensible direct correlation between an exempt organization that is governed in accordance with "good governance" practices and its

---

[56] A commentary on this check sheet is in Chapter 7, text accompanied by note 154.

compliance with the federal tax law.[57] The IRS endeavored to prove that point, initially by analyzing information collected by its agents by means of the check sheets.

The results of this analysis were publicly presented by the-then director of the Exempt Organizations Division in a speech delivered on April 19, 2012.[58] The preliminary findings were said to indeed suggest that exempt organizations with proper governance practices are more likely to be in compliance with the tax law.

This study found a valid relationship between four of the questions on the check sheet and this mode of compliance. That is, tax-exempt organizations are more likely to be tax-law compliant if they have a written mission statement, use comparability data in setting amounts of compensation, have procedures in place for the proper use of charitable assets, and where the annual information return was reviewed by the full governing board. By contrast, organizations with control vested in one individual, or a small group, were less likely to be tax compliant. Some of the answers to the questions on the check sheet triggered no significant correlation with compliance with the federal tax law, such as whether an entity adopted a conflict-of-interest policy, never or only occasionally used comparability data in determining compensation amounts, and the fact of family relationships and/or business relationships with other board members (or officers or key employees).[59]

It was said on that occasion that the IRS is planning on future studies of this nature but, to date, none have occurred or, at least, the results of any such study have not been made public.[60]

---

[57] See the text accompanied by *supra* note 1.

[58] A summary of this speech was posted on May 14, 2012, by Ellis Carter in an issue of *Charity Lawyer*. This summary also appeared in an online newsletter published by Law For Change.

[59] A commentary on this data is in Chapter 7, text accompanied by notes 155-159.

[60] This is due, in considerable part, because the IRS's top management staff have been decimated in the aftermath of a major controversy generated by what some are casting as a major scandal concerning the processing of applications for recognition of exemption submitted by Tea Party and other political advocacy groups. The alleged "discriminatory" handling of these applications was first disclosed by the then-Director of the Exempt Organizations Division (Lois Lerner), when she disclosed the problem in the course of a speech on May 10, 2013. The disclosure came on the eve of a critical report from the Treasury Department, which

concluded that the IRS used "inappropriate criteria" in its processing of these applications (Treasury Inspector General for Tax Administration report 2013-10-053 (May 14, 2013)). TIGTA subsequently concluded that the IRS has significantly improved the application process (TIGTA report 2015-10-025 (March 27, 2015)). But this brouhaha continues (e.g., "The Internal Revenue Service's Processing of 501(c)(3) and 501(c)(4) Applications for Tax-Exempt Status Submitted by 'Political Advocacy' Organizations from 2010–2013" (S. Rep. No. 114–119, 114th Cong., 1st Sess. (2015); this report is from the Senate Finance Committee). Courts have not been sympathetic to the IRS in this regard. A federal court of appeals referenced the "unequal treatment" of "victim" applicant organizations by the IRS, the agency's "unconstitutional acts," the IRS's "discriminatory processing and delay," and viewpoint discrimination on the part of the IRS (True the Vote, Inc. v. Internal Revenue Service, 831 F.3d 551, 555, 559, 561 (D.C. Cir. 2016)). Another federal appellate court was equally blunt, repeating the findings of the Treasury Inspector General for Tax Administration that the IRS used "political criteria to round up applications for [recognition of] tax-exempt status" filed by various groups, serving the applicants with "crushing demands" for "unnecessary information" (United States v. NorCal Tea Party Patriots, 817 F.3d 953, 995 (6th Cir. 2016)).

6

IRS Private Letter Ruling Policy

> Tax-exempt public charities must have members who are "representative of the community" and must have a "system for public oversight."
>
> *Internal Revenue Service*

To reiterate, the positions of the IRS on the matter of nonprofit governance are not based on a federal statute, nor reflected in regulations promulgated by the Department of the Treasury. There is one IRS revenue ruling that barely addresses the point.[1] Some of the agency's views in this regard are found in the basic annual information return and its accompanying instructions.[2] Mostly, however, the IRS positions as to nonprofit governance are reflected in private letter rulings.[3] These positions are almost always predicated on application of the private benefit doctrine.[4]

Two categories of IRS private letter rulings principally dominate the agency's policy regarding nonprofit governance. One category of these rulings [28] concludes that the existence of a small (however defined) board, usually of a public charity, is inherently provision of a form of private benefit.[5] The other category of these rulings, numbering [23], holds that a board, again usually of a public charity, dominated by related individuals is likewise inherently a manifestation of private benefit.[6] (Often these two notions are combined in a single ruling because of the existence of small boards

---

[1] See Chapter 3, text accompanied by note 84.
[2] See Chapter 5, text accompanied by notes 12–47.
[3] These rulings are not entitled to any judicial deference (see Chapter 2, text accompanied by notes 130–141.
[4] See Chapter 3, text accompanied by notes 28–41.
[5] See text accompanied by *infra* notes 12–66.
[6] See text accompanied by *infra* notes 67–98.

dominated by, or often consisting wholly of, related individuals.) A third, smaller, category of these rulings (seven) consist of findings by the IRS that a public charity is not entitled to tax-exempt status because it refused to adopt a particular policy.[7] The IRS has ceased issuing rulings of this third type, presumably on the ground that to continue to do so would be blatantly inconsistent with the views of IRS officials as expressed in other contexts, such as the requirements inherent in the process for securing recognition of tax exemption, which clearly do not include adoption of certain policies.[8]

Three IRS private letter rulings are inconsistent with the foregoing three categories of rulings.[9]

This chapter constitutes the database, as to IRS ruling policy in this regard, underlying the book. These rulings began to be made public in 2007; the most recent of them was made public on [September 30, 2016].

Board Size

It is the view of the IRS, as expressed in many private letter rulings, that a small board of a nonprofit organization (almost always a putative public charity) is per se evidence of violation of the private benefit doctrine, thus precluding recognition of tax-exempt status of the entity.[10]

This ruling policy commenced with heavy emphasis by the IRS on board control of an organization. This is rather peculiar, inasmuch as governing boards of tax-exempt organizations almost always control the entities.[11] Nonetheless, the IRS would repeatedly

---

[7] See text accompanied by *infra* notes 99–112.

[8] See Form 1023, Part V, note accompanying question 5.

[9] See text accompanied by *infra* notes 113–121.

[10] The IRS issued three private letter rulings holding that the existence of a small governing board of a charity, by itself, is an insufficient basis for denial of recognition of exemption (see *supra* note 9). These discrepant rulings conform to the state of the case law on the topic. See Chapter 3, text accompanied by notes 94–102.

[11] It is possible (but unlikely) that a nonprofit organization could be controlled by an energetic and engaged membership. Otherwise, situations where true control of a

lament "unfettered control" at the board level, focusing on small boards. Not content with the view that small boards automatically translate into instances of private benefit, the IRS soon began insisting that, for tax exemption to be available, boards (usually of public charities) had to be sufficiently large as to be "representative of the community." This, in turn, quickly morphed into the view that public charities and other nonprofit entities, to be exempt, had to be subject to "public control." The most recent iteration of this nonsense is that the governing board of an exempt organization has to qualify as an "independent oversight board."

It Began with Fertility Services

The first of the IRS private letter rulings addressing the matter of governance was released by the federal government in 2007.[12] This ruling, like so many of those that were to follow, did not solely concern the governance issue.

Indeed, in this ruling, the governance issue was largely overshadowed by another question, which was whether the provision of fertility services at no cost to married and single women who desire to have children and have chosen to become pregnant by artificial insemination is a charitable activity. This was a delicate issue for the IRS. The organization maintained a sperm bank, consisting of sperm donated to it. At the time of the ruling, however, only three men had contributed sperm; one of them donated 88 percent of the sperm. The organization maintained a website describing its services and soliciting applications from women seeking to become recipients of donated sperm. This website included an extensive biography of this donor, without including any biographical information about any other donor. This donor was a founder of the organization, a director and officer of it, and its only financial supporter.

---

nonprofit entity is elsewhere than with its board will probably be confined to instances where it is a subsidiary of a controlling parent.

[12] Priv. Ltr. Rul. 200736037 (June 15, 2007). Thus, this ruling was being written about the time that then-Commissioner Miller was contemplating his historic speech (see Chapter 1, text accompanied by note 2).

The IRS appeared uncomfortable with this arrangement, perhaps uncertain as to this founder's motives. The ruling referenced a questionnaire sent to prospective sperm recipients to determine their suitability to receive sperm donations; the IRS observed that the organization had "not demonstrated that the standards [the organization] use[d] for evaluating applicants or selecting recipients have any medical, psychological or social underpinnings." The agency noted that the founder/principal donor had the ability to "subjectively overrule" the initial screening decision. The IRS then ruled that the organization did not serve the requisite "public purpose."

In pursuing recognition of tax exemption, this organization relied on an IRS revenue ruling holding that an organization that collected and distributed human blood and blood products for the benefit of the public and conducted related research qualified for exemption as a charitable entity, noting that this organization served a "public purpose."[13] The IRS, however, differentiated between the blood distribution entity and the sperm distribution entity, noting that the former obtained blood from many professional and volunteer donors; supplied blood to a wide variety of recipients, including hospitals, government agencies, physicians, clinics, and commercial laboratories; supplied blood free for indigent and charity patients; gave blood to other institutions for research purposes; provided a variety of services relating to the provision of blood in medically necessary situations; and engaged in the provision of related educational services.

These elements of this differentiation exercise had nothing to do with governance. The IRS, nonetheless, relied on one other differentiating factor. This was that the blood distribution organization's board of trustees was "comprised predominantly of public members who were not otherwise associated with the organization." By contrast, the sperm distribution organization's board of directors consisted of two individuals, who are father and son; these two individuals were also the organization's two officers. It was also "significant" to the IRS that one of these individuals was

[13] Rev. Rul. 66-323, 1966-2 C.B. 216.

also, as noted, the organization's founder, sole financial donor, and principal sperm donor.

In this private letter ruling, the IRS emphasized that the organization involved was controlled by one individual, who was the entity's founder, its sole financial donor, one of two related trustees, and one of two related officers. Thus, the IRS ruled, "taking into account [the entity's] structure, governance and operations, [the organization's] activities result in the provision of more than an incidental level of private benefit to [this controlling individual] and his family." Consequently, the organization was held to be violating the prohibition in the tax regulations against "impermissible private benefit."

Therefore, with this private letter ruling, the IRS laid its claim to a basis for ruling as to a nonprofit organization's "structure" and "governance," notwithstanding the fact that the federal tax law generally says nothing about the composition of an entity's governing board as a criterion for tax exemption, and placed the IRS on its path for taking the position that an organization's "small" board and/or its "related" board are bases for denying recognition of tax-exempt status. Moreover, it rested its authority for these sweeping propositions on application of the private benefit doctrine, even though there was no precedent for applying the doctrine in that manner.

This was a radical move on the part of the IRS, one that, at the time, generated little notice. Commentators focused on the sperm donation program and offered jokes about the organization's founder's intentions but failed to take note of what this ruling portended for the future, as the IRS embarked on its campaign to import governance of exempt organizations into its realm of authority.[14]

---

[14] This ruling was republished as Priv. Ltr. Rul. 200737044 (June 18, 2007). This case was litigated, with the government prevailing, although the governance aspects of the case were not pursued as part of the litigation and thus not reflected in the court's opinion (Free Fertility Foundation v. Commissioner, 135 T.C. 21 (2010)).

Ostensibly Unwarranted Control

The IRS thereafter embarked on a multi-ruling analysis of nonprofit governance cases, focusing intently on the matter of *control*, particularly at the board level. This was all quite odd because, for most charitable and other tax-exempt organizations, the board level – irrespective of the number of board members – is where control is generally supposed to be.

The agency considered a nonprofit organization's efforts to be recognized as an exempt charitable organization, where the principal issue was whether the entity qualified as a provider of low-income housing; the IRS ruled that it was ineligible for exemption.[15] At issue, however, were governance matters, including the size of the organization's board of directors. The founder of the organization was designated as the sole "Founding Director" and the entity's president. The IRS was concerned with the degree of authority vested in this individual, observing that he had "significant control" over the affairs of the organization.[16] Two other directors were named; the IRS, "[i]n light of the degree of authority vested in" the founder and the "absence of documentation of the board's participation in decision making to date," stated that "there is nothing to indicate that the other two directors have had or will have significant input." Also, the IRS wrote that "it is questionable whether the other two board members will be able to objectively review decisions and arrangements made prior to the date of that [sic] any [recognition of] exemption may be granted to" the organization. The IRS concluded that this organization was not being operated for public interests but rather for the non-exempt purpose of benefiting its founder.

---

[15] Priv. Ltr. Rul. 200828029 (April 18, 2008).

[16] This individual was the only director who could be removed only for cause. His term of service on the board exceeded that of the other directors and, since board members may serve unlimited successive terms, his term, the IRS remarked, "may be considered perpetual." He financed the organization's activities and was its sole incorporator.

The IRS reviewed the operations of an organization and concluded that it did not qualify as a tax-exempt church.[17] The entity's board consisted of four, related individuals. The IRS concluded that this "family exercises complete control over your organization and its assets could be used to benefit the family." The IRS added: "The structure of your organization indicates that it can be used to benefit private individuals, such as [this family], and you lack safeguards that would help to prevent such use."[18]

A nonprofit organization attempted to qualify for recognition of exemption as a church; the IRS ruled that the organization failed to qualify for church status.[19] Also at issue, however, was application of the private benefit doctrine, inasmuch as the organization had two directors, who were also its two officers; one of these individual's was also the entity's pastor. The IRS, observing that these two individuals had "absolute control" over the organization, concluded that the organization thus was being operated to serve their private interests.

An organization failed in its efforts to be recognized as a tax-exempt charitable entity, in part because it did not adequately describe its activities during the application process and indicated that it would be operating in a commercial manner.[20] Another disqualifying aspect of this entity was its board of three individuals, who were characterized by the IRS as having "unfettered control" over the organization and its assets. The organization was said by the IRS to have not established that the entity will not be operated for the "personal benefit" of the three directors. These facts were ruled to demonstrate violations of the private inurement and private benefit doctrines.

A nonprofit organization was established for the purpose of acquiring and operating a house of worship. It appeared that one of the principal purposes of its formation was to purchase a parcel of real property from one of its trustees. Overall, the organization was

---

[17] Priv. Ltr. Rul. 200830028 (April 28, 2008).

[18] The IRS did not cite any authority for a requirement in law for such "safeguards." This is because there is none.

[19] Priv. Ltr. Rul. 200843032 (August 1, 2008).

[20] Priv. Ltr. Rul. 200845053 (August 11, 2008).

not forthcoming in its submission of information to the IRS, including provision of vague and misleading answers to the agency's follow-up questions. The IRS was clearly suspicious that one or more acts of private inurement had been committed or would be in the immediate future. The organization had a governing board of three individuals, characterized by the IRS as a "small, related" board. The IRS denied recognition of tax exemption to this entity; one of the principal reasons for doing so was that it has "not demonstrated that your trustees use their control for exempt rather than private purposes."[21]

A nonprofit organization was formed with a governing board consisting of three individuals, all related: its founder, the founder's spouse, and the founder's father. The IRS wrote that a "governing board that consists solely of immediate family members does not constitute an independent body, and has an inherent conflict of interest when placed in a position to approve financial transactions involving other family members."[22] The agency added that the organization's records "evidenced the fact that operating under the control of one person or a small, related group suggests that an organization operates primarily for non-exempt private purposes." Indeed, the IRS inventoried a host of private inurement issues and private benefit transactions that were caused by reason of the fact that the organization was "under the control of one person with a family-based governing board."

Another nonprofit organization had a board of three individuals. The articles of incorporation and bylaws of this entity provided that one of these board members (the organization's chief executive officer) could not be removed from office by the board. The IRS asked this organization to expand its board but it refused. The agency denied recognition of exemption in this case on the ground that "private interests" are being served.[23]

---

[21] Priv. Ltr. Rul. 200846040 (August 21, 2008).

[22] Priv. Ltr. Rul. 201113041 (January 7, 2011). As to the fact that the IRS's jurisdiction does not extend to adjudication of matters concerning nonprofit organizations and conflicts of interest, see Chapter 1, text accompanied by notes 96 and 97; Chapter 7, note 65.

[23] Priv. Ltr. Rul. 201218041 (February 7, 2012).

A nonprofit corporation sought recognition of exemption as a charitable and religious entity, and public charity status as a church. It did not, however, meet the IRS criteria for church status. As to tax-exempt status, the IRS found that a substantial part of this organization's activities was creation and promotion of its founder's book and seminar activities, which were non-exempt functions.[24] The IRS, however, was concerned about the organization's three-individual board. The IRS concluded that this governance factor, combined with the activities showing private inurement, "creates greater cause to believe that you are operated for private, rather than public, interests."

A nonprofit organization endeavored to be recognized as a religious, educational, and charitable entity. It failed in this regard, due to the facts that it did not engage in exempt functions and had a two-person board of directors.[25] As to the latter, the IRS wrote that these directors have "unlimited control" and "complete control" over the operation of the organization. They were said to have a "personal and private interest" in the organization's activities. The IRS added that this control element "allows for the potential for excess benefit" because the directors may be compensated.

An organization sought recognition of tax exemption on the ground that it is a synagogue. The IRS concluded that the entity did not meet the agency's criteria for qualification as a church and that it failed to respond openly and candidly to the IRS's inquiries; the IRS thus issued an unfavorable ruling.[26] The governance aspects of this ruling were that the organization had three trustees, but no bylaws, causing the directors to, in the words of the IRS, have "unlimited control and terms." The IRS wrote: "The ability of your three current officers to remain in office until they choose to remove themselves and be replaced by someone of their own choosing provides a window of opportunity for private benefit."

A nonprofit organization was formed to guide young people and their families in Christian activities, with programming involving teacher colleges, a teaching institute, and a teaching hospital. The

---

[24] Priv. Ltr. Rul. 201232034 (May 16, 2012).
[25] Priv. Ltr. Rul. 201236033 (June 12, 2012).
[26] Priv. Ltr. Rul. 201242014 (July 24, 2012).

IRS denied recognition of tax exemption as a charitable entity to this organization, largely on the grounds that the entity did not provide sufficient information as to its proposed activities and that it was operated for the benefit of its founder by promoting her copyrighted materials and providing funds to repay her personal loans.[27] The IRS noted, however, that the fact the organization has a five-person compensated board is inherently a form of private inurement. The agency wrote that this entity was "formed by a small group of individuals who have exclusive control over the management of your funds and operations" and, as a result of this exclusive control, these founders "benefit through the use of your facility, [and] the setting of compensation based on their needs [,] as well as your operations."

An organization sought recognition of tax exemption as a charitable entity, on the ground that it functions as a social network facilitating contributions from individuals to public charities. The IRS denied recognition of exemption to this entity, primarily on the ground that it is operating in a commercial manner by providing fundraising and public relations services.[28] The IRS noted, however, that this organization has a three-person governing board. A for-profit company is providing various services to this nonprofit entity; the three directors also control the for-profit organization. The IRS decided that this organization is being operated "primarily as a conduit" of business to the "related for profit." The IRS added: "This is particularly concerning when the board is a small group of entirely related individuals."

Another nonprofit organization was established for the purpose of providing online fundraising services to public charities. These services were provided on a fee-for-service basis, although the organization sought to convince the IRS that its fees were "very competitive" in comparison to for-profit fundraising companies. This effort proved unsuccessful, with the IRS ruling that the organization did not qualify for tax exemption as a charitable entity because it was primarily operating in a commercial manner. [29] This organization's board is composed of three members, namely, its

[27] Priv. Ltr. Rul. 201421022 (February 27, 2014).
[28] Priv. Ltr. Rul. 201452017 (October 2, 2014).
[29] Priv. Ltr. Rul. 201507026 (October 22, 2014).

founder, the founder's spouse, and the organization's accountant. The IRS asked the organization to expand its board to include unrelated members; the organization declined to do so. The matter of board size (or composition) is not discussed in the ruling as a basis for the denial of recognition.

A nonprofit organization was formed to offer spiritual, emotional, and other support to individuals who are grieving; it also will address the "systemic injustices within our society that are the source of grief for persons who are poor and marginalized." The IRS concluded that, inasmuch as this entity's primary activities consist of selling published materials and manufactured ceramic items, it is operating in a commercial manner.[30] The fact that two directors shared in royalty arrangements and lived without charge in the organization's facilities give rise to charges of private inurement. Not surprisingly, this organization was denied recognition of tax exemption. This entity started with a board of three (two related), then acceded to the IRS's request to add four unrelated board members. This concession did not advance the organization's objectives, although its board size was not cited as a factor in its failure to qualify for exemption.

The IRS ruled that a situation where an individual is an organization's founder, and also its executive director, president, sole employee, and one of three board members,[31] a violation of the private inurement doctrine occurred because she is in "complete control" of the entity.[32] There is no indication in the ruling that this individual somehow dominated the boards' operations or that the other two directors[33] are related to her. Thus, as a matter of law,

---

[30] Priv. Ltr. Rul. 201526020 (April 2, 2015).

[31] This individual is also a certified body talk practitioner, an animal talk practitioner, a fuji-san practitioner, a complete mind and body instructor, a hypnotherapist, a Reiki Master, and a breakthrough facilitator for body talk.

[32] Priv. Ltr. Rul. 201540019 (July 7, 2015).

[33] One of these other directors is a certified yoga practitioner, a flower essence practitioner, and a long-time devotee of natural healing remedies. The third director is a singer and a song writer.

there was no basis for the IRS to conclude that this founder, only one of three directors, controlled the organization.[34]

An organization seeking recognition of exemption as a charitable entity had a three-individual board (two of whom were related by marriage). The organization's founder/president and its secretary were married to principal officers of a related organization. One of the reasons the IRS denied recognition of exemption to this entity was its board structure. On the point, the IRS ruled that the existence of "this small group of individuals" was a fact that "suggests" that the organization "operates primarily for non-exempt private purposes."[35]

An organization sought qualification as a tax-exempt social club.[36] The IRS ruled that this entity was not eligible for exemption, principally on the ground that it did not meet the basic tax law requirements for exempt social clubs.[37] The IRS noted, however, that this organization has a four-person board of directors, all selected by its founder. The board was said to "exercise exclusive control over your management and day-to-day operations." The members of the organization, the IRS observed, do not exercise any control over the entity and lack a voice in the management of the club.

The IRS thus came to equate "absolute control" by a charity's small board as evidence that the organization was being operated to serve these individuals' private interests, even though in most tax-exempt organizations control is always vested in a governing board.

---

[34] Given the talent on this board (see *supra* notes 31 and 33), the IRS should have recognized it as a most exemplary governing board (except the IRS does not have the authority to do that).

[35] Priv. Ltr. Rul. 201634029 (May 26, 2016).

[36] That is, an organization that is exempt pursuant to IRC § 501(a) as an organization described in IRC § 501(c)(7).

[37] Priv. Ltr. Rul. 201451030 (September 25, 2014).

One-Individual Boards

Organizations with a one-individual board are, in the view of the IRS, ineligible for tax exemption.[38] This point is manifested in one of the few IRS private letter rulings applying governance principles outside the public charity setting. As usual, the reasons for denial of recognition of exemption involve facts that have nothing to do with the matter of governance. In this ruling, an organization attempted to qualify as an exempt business league,[39] claiming that its purpose is to improve the business conditions in the health care professionals' industry. The IRS concluded, however, that the real purpose of the organization was to market its founder's financial planning seminars and direct business to a for-profit business, wholly owned by this individual, for the purchase of financial products. The organization was ruled to be ineligible for exemption because it was formed to provide particular services for individuals and was, therefore operated in a manner similar to a for-profit business, benefiting this individual and his for-profit business.[40]

This ruling pertains to nonprofit governance, however, because the founder of the organization involved was the sole member of its governing body and "holds all positions in the organization." A form of private benefit was found in this context,[41] with the IRS writing that the organization was "controlled by your founder, and your founder will benefit either directly through your operation or indirectly through expanded business to" the founder's for-profit company.

---

[38] This is the case even where state corporation law permits one-individual boards, such as Ohio (see Chapter 3, text accompanied by notes 109-111. Even California, the states with the most rigorous of nonprofit governance laws (see Chapter 4, text accompanied by note 12) permits, by statute, one-individual boards.

[39] That is, an organization that is exempt from federal income tax pursuant to IRC § 501(a) as an organization described in IRC § 501(c)(6).

[40] Priv. Ltr. Rul. 201242016 (July 27, 2012).

[41] A legitimate argument may be made that the private benefit doctrine only applies with respect to tax-exempt charitable entities. The IRS, however, is of the view that the doctrine applies with respect to other categories of exempt organizations, and has so ruled in cases involving exempt social welfare organizations, business leagues, and social clubs.

A nonprofit organization was denied recognition of exemption as a charitable entity, largely for reasons having nothing to do with governance. This entity, however, had one director, who, the IRS wrote, "controls all aspects of your operations."[42]

An organization was unsuccessful in its attempt to be recognized as a tax-exempt charitable entity.[43] The IRS noted that the organization has one director, who is also the sole officer and sole employee, but did not allude to this governance arrangement as a reason for the denial.[44]

Concept of Community Representation

Building on this base of rulings focused on the control factor, ostensibly buttressed by the private benefit doctrine, the IRS began insisting that the state of the law was such that tax exemption for public charities hinged on whether their boards have members who are "representative of the community."

Apparently the first of the IRS rulings emphasizing this ostensible need for *community representation* was one released in mid-2008.[45] The IRS was concerned about the ostensible dominance of the organization's president, who was portrayed as having "significant control" over the entity's affairs. The IRS lamented that the other board members "have been selected based upon their business experience."[46] Moreover, the IRS wrote, the organization is "not operated by through [sic] a community-based board of directors, and there is no indication that community groups have input into the your [sic] operations." The IRS did not cite any authority for this ostensible requirement of a community-based governing board or

---

[42] Priv. Ltr. Rul. 201443021 (July 29, 2014).

[43] Priv. Ltr. Rul. 201525014 (March 24, 2015).

[44] Also Priv. Ltr. Rul. 201252021 (September 13, 2012).

[45] Priv. Ltr. Rul. 200828029 (April 18, 2008).

[46] This criterion is usually considered a positive and major one in the pantheon of board credentials.

for a requirement that community groups must have some form of input into charitable organizations' operations.[47]

A nonprofit organization was formed to "develop and implement targeted initiatives to improve the safety, quality, accessibility and cost effectiveness of healthcare" in its state. It has three organization founders: a for-profit company (the "insurance founder"), a tax-exempt trade association, and a public charity (the "research founder"). The IRS denied recognition of exemption to this organization on the grounds of private inurement and private benefit.[48] As to the former, the IRS stated that the organization's "structural and governance relationship with two non-charitable entities presents an opportunity for inurement to them." The IRS stated that this governance structure "gives control to your non-charitable founders." These two founders were said to have "independent financial interests in your activities." The IRS stated that "[n]one of your officers or directors represent the broader interest of the community."

Requirement of Public Control

Indeed, in some of its rulings, the IRS asserted that "charitable organizations serving a public interest" are to be subject to "public control." In one of these instances, the IRS asserted that an organization "lack[ed] the ... public control that [is] characteristic of a charitable organization seeking to serve the public" and that it "shows none of the public involvement that characterize organizations serving a public interest."[49] Nothing was cited by the

---

[47] During the application processing stage, the IRS tried to force this organization to expand its board of directors to include individuals unrelated to the applicant's sole director; the organization replied that it would do so only after receipt of a favorable determination letter. This practice of the IRS, pushing for board expansion as a condition of exemption, was commonplace during this time (e.g., Exploratory Research, Inc. v. Commissioner, 95 T.C.M. 1347, 1348-1349 (2008)). In this case, the IRS stated that it was seeking to "insure that ... [the] organization will serve public interests" (at 1348).

[48] Priv. Ltr. Rul. 201436050 (June 12, 2014).

[49] E.g., Priv. Ltr. Rul. 201429027 (December 12, 2012).

IRS in support of these concepts of *public control* and/or *public involvement*.[50]

During the course of processing an application for recognition of exemption filed by an organization seeking status as a charitable entity, the IRS sent a letter to the organization stating: "To insure that your organization will serve public interests[,] changes should be made to the bylaws whereby control is vested in a Board of Directors consisting of a majority of unrelated persons." Apparently the organization declined to expand its board as the IRS requested. The ruling states: "Despite repeated requests to expand control, any efforts made in responding to such requests have been superficial and ineffectual."[51]

An organization sought recognition of tax exemption as a charitable organization on the ground that its principal purpose is to increase the level of charitable giving by younger donors. To that end, its emphasis is on the adaptation of technology popular among these donors, principally the use of wireless mobile telephones. The IRS, however, saw private benefit and commercial activity.[52] Private benefit was found in the relief of administrative burdens of the wireless mobile telephone carriers who participate in the fundraising campaigns. Commercial activity was seen in the services provided by the organization in collecting and storing data regarding transactions between donors, the mobile carriers, and the recipient charities. The IRS observed that this organization "lack[s] the public support and public control that are characteristic of a charitable organization seeking to serve the public" and "shows none of the public involvement that characterizes organizations serving a public interest." As illustrations, the organization was faulted for not having representatives from public charities and "civic groups" on its board and for allowing the directors to also serve as its officers.

Another nonprofit organization was established for the purpose of providing online fundraising services to public charities. These services were provided on a fee-for-service basis, although the

---

[50] There is no such law.
[51] Priv. Ltr. Rul. 200843032 (August 1, 2008).
[52] Priv. Ltr. Rul. 201429027 (December 12, 2012).

organization sought to convince the IRS that its fees were "very competitive" in comparison to for-profit fundraising companies. This effort proved unsuccessful, with the IRS ruling that the organization did not qualify for tax exemption as a charitable entity because it was primarily operating in a commercial manner.[53] This organization's board is composed of three members, namely, its founder, the founder's spouse, and the organization's accountant. The IRS asked the organization to expand its board to include unrelated members; the organization declined to do so. The matter of board size (or composition) is not discussed in the ruling as a basis for the denial of recognition.

Concept of Independent Oversight Board

References began appearing in these rulings to a requirement for an "independent oversight board." In one of its private letter rulings, the IRS stated: "The close control held by a few individuals, without a system for public oversight, creates an environment for potential abuse and insider benefit as there are no defined roles or responsibilities for your board or policies setting forth their duties and the handling of your finances."[54]

In one instance, the IRS called on charities seeking recognition of exemption to have a "system for public oversight."[55] On this occasion, the IRS declared that the "close control held by a few individuals ... creates an environment for potential abuse and insider benefit." The agency also wrote that "undue control of the organization by a related board causes the organization to serve private interests."

In another instance, the IRS recognized the tax exemption of an organization that was said to provide psychological counseling and therapy to individuals and families affected by drug addiction, alcohol, or violence. In reality, the operation was a commercial psychiatric practice. Also, on examination, the IRS found many

---

[53] Priv. Ltr. Rul. 201507026 (October 22, 2014).
[54] Priv. Ltr. Rul. 201242014 (July 24, 2012).
[55] E.g., Priv. Ltr. Rul. 201325017 (March 28, 2013).

forms of private inurement, with the psychiatrist involved treating the organization as, in the words of the IRS, "her personal checking account."[56] This individual was the entity's sole director, she held all of the officer positions, and controlled the organization's bank accounts. Despite the lack of an exempt function and rampant private inurement, the IRS observed that the "most significant problem observed during the examination was the complete lack of any oversight or internal controls." The IRS stated that "[t]here was no independent oversight board in place with the organization to provide guidance to the officers." "These conditions," the IRS concluded, "lent themselves to financial problems," with this lack of oversight by an independent board "result[ing] in an environment where [the psychiatrist] could do as she pleased without having to answer to anyone." The IRS examiner wrote that a tax-exempt organization, to remain exempt, "must put precautions in place to protect the assets of the organization,"[57] noting that the organization "fell completely flat on this."[58] The IRS revoked the exempt status of this entity.

A similar situation subsequently arose. An organization sought recognition of exemption as a synagogue but it did not meet the IRS criteria for church status and was not sufficiently responsive in responding to the IRS's requests for information. This organization had a board of three individuals, two of which were related. The IRS wrote: "The close control held by a few individuals, without a system for public oversight, creates an environment for potential abuse and insider benefit as there are no defined roles or responsibilities for your board or policies setting forth their duties and the handling of your finances."[59]

An organization sought qualification as a tax-exempt business league. The IRS ruled that this entity was not eligible for exemption on the ground that its members, who are non-voting, are not

---

[56] Priv. Ltr. Rul. 201252021 (September 13, 2012).

[57] No citation of any authority was provided for this assertion.

[58] Indeed, the IRS wrote that, "[b]ecause of the manner in which [the psychiatrist] set up the organization without oversight or controls and the manner in which [she] routinely pilfered the accounts of the organization[,] fraud was seriously considered."

[59] Priv. Ltr. Rul. 201325017 (March 28, 2013).

involved in the organization's activities at a meaningful level.[60] The IRS noted that this entity had a three-person self-perpetuating board. The agency noted that, in the case, "[t]here is no oversight of an independent board."

Religious Institutions

The IRS has taken the position that its rule that an exempt organization's board must have a majority of unrelated persons has been extended to entities seeking recognition of exempt status as synagogues.

Initially, this governance issue was not raised. An organization applied for recognition of tax exemption as a synagogue. It failed in this regard because it provided incomplete and contradictory information to the IRS in response to follow-up questions. The IRS observed that this organization has a self-perpetuating board of three individuals. The IRS, however, stated: "The close control held by a few individuals, without a system for public oversight, creates an environment for potential abuse and insider benefit as there are no defined roles or responsibilities for your board or policies setting forth their duties and the handling of your finances. The ability of your three current officers [sic] to remain in office until they choose to remove themselves and be replaced by someone of their own choosing provides a window of opportunity for private benefit."[61]

In a similar situation, an organization failed to qualify as a tax-exempt synagogue because it did not provide sufficient information to the IRS. Nonetheless, the IRS fixed on this organization's board of trustees, which at the outset consisted of three related individuals. During the processing of the application, one of these directors resigned; this position was filled by an individual unrelated to the other two. The IRS sagely wrote that, "[d]espite having one board member resign, two of the three are still related." The IRS added:

---

[60] Priv. Ltr. Rul. 201349021 (July 2, 2013).

[61] Priv. Ltr. Rul. 201242014 (July 24, 2012).

"Your addition of a fourth, unrelated board member does not eliminate the control of the board by the majority-related board."[62]

A third situation was quite similar to the foregoing two (although in this case the IRS also concluded that the organization did not qualify as a tax-exempt church). As to governance, this entity had three board members. The IRS observed that this entity has a "small board," adding that "there is no indication that the board members have an active role in your operations."[63]

The IRS denied recognition of exemption to an Islamic religious organization, largely due to its inability to satisfy the IRS's requests for information. Nonetheless, this entity had a three-individual board, a fact that the IRS dwelled on. At the time of application, this organization's board consisted of two related individuals; during the application process a third, unrelated individual was added to the board. The IRS wrote: "Your inability to adequately explain your activities is particularly troubling in light of the fact that such activities are controlled by two related persons." The IRS concluded the governance aspect of this ruling by disparaging the qualifications of the unrelated director, stating that "it is questionable whether a person who works in the field of automobile insurance will have a significant voice in the affairs" of a religious organization.[64] The IRS added that this organization has "not demonstrated that there are sufficient safeguards in place to prevent your net earnings from inuring to the benefit of [the two related directors], or to prevent you from operating for their private benefit."[65]

It is doubtful that any tax-exempt church, synagogue, mosque, or similar religious institution has a "system for public oversight," and quite likely that an attempt by a government to force such a governance structure on a religious institution would be a violation of First Amendment principles.

---

[62] Priv. Ltr. Rul. 201325017 (March 28, 2013).

[63] Priv. Ltr. Rul. 201427018 (April 7, 2014).

[64] The IRS has no authority to evaluate the qualifications of an individual to sit on the board of a nonprofit organization or to evaluate the extent or effectiveness of an individual's participation in board functions.

[65] Priv. Ltr. Rul. 201332013 (May 17, 2013).

Health Care Exception

A nonprofit corporation was formed to support quality and cost improvements in pediatric health care, particularly pediatric health care provided to the Medicaid population. Overall, this organization seeks to improve the quality of and access to Medicaid services for children. The organization has a governing board of 28 individuals. Nine of them specialize in pediatrics or represent pediatric hospitals or large-group practices. Eight of them are at-large directors, albeit having knowledge about pediatric services. Three directors are ex officio. The IRS observed that this organization has a "very large board of directors," lamenting, nonetheless, that "none of the directors will represent the broad interests of the community." The IRS wrote that it "must assume" that if these "private individuals" have control, the organization "will further their profit-seeking motives." These directors, it was written, have "no obligation to put charitable purposes ahead of profit-making objectives." This organization was denied recognition of tax exemption.[66]

Related Boards

It is the view of the IRS, as expressed in private letter rulings, that a board of a nonprofit organization (almost always a putative public charity), consisting entirely or primarily of related individuals, is per se evidence of violation of the private benefit doctrine, thus precluding recognition of tax-exempt status of the entity.

The first organization to be determined by the IRS to not qualify as a tax-exempt public charity, in part because it had a related board (father and son), was the sperm bank organization discussed

---

[66] Priv. Ltr. Rul. 201440020 (July 8, 2014). Facially, this may well be the most preposterous of the IRS private letter rulings finding private benefit on the basis of governing board size. It is likely, however, (although the ruling is silent on the point) that this holding is part of the IRS's traditional practice of not allowing physician-controlled entities in the tax-exempt health care field (Hyatt and Hopkins, *The Law of Tax-Exempt Healthcare Organizations, Fourth Edition* (John Wiley & Sons, Inc.: 2013) § 33.4). See Chapter 3, text accompanied by note 82.

earlier.[67] This private letter ruling, however, focused primarily on board size.

The first IRS private letter ruling where the matter of a related board become a major factor precluding tax exemption arose when a nonprofit organization applied for recognition of exemption as a church. The IRS denied recognition of exemption, in part because the entity did not meet the IRS's criteria for an exempt church.[68] The IRS, however, also invoked the private benefit doctrine, based on the fact that all of the members of the entity's four-person board of directors were members of the same family. One of these directors was the organization's founder. The IRS wrote that this family exercises "complete control" over the organization. The agency stated that the "structure of [the] organization indicates that it can be used to benefit private individuals," namely, members of the family. The entity was said to "lack safeguards that would help prevent such use." The IRS stated that the organization "provided no evidence that [it] will not be used for the benefit of private individuals."

An organization seeking to qualify as an exempt church was denied recognition of exemption solely because of the fact of its two-person related board of directors.[69] This husband-and-wife team was said by the IRS to have "absolute control" over the entity. The IRS wrote that the organization failed to demonstrate that it was "not operated to serve the private interests" of the two individuals. In this case, the IRS made what the agency termed "repeated requests to expand control;" during the processing of the application, the IRS wrote to the organization stating that, "[t]o insure that your organization will serve public interests [,] changes should be made to the bylaws whereby control is vested in a Board of Directors consisting of a majority of unrelated persons."

As noted, the IRS declined to extend tax exemption to a nonprofit organization that was established for the purpose of acquiring and operating a house of worship, with the IRS suspicious that the true purpose of its formation was to purchase a parcel of

---

[67] See the text accompanied by *supra* notes 12, 14.

[68] Priv. Ltr. Rul. 200830028 (April 28, 2008).

[69] Priv. Ltr. Rul. 200843032 (August 1, 2008).

real property from one of its trustees.[70] In that case, the organization had a three-individual board of trustees, which the IRS characterized as related parties because these three persons were also partners in a for-profit business. This "structure of control" was said by the IRS to "create[] the potential for abuse of exemption provisions."

Thus, the IRS often will state that the board of directors of a tax-exempt charitable organization must consist of a "majority of unrelated persons." This occurred in a case where an organization, with two trustees, was seeking recognition of tax exemption as a church.[71] There, the IRS observed that "there is no independent oversight of [the] organization's activities nor is there an independent process for determining and approving the level of compensation."

Another organization with a board of related individuals would not have qualified for exemption in any event inasmuch as its planned operations were those of a genealogical society.[72] This organization had as its primary purpose the promotion of an individual's legacy, which was held by the IRS to be serving the private interests of a particular family.[73] The board of this organization (the number of members of which was not stated) was comprised entirely of nephews and nieces of this individual. The IRS concluded that this organization was "primarily operated" to serve the "private interests" of this family, observing that the family "could, without challenge, dictate the organization's programs, operations, budget, and spend its funds."

An organization sought recognition of exemption as a charitable entity. It was unsuccessful in this regard, in considerable part because its operations were commercial in nature, so that it failed the operational test.[74] Also, the entity's three-person board of directors consisted of three family members, who were said by the

---

[70] See the text accompanied by *supra* note 21.

[71] E.g., Priv. Ltr. Rul. 200843032 (August 1, 2008).

[72] This type of organization generally is precluded from tax exemption as a charitable or educational entity on the ground of the private benefit, in the form of genealogy research services, extended to its members. E.g., Callaway Family Association v. Commissioner, 71 T.C. 340 (1978).

[73] Priv. Ltr. Rul. 200916035 (January 23, 2009).

[74] Priv. Ltr. Rul. 201016088 (January 29, 2010).

IRS to "hold complete control" of the organization. This fact was said by the IRS to violate the private benefit doctrine, which was the second basis for denial of exemption.

A tax-exempt organization was audited by the IRS. As the consequence, its exemption was revoked because the entity's president was found to have repeatedly engaged in private inurement and excess benefit transactions.[75] The governing board of this entity consisted of its president, his father, and his wife. The IRS wrote that all of these inappropriate transactions took place because the organization was under the control of the president and the entity had a "family-based governing board." The IRS wrote: "A governing board that consists solely of immediate family members does not constitute an independent body, and has an inherent conflict of interest when placed in a position to approve financial transactions involving other family members." It added: "The records of the organization evidenced the fact that operating under the control of one person or a small, related group suggests that an organization operates primarily for non-exempt private purposes."

A nonprofit organization failed to secure a determination that it is a charitable and educational entity primarily because it operated in a commercial manner and otherwise failed the operational test.[76] The majority of this organization's governing board was related, by family and business relationships. The founder of the organization, one of the board members, was said by the IRS to have "unchecked control" over the board and the organization. These facts, the IRS wrote, "demonstrate" that the organization is serving "private interests."

A nonprofit corporation failed, for several reasons, to secure recognition of exemption as a charitable entity.[77] The IRS observed that the organization's operations "are controlled by and are dependent upon members of" a family. The majority of the board consisted of family members; the remaining board members were cast as "professional friends" of the organization's president. The IRS concluded that this entity failed to establish that it is not organized and operated for the benefit of private interests.

---

[75] Priv. Ltr. Rul. 201113041 (January 7, 2011).
[76] Priv. Ltr. Rul. 201203025 (October 26, 2011).
[77] Priv. Ltr. Rul. 201209011 (December 8, 2011).

Another nonprofit entity was unsuccessful in obtaining recognition of tax exemption as a charitable entity, because of lack of exempt functions and various private inurement transactions. [78] This organization had a three-person board of directors, two of whom were related. The organization's articles of incorporation state that its chief executive officer, one of the board members, cannot be removed from the board. When asked to explain this provision, she replied that it was added to, as stated in the ruling, "insure that she can protect her interest in the organization." The IRS stated that it asked the organization "multiple times" to expand its governing board but it failed to do so. The IRS added that the organization has "structured its board so that private interests are protected."

An organization was denied recognition of tax exemption as a religious organization and classification as a church. [79] It has a governing body of five, who are selected by the organization's membership. Two of the trustees are, in the language of the ruling, married to and "live with" each other; two of the other trustees have the same relationship. This board of trustees was cast as having a "closely related" nature. The organization was said to have not met the burden of establishing that its activities will not serve to benefit private interests. Indeed, the IRS wrote that the "potential for private benefit clouds every aspect of [the] organization's operations." The agency stated that this issue of board composition was "identified early in the process of developing your case," and the organization had "ample time and opportunity to address it." Even though private benefit has not occurred at the time the ruling was issued, the IRS wrote that the relationships on the board "could readily facilitate the types of future abuses" contemplated by the private benefit prohibition.

As noted, a nonprofit corporation was denied recognition of exemption as a charitable and religious organization, with its founder's book and seminar promotion as its primary activity, in part because its governing board was small.[80] This board consisted of the organization's founder and her brother and daughter. The private benefit activities and the board of related individuals were

---

[78] Priv. Ltr. Rul. 201218041 (February 7, 2012).

[79] Priv. Ltr. Rul. 201221022 (March 1, 2012).

[80] See the text accompanied by *supra* note 24.

combined by the IRS in reaching its conclusion that exemption was precluded because the organization was being operated for "private, rather than public, interests."

An organization was denied recognition of exemption as a religious organization on the ground that it did not engage in any religious activities.[81] Another reason given by the IRS for this conclusion was that the organization has a two-person board, with these individuals "related through marriage." The IRS asked this entity to expand its board of directors but the two directors were unwilling to do so "because at this time no one shares in our vision." The IRS wrote that the two directors have a "personal and private interest" in the organization's activities, and will have "unlimited control over [its] operations and finances." The IRS concluded that this board arrangement "allows for the potential for excess benefit through compensation as well as the use of the facility and other assets."

A nonprofit organization was denied recognition of tax exemption on private inurement doctrine grounds.[82] One reason for the conclusion as to private inurement was that substantially all of the grants made by the entity to date were made to a for-profit company owned by the son of two of the three board members. Private inurement was also, in the wording of the ruling, "indicated" by the fact that the three-person board of directors of the organization are all members of the same family and "control all aspects of the grant program."

As noted, an organization was denied classification by the IRS as a tax-exempt synagogue, in part because it had a small board.[83] Two members of a three-individual board were related. The IRS stated: "The close control held by a few individuals, without a system for public oversight, creates an environment for potential abuse and insider benefit as there are no defined roles or responsibilities for your board or policies setting forth their duties and the handling of your finances." The agency concluded that the "undue control of the

---

[81] Priv. Ltr. Rul. 201236033 (June 12, 2012).
[82] Priv. Ltr. Rul. 201302040 (October 19, 2012).
[83] See the text accompanied by *supra* note 59.

organization by a related board causes the organization to serve private interests and thus fail the operational test."

An organization was formed by two individuals. It governing body consisted of three individuals who are related to or are friends of the founders. This organization failed in its attempt to gain recognition as a tax-exempt charitable entity but for reasons unrelated to the board composition. Nonetheless, the IRS recited this fact in its ruling.[84]

As noted, an organization was denied recognition of tax exemption because it did not sufficiently engage in exempt functions, operated for the benefit of its founder by promoting her publications and paying her loans, and had a five-individual compensated board.[85] This governing board consisted of five family members. The IRS ruled that this organization was violating the private benefit doctrine because it is governed by a "small group of individuals who have exclusive control over the management of [its] funds and operations."

As noted, an organization failed to achieve recognition in large part because its operation of a social network connecting donors with public charities was found to amount to the provision of fundraising and public relations services on a commercial basis.[86] Another reason for denial of recognition, however, was that this organization has a three-individual board. These board members are related in that they are the owners of a business and two of them are married to each other. Concluding that the primary purpose of this organization was to serve as a conduit of business to the for-profit company, the IRS wrote that these operations are "particularly concerning when the board is a small group of entirely related individuals."

Again, an organization conducting a mobile giving program in hopes of stimulating charitable giving by younger donors was denied recognition of tax exemption on the ground that it is violating the private benefit doctrine.[87] Part of this organization's inability to

---

[84] Priv. Ltr. Rul. 201411038 (December 19, 2013).

[85] See the text accompanied by *supra* note 27.

[86] See the text accompanied by *supra* note 51.

[87] See the text accompanied by *supra* note 28.

achieve exemption was tied to the fact of its two-individual board. The IRS, as part of the application review process, forced this entity to add three unrelated individuals to its governing board. The organization's board meeting minutes showed that there were never more than four members in attendance at any meeting, and that the two founding board members attended and voted at all of the meetings. The IRS wrote that this organization "shows none of the public involvement that characterizes organizations serving a public interest."

Further, as noted, an organization was denied recognition of tax exemption as a charitable entity because its activities, the provision of online fundraising services to public charities, were conducted in a commercial manner.[88] The size or composition of this organization's governing board was not identified by the IRS as a basis for the adverse ruling. The board is, however, comprised of three individuals, namely, the organization's founder, the founder's spouse, and the organization's accountant. The IRS asked the organization to expand its board to include unrelated members; the organization declined to do so. The entity's founder told the IRS that we "feel it [is] best to keep the board small, making the decision making involved with rolling out the organization simpler."

Likewise, an organization did not succeed in its pursuit of tax exemption as a charitable entity because it was operated in a commercial manner.[89] This entity commenced operations with a governing board of three (two of which are related), then agreed to the IRS's request to add four unrelated board members. The organization's board composition was not cited as a factor in its inability to qualify for exemption.

An organization endeavored to gain recognition as a tax-exempt business league. It failed in this regard, principally because it has ceded control of its operations to a for-profit company and the members of the entity are not involved in its activities at a meaningful level.[90] The IRS observed, however, that this organization has a self-perpetuating board, the members of which are not selected by the organization's members. The board consists of three individuals, two

---

[88] See the text accompanied by *supra* note 29.
[89] See the text accompanied by *supra* note 58.
[90] Priv. Ltr. Rul. 201349021 (July 2, 2013).

of whom are related. The IRS noted, without ruling on the point, that "[t]here is no oversight of an unrelated board."

An organization was denied recognition of tax exemption because it engaged in private inurement and commercial transactions. As part of the process of reviewing the application for recognition, the applicant organization, which started with a board of three (two of which were related), acceded to the IRS's request to add four unrelated board members.[91]

During the process by which an organization secured recognition of exemption as a charitable entity, the IRS forced the entity to expand its board of directors from one individual to three unrelated individuals and add another individual as an officer.[92]

An organization had its charitable tax-exempt status revoked because of its practices that, according to the IRS, violate the private benefit and commerciality doctrines. The organization's board of directors consists of three individuals, two of whom are related by marriage. The organization's founder and president, and its secretary, are married to principal officers of a for-profit company (who are also related). The IRS observed that this organization is "governed by a small group of individuals in which two of the three officers are related by marriage." The IRS continued: "While this fact alone may not necessarily disqualify [the organization] for exemption, it provides an opportunity for abuse of the claimed tax-exempt status and suggests that [the organization] operates primarily for non-exempt private purposes, rather than exclusively for public purposes."[93]

A nonprofit organization was formed as a "sweat equity housing cooperative association" in accordance with a state statute. Its "precept," according to this ruling, is to "preserve and rehabilitate rural properties of historic value that serve simultaneously as family businesses and family homes." This organization's governing board is comprised of five individuals, who are also its officers; they are

---

[91] Priv. Ltr. Rul. 201526020 (April 2, 2015).

[92] Priv. Ltr. Rul. 201541013 (May 29, 2014).

[93] As authority for those conclusions, the IRS cited Church of Ethereal Joy v. Commissioner, 83 T.C. 20 (1984) (summarized in Chapter 3, text accompanied by notes 103-10]) and Rev. Rul. 55-656, 1955-1 C.B. 262 (summarized in Chapter 3, text accompanied by note 86).

related to one another. Each board member is to have a possessory interest in one of the entity's residential units and possessory interest in common with other members of real and personal property not constituting residential units. This interest will be that of landlord and tenant. Each member must contribute equally for the buy-in of stock. At the time of dissolution, there may a cash distribution to members. Although the IRS ruled that this organization is not entitled to exemption on the ground of private inurement, stating that the entity has a "substantial non-exempt purpose of operating a cooperatively owned property rehabilitation organization, which destroys [its] claim for exemption," the IRS observed that the organization is "operat[ed] for the benefit of your creators, who are also all family members."[94]

It is noted that, although the private benefit doctrine is equally applicable to public charities and private foundations,[95] the IRS – without explaining how this can be – applies its position that related boards equal private benefit in the public charity setting but not in the private foundation setting.[96] There is no principled basis for this distinction.[97] Thus, for example, the IRS was not in the least troubled by a governing board of a private foundation that was a small one (four individuals), with all of its members being members of the same family.[98]

---

[94] Priv. Ltr. Rul. 201640022(July 7, 2016).

[95] See Chapter 3, text accompanied by notes 28–41.

[96] See Chapter 7, text accompanied by note 136.

[97] It may be contended that the law as to private foundations is such that the private benefit doctrine is of less concern because of the applicability of the self-dealing rules (IRC § 4941). But (1) there is no authority for this watering-down of the private benefit doctrine; (2) the IRS has applied the private benefit doctrine in the private foundation context, the self-dealing rules notwithstanding (e.g., Priv. Ltr. Rul. 201641023 (March 2, 2016); and (3) the excess benefit transaction rules (IRC § 4958) play essentially the same role in the realm of public charities as the self-dealing rules do in the area of private foundations.

[98] Priv. Ltr. Rul. 201244020 (August 10, 2012).

Lack of Governance Policies

To date, the IRS has issued [seven] private letter rulings taking the position that the failure of the board of a nonprofit organization (almost always a putative public charity) to adopt a particular governance policy is a basis in law for preclusion of recognition of tax-exempt status of the entity.

The first of these rulings involved an organization that did not have a conflict-of-interest policy suitable to the IRS. The IRS tried its best to reshape the governance structure and practices of this entity. First, the IRS tried to force the organization, as a condition of exemption, to "expand [its] board so that it is more representative of the community that it serves."[99] Then, the IRS asked the organization to amend its draft conflict-of-interest policy "so that certain language related to possible conflicts of interest could be added."[100] That is, the IRS wanted to the scope of the policy widened to encompass independent contractors and family members. The organization responded that, once a determination letter recognizing tax-exempt status was issued, it would expand its board and adopt the IRS-recommended policy. The IRS, however, denied recognition of exemption, in part because the organization had a small governing board.[101]

Likewise, an organization failed to qualify with the IRS as a tax-exempt religious entity largely because it did not meet the agency's criteria for an exempt church. The organization was also faulted for having a small board. Further, the IRS observed that this organization had "not adopted bylaws or provided specific information about the governance of your organization, nor have you adopted a conflict of interest policy."[102] The IRS concluded that the "structure" of this organization "indicates that it can be used to benefit private individuals." This entity was said to be ineligible for

---

[99] See text accompanied by *supra* notes 43–46.

[100] The revised Form 990 has always stated on its face that a conflict-of-interest policy (and other policies) is not required as a condition of recognition of tax-exempt status.

[101] Priv. Ltr. Rul. 200828029 (April 18, 2008).

[102] Priv. Ltr. Rul. 200830028 (April 28, 2008).

tax exemption "even if you did conduct activities in furtherance of an exempt purpose."

In a similar situation, an applicant for recognition of tax exemption did not have a conflict-of-interest policy. It was a religious organization; it advised the IRS, after a conflict-of-interest policy was demanded, that its "integrity will keep [it] from having conflict of interest problems." Undeterred, the IRS stated to this organization that the "absence of bylaws and a conflict of interest policy" is "problematic" because it "lack[s] the basic procedural safeguards necessary to prevent impermissible private benefits from flowing to your members."[103] The very fact that compensation of individuals "will be determined by the individuals being compensated" and others on its "closely-related governing body" was seen by the IRS as a conflict of interest, leaving "open the possibility of private inurement." The IRS wrote that "even if no benefit has flowed to individual members up to this point, the pervasiveness but ambiguous relationship" between this organization and two other churches, "coupled with the lack of procedural safeguards," ... "could readily facilitate ... types of future abuses." The IRS concluded: "The potential for private benefit clouds every aspect of your organization's operations."

An applicant organization was denied recognition of tax exemption essentially because it did not sufficiently explain its activities and finances to the IRS.[104] The organization did not have bylaws.[105] This entity had not held any board meetings.[106] It did not have any "written policies setting forth the duties and responsibilities" of its directors. In response to an IRS inquiry as to how this organization operates, it responded that the "organization conducts itself as a regular synagogue six days per week with the board of directors managing the smooth operations of the facility." The IRS lamented the fact that the organization had a self-

---

[103] Priv. Ltr. Rul. 201221022 (March 1, 2012).

[104] See Chapter 3, text accompanied by notes 54-64.

[105] There is no requirement in the federal tax law that a tax-exempt organization have bylaws.

[106] There is nothing in the federal tax law that requires that a board of a tax-exempt organization have meetings.

perpetuating board and did not have term limits.[107] This lack of "formal structure" was said to provide a "window of opportunity for private benefit." The IRS concluded: "You lack internal controls for your everyday operations."[108]

Another applicant organization was found by the IRS to have an inadequate conflict-of-interest policy, along with lack of bylaws for a period of time. The conflict-of-interest policy that the organization adopted did not contain all of the definitions and did not embrace all of relationships the IRS desired. The IRS stated that "it is unclear how such a policy would apply" ... "to ensure that no inurement or improper private benefit will occur."[109] "In sum," the IRS wrote, "you have not demonstrated that there are sufficient safeguards in place to prevent your net earnings from inuring to the benefit of [insiders], or to prevent you from operating for their private benefit."[110]

An organization that also failed to qualify for exemption as a charity was the subject of an IRS ruling that observed that the entity did not have a conflict-of-interest policy, nor did it have a policy as to the establishment of executive compensation or "procedural safeguards to prevent [the organization's] assets from being diverted for private purposes." These latter two elements of fact were referenced as part of a set of reasons for the denial of recognition of exemption.[111]

The IRS in one private letter ruling, while not revoking exemption on this basis, went out of its way to highlight the fact that an organization does not have a conflict-of-interest policy or a document retention and destruction policy, noting also that it lacks any internal control reports, an annual report, or audited financial statements.[112]

---

[107] There is nothing in the federal tax law that prohibits either of these features of nonprofit governance, both of which are common.
[108] Priv. Ltr. Rul. 201242014 (July 24, 2014).
[109] The function of a conflict-of-interest policy is to identify and disclose conflicts of interest; it is not to deter transactions involving private inurement or unwarranted private benefit.
[110] Priv. Ltr. Rul. 201332013 (May 17, 2013).
[111] Priv. Ltr. Rul. 201525014 (March 24, 2015).
[112] Priv. Ltr. Rul. 201543019 (July 29, 2015).

Discrepant IRS Rulings

The vast majority of the IRS rulings concerning nonprofit governance hold that, as summarized above, the existence of a small board and/or a related board is per se evidence of violation of the private benefit doctrine. As discussed throughout, these positions of the IRS are not consistent with the correctly decided case law and are incorrect. Interestingly, there are three IRS private letter rulings that are consistent with the case law, are inconsistent with the general IRS ruling policy, and thus that are correct.

In the first of these rulings, an organization applied to the IRS for recognition of tax exemption and classification as a church. In the view of the IRS, this entity did not qualify as a church and was "not forthcoming" in its responses to the IRS's requests for additional information; the IRS thus ruled that this organization was not entitled to tax-exempt status.[113] The organization had three trustees, who were partners in a for-profit business. Nonetheless, the IRS did not deny recognition of exemption based on board composition. Indeed, the IRS wrote that a "small, related board provides [the] potential for abuse of the exemption provisions" and that an applicant "must openly and candidly disclose all facts bearing on the finances and operation of the organization."[114] Then the IRS quickly pivoted position and wrote that a "small, related board provides [the] potential for abuse of the exemption provisions" and that an applicant "must openly and candidly disclose all facts bearing on the finances and operation of the organization."[115] The IRS added: "Where, as here, an organization is completely controlled by its creators, without participation by members, the community or even the oversight of a religious denomination, the opportunity for abuse makes vital an open and candid disclosure of all the facts about the organization and its operations, so that the Court can be assured that

---

[113] Priv. Ltr. Rul. 200846040 (Aug. 21, 2008).

[114] The IRS cited *Bubbling Well Church* as authority for this statement (see Chapter 3, text accompanied by notes 94-102.

[115] The IRS cited *Basic Unit Ministry* as authority for this statement (see Chapter 3, text accompanied by note 99.

it is not sanctioning an abuse of the revenue laws."[116] The IRS ruled that the entity has "not demonstrated that [its] trustees use their control for exempt rather than private purposes."

In the second of these rulings, an organization was denied classification as a church and was denied recognition of tax exemption on the ground of private inurement. The board of directors of this entity consisted of three members of a family. The IRS observed that this governing board is "small and closely related by family ties." But, the IRS added, "This factor alone is not enough to deny exemption."[117] Yet, the agency asserted that the factor, combined with elements of private benefit found by the IRS, "creates greater cause to believe that you are operated for private, rather than public, interests." Indeed, the IRS wrote that a "community based board of people with no financial interests in the entity can help prevent it from operating for private rather than public benefit."

The third of these rulings may be considered the "crown jewel" of all of the IRS's private letter rulings on nonprofit governance issued to date. It may be so regarded because, unlike the vast majority of the IRS's rulings in this area, it is wholly correct as a matter of law. One wonders how this ruling (and its two predecessors) made it through the IRS process.[118]

In this third ruling, an organization was unsuccessful in its efforts to obtain recognition of tax exemption because the IRS held it was not engaging in exempt functions and did not adequately respond to the agency's requests for additional information.[119] This organization's board originally consisted of two related individuals; it subsequently added a third, unrelated individual to the board.[120] The IRS did not state in this ruling that control of an organization by

---

[116] The IRS cited *Bubbling Well Church* (see *supra* note 114) as authority for this statement.

[117] Priv. Ltr. Rul. 201232034 (May 16, 2012). The IRS cited *Bubbling Well Church* (*supra* note 114) in support of this conclusion.

[118] One also wonders whether its author remains employed at the IRS.

[119] Priv. Ltr. Rul. 201332013 (May 17, 2013).

[120] The IRS disparaged this move, observing that, inasmuch as the organization will be operating a satellite television network and this third board member works in the field of automobile insurance, "it is questionable whether" this individual "will have a significant voice in the affairs of" the organization.

related individuals is private benefit precluding exemption. The agency only said that an application for recognition of exemption in this type of case "calls for open and candid disclosure of all facts bearing upon [an applicant's] organization, operations, and finances so that ... [it] can be assured that it is not ... an abuse of the revenue laws."[121]

---

[121] The IRS cited *Bubbling Well Church* (*supra* note 114) in support of this statement.

7

IRS Lacks Jurisdiction to Regulate Nonprofit Governance

> A federal court of appeals characterized a federal agency's attempt to dictate the composition of the board of directors of a nonprofit organization as an "unprecedented invasion of internal corporate governance."
>
> *California Independent System Operator Corporation v. Federal Energy Regulatory Commission (2004)*

The efforts of the IRS to regulate the governance of public charities and other types of tax-exempt organizations are what the Supreme Court termed an "assertion of authority not conferred."[1] Thus, the acts the agency has taken and is taking in this regard are "ultra vires."[2] The IRS's attempts to engage in nonprofit governance regulation exceed, in the words of the Court, the "scope of its regulatory authority (that is, its jurisdiction)."[3] These conclusions of law are based, not only on IRS actions that are outside the scope of relevant statutory law (the basis of its jurisdiction), but also an astonishing lack of requisite expertise at the agency, the latter buttressed by five sets of facts.[4]

---

[1] City of Arlington, Texas v. Federal Communications Commission, 133 S. Ct. 1863, 1869 (2013).

[2] *Id.*

[3] *Id.* at 1866.

[4] The *City of Arlington* decision, with its distinction between agencies' assertion of authority not conferred and agencies' incorrect application of their authority, is the basis for this book's analysis, which is rested on both of these two elements (the first element being addressed in this chapter and the second element addressed in Chapter 8). The Court majority ruled that the *Chevron* mode of deference is applicable in both contexts. It rejected the argument that there are two distinct classes of agency interpretations, namely, the "big, important" ones (pertaining to agencies' jurisdiction) and "humdrum, run-of-the-mill stuff" (applications of

Application of Law

As discussed, the conventional approach when assessing the boundaries of an agency's jurisdiction is to commence the analysis from the standpoint of the legislative branch of the government involved.[5]

General Rules

The appropriate branch has the initial responsibility to define the purpose and duties of an agency within the overall governmental system. At the federal level, determination of the jurisdiction of a government agency normally begins with review of one or more actions by Congress, which by statute creates federal governmental agencies, and defines their purposes and responsibilities.

Also, as discussed, there often are several statutes involved. Usually, as the Supreme Court has noted, a governmental agency is the subject of an organic statute, which fixes the general range of an agency's jurisdiction.[6] Other statutes may confer jurisdiction with respect to narrower matters. This analysis is much more difficult, when judging IRS jurisdiction with respect to nonprofit governance, because there is no statute creating the IRS, although its general equivalent can be extrapolated from provisions in the Internal

---

jurisdiction the agency plainly has), with the first of these interpretations thus not subject to *Chevron* deference (*id*. at 1868). This distinction between "jurisdictional" and "nonjurisdictional" interpretations was labeled by the Court majority as a "mirage" (*id.*) and an effort to circumscribe the reach of, if not overturn (implicitly or otherwise), *Chevron* (at 1873). These competing points of view have been the basis of a quarrel between Justice Scalia (who wrote the majority opinion in *City of Arlington*) and Justice Breyer. The aspect of this feud, which pits the view that the courts should decide the "big" jurisdictional issues against the view that that task is best suited to the agency involved, are detailed in Sunstein, "Chevron Step Zero," 92 *Va. L. Rev*. (No. 2) 187 (April 2006)). With this in perspective, it is notable that the Court recently upheld a regulation promulgated by the Department of Housing and Urban Development, construing provisions of the Fair Housing Act, without application of *Chevron* (Texas Department of Housing and Community Affairs v. Inclusive Communities Project, Inc., 135 S. Ct. 2507 (2015)).

[5] See Chapter 2, text accompanied by notes 17–30.

[6] *Id*., text accompanied by note 34.

Revenue Code.[7] The IRS also derives jurisdiction from collateral, narrower statutes, such as the regulation of those who practice before it.[8]

As the Supreme Court has stated, the "question a court faces when confronted with an agency's interpretation of a statute it administers is always, simply, *whether the agency has stayed within the bounds of its statutory authority*."[9] The Court wrote that, as to agencies charged with administering congressional statutes, their "power to act and how they are to act is authoritatively prescribed by Congress."[10] The question in this regard "is always whether the agency has gone beyond what Congress has permitted it to do."[11]

Review of an agency's organic statute when determining the scope of an agency's jurisdiction is central to Supreme Court jurisprudence on the point. Thus, in the FCC case, the Court reviewed the Communications Act of 1934;[12] in the FPC case, the Court evaluated the Power and Gas Acts;[13] and the Court's analysis of the role of the FEC was based on elements of the Federal Election Campaign Act.[14] As to the IRS's "organic statute," which gives it the jurisdiction to administer, conduct, and supervise the execution and application of the internal revenue laws and related statutes and tax conventions,[15] it says nothing about any agency jurisdiction to regulate nonprofit governance. As a Justice of the Supreme Court recognized, in a concurring opinion, the "business" of the IRS is, essentially, to "administer laws designed to produce revenue for the Government."[16] This fact is explicitly stated in the federal tax regulations[17] and repeatedly by the IRS itself.[18] Thus, to

---

[7] See Chapter 1, text accompanied by notes 35–48.
[8] See Chapter 2, text accompanied by notes 191–202.
[9] City of Arlington, Texas v. Federal Communications Commission, 133 S. Ct. 1863, 1868 (2013).
[10] *Id.* at 1869.
[11] *Id.*
[12] See Chapter 2, text accompanied by notes 32–42.
[13] See *id.*, text accompanied by notes 62–74.
[14] See *id.*, text accompanied by notes 75–93.
[15] See Chapter 1, text accompanied by note 44.
[16] Bob Jones University v. United States, 461 U.S. 574, 611 (1983).
[17] See Chapter 1, text accompanied by note 49.
[18] See *id.*, text accompanied by notes 50–52.

be definitive, there is no reference whatsoever in the statutory law comprising the basis of the IRS's jurisdiction, or its legislative history or in any interpretation from the Department of the Treasury or the IRS, according the IRS jurisdiction over the regulation of the governance of tax-exempt organizations.

The parallels in the case law are striking. The Supreme Court upheld the discretion exercised by the FCC when it, in interpreting a "public interest" standard, *declined* to impose a greater obligation to provide special programming for the hearing impaired on a public television licensee than on a commercial licensee.[19] The Court in the CSC case first described the "business" of that agency – promotion of the efficiency of the federal civil service – then chided the agency for seeking responsibility for foreign affairs, treaty negotiations, and other policy matters outside the scope of its jurisdiction.[20] In the FPC case, the Court stated that the job of that agency is to promote the orderly production of supplies of electric energy and natural gas, and not to eliminate employment discrimination.[21] The Court harshly criticized the FEC for using its position as administrator and enforcer of the federal election laws to evolve into a "censor" and a licensor dictating when persons can engage in their rights of free speech.[22] As a dissenting Justice stated, the "business" of the IRS is to "administer laws designed to produce revenue for the Government, not to promote 'public policy.'"[23]

Organic statutory law aside, there is no collateral statute that addresses the matter of nonprofit governance by the IRS. The agency has the jurisdiction to review applications for recognition of exemption filed by nonprofit organizations and issue favorable determination letters when these entities qualify for exemption, and otherwise administer and enforce the law of tax-exempt organizations.[24] This body of law includes two instances where Congress has briefly and narrowly legislated in the area of nonprofit

---

[19] See Chapter 2, text accompanied by notes 32–42.
[20] See *id.*, text accompanied by notes 43–57.
[21] See *id.*, text accompanied by notes 62–74.
[22] See *id.*, text accompanied by notes 75–93.
[23] Bob Jones University v. United States, 461 U.S. 574, 611 (1983).
[24] See Chapter 3, text accompanied by notes 1–19.

governance.[25] Nothing in these laws, however, remotely suggests that Congress has accorded the IRS the jurisdiction to generally regulate in the field of nonprofit governance. Any argument to the contrary must fail.[26] As the Supreme Court has stated, it is fundamental that an agency "may not bootstrap itself into an area in which it has no jurisdiction."[27]

Consequently, it is asserted that the IRS, in its efforts to regulate nonprofit governance, is acting outside the scope of its permissible jurisdiction. This conclusion is based, in large part, on the argument that the IRS is acting in ways that have taken it and continues to take it beyond the bounds of its jurisdiction as fixed by statute.[28]

A surprising number of cases support the assertion that the IRS is, in its regulation of nonprofit governance, acting beyond its statutory role.[29] One court addressed this matter by concluding that a federal department lacked "statutory rulemaking authority" to promulgate a rule.[30] (Of course, as to nonprofit governance, the IRS has never promulgated a formal rule. Inasmuch as, however, the IRS is precluded from lawfully issuing a rule as to nonprofit governance, it is certainly precluded from lawfully issuing private letter rulings on the point.)

---

[25] See *id.*, text accompanied by notes 66–72.

[26] The IRS has never asserted that its ostensible jurisdiction over the regulation of nonprofit governance is based on a statute.

[27] Federal Maritime Commission v. Seatrain Lines, Inc., 411 U.S. 726, 745 (1973).

[28] As the Court observed, "courts must presume that a legislature says in a statute what it means and means in a statute what it says there" (Connecticut National Bank v. Germain, 503 U.S. 249, 253–254 (1992)).

[29] It may be anticipated that some will contend that the IRS has the requisite jurisdiction (or authority) to regulate nonprofit governance as a logical (or perhaps unavoidable) extension of its role in processing applications for recognition of exemption and examining tax-exempt organizations. That contention is, of course, rejected in this book. The cases that follow (text accompanied by *infra* notes [30–95]) illustrate the fine line-drawing courts can make when assessing the bounds of an agency's jurisdiction, buttressing the argument that the IRS's authority to administer these aspects of the law of tax-exempt organizations is an insufficient justification for the agency to stretch its regulatory authority into the realm of nonprofit governance.

[30] Pharmaceutical Research & Manufacturers of America v. Department of Health and Human Services, 43 F. Supp. 3d 28, 37 (D.D.C. 2014).

In one instance, although Congress accorded the Attorney General of the US rulemaking power to promulgate regulations under the Controlled Substances Act in two specific areas, the Attorney General issued a rule which the Supreme Court found exceeded this official's statutory rulemaking authority because, *inter alia*, the CSA "does not grant the Attorney General this broad authority to promulgate rules."[31] The Court stated that the "idea that Congress gave the Attorney General such broad and unusual authority through an implicit delegation in the CSA's registration provision is not sustainable."[32] Likewise, it is too much of a stretch to conclude that the IRS's statutory authority to administer and enforce the federal tax laws somehow impliedly gives the agency a "broad and unusual authority" to regulate the governance of tax-exempt organizations.

Congress gave the Urban Mass Transportation Administration specifically delegated authority; an appellate court held that a rule promulgated by the UMTA was outside the scope of that authority and thus was unauthorized agency action.[33] This court of appeals wrote that, "[w]here Congress prescribes the form in which an agency may exercise its authority ... [a court] cannot elevate the goals of an agency's action, however reasonable, over that prescribed form."[34]

In another instance, Congress, under the Telecommunications Act of 1996, only required the Federal Communications Commission to prepare a report on a topic. The FCC nonetheless implemented rules pertaining to that topic. The rules were vacated by this court because the FCC could "point to no statutory provision that gives the agency authority to mandate" the rules in question.[35]

---

[31] Gonzales v. Oregon, 546 U.S. 243, 259 (2006). A court summarized the Court's ruling by stating that the "two specific grants of rulemaking authority could not be stretched to include such broad, expansive rulemaking authority" (Pharmaceutical Research & Manufacturers of America v. Department of Health & Human Services, 43 F. Supp. 3d 28, 38 (D.D.C. 2014)).

[32] Gonzales v. Oregon, 546 U.S. 243, 267 (2006).

[33] Amalgamated Transit Union v. Skinner, 894 F.2d 1362 (D.C. Cir. 1990).

[34] *Id.* at 1364.

[35] Motion Picture Association v. Federal Communications Commission, 309 F.3d 796 (D.C. Cir. 2002).

On another occasion, this appellate court "categorically" rejected the FCC's argument that "it possesses *plenary* authority to act within a given area simply because Congress has endowed it with *some* authority to act in that area."[36] The court invalidated a regulation implemented by the Secretary of Labor regarding interim relief for mining companies because there was no statutory grant of authority to the Secretary to do so and there was strong evidence that "Congress did not intend to authorize the Secretary to grant [the relief] as a matter of course."[37] A district court followed this line of case law in invalidating a regulation because the "statutory provisions [the department] has strung together to give it rulemaking authority are ... specific grants of authority that do not authorize" the rule at issue.[38]

Singular Governance Case

Research has revealed only one case involving the issue of the scope of jurisdiction of a federal agency specifically in the context of corporate governance. The case, concerning the Federal Energy Regulatory Commission, has striking parallels to the IRS's efforts to regulate nonprofit governance. An appellate court held that the FERC did not have the statutory authority to make or enforce its order endeavoring to dictate the composition of the board of a public benefit corporation, a form of nonprofit corporation.[39]

Around the time of this decision, as the court explained, vertically integrated electric utilities sold generation, transmission, and distribution services as a single bundled package. Changes in regulatory laws and technological advances led to increased entry into the wholesale electric power generation markets. Because the

---

[36] E.g., American Library Association v. Federal Communications Commission, 406 F.3d 689, 708 (D.C. Cir. 2005).

[37] United Mine Workers of America v. Mine Safety & Health Administration, 823 F.2d 608, 617 (D.C. Cir. 1987).

[38] Pharmaceutical Research & Manufacturers of America v. U.S. Department of Health & Human Services, 43 F. Supp. 3d 28, 39 (D.D.C. 2014).

[39] California Independent System Operator Corporation v. Federal Energy Regulatory Commission, 372 F.3d 395 (D.C. Cir. 2004).

transmission market had remained restricted and difficult to enter, utilities owning or controlling transmission facilities have enjoyed a natural monopoly which they could exploit to favor their own generation and exclude or burden their competitors.

The FERC found that the vertically integrated electric utilities were using their monopoly control over interstate transmission facilities to disadvantage potential competitors and thus thwart competition, to the detriment of the public interest. The agency sought to remedy this market burden by requiring these utilities to unbundle wholesale electric power services and to file open-access nondiscriminatory transmission tariffs. Public utilities were encouraged by the FERC to participate in independent system operators. An ISO conducts the transmission services and ancillary services for all users of the system, replacing the conduct of the services by the system owners – that is, the integrated electric utilities the market power of which the FERC was attempting to control by encouraging the creation and operation of ISOs. The FERC deemed, by order, it critical that an ISO be independent of the market participants so that decisions of policy, operation, and dispute resolution would be free of any discriminatory impetus.

The California Independent System Operator Corporation (CAISO) was created by the state of California by statute in 1996. This legislation created a California Electricity Oversight Board and directed it to incorporate CAISO as a public benefit corporation to operate electric grid facilities in the state for the purpose of ensuring efficient use and reliable operation of the transmission grid. The statute directed the CEOB to put in place procedures for selecting a board of directors for this new corporation composed exclusively of California residents and including representatives of eleven stakeholder classes. Further, this legislation mandated creation of a power exchange.

To implement his restructuring, the three largest investor-owned electric utilities in California filed an application with the FERC to transfer control of their transmission facilities to CAISO and to sell electricity to the power exchange. The application was conditionally granted by the FERC, including generally approving the proposed governance structure as consistent with the principles of ISOs under its order, but the agency ruled that the proposed California residency requirement was discriminatory.

California underwent, in the summer and fall of 2000, a period of considerable turmoil in the electricity market. The FERC, the legislature and the governor of California, and the CAISO concluded separately that a new board structure was needed for the CAISO in light of the turmoil. In late 2000, the FERC proposed a seven-member board selected from candidates identified by an independent search firm. In December, the FERC ordered that, of a consensus is not reached as to an acceptable means of selecting new ISO board members, the method proposed by it would be carried out.

In January 2001, also in response to the electricity crisis, the California legislature, by statute, replaced the CAISO board with a five-member board appointed by the governor. Pursuant to those procedures, a board was appointed. Also at that time, the governor authorized the state's Department of Water Resources to purchase energy. Shortly after that, the DWR become a major market participant in the California wholesale energy markets.

Thereafter, the CAISO filed, with the FERC, a comprehensive market redesign proposal to improve the state's energy markets. The FERC responded with an order that the procedures it had proposed in 2000 to replace CAISO's board be implemented. The FERC's primary concern with the CAISO board composition was that having CAISO run by a state-appointed board conflicted with the principles, expressed in the FERC's orders, that ISOs should be independent of market participants. Because the California governor appointed the board and because California, through the DWR, had been a major market participant in the electricity market administered by CAISO, the composition of the board, the FERC reasoned, violated these principles of independence.

CAISO, the Public Utility Commission of California, and the CEOB sought court review of the FERC's order. This review was granted because, in the words of the court, the FERC "has no authority to replace the selection method or membership of the governing board of an ISO, let alone to compel a corporation created by state law to employ a governing board chosen in violation of that law."[40]

The court opened its analysis with the observation that, "lest there be any mistake, FERC has done nothing less than order a public utility subject to its regulation to replace its governing board."[41] It found no precedent for the FERC's order, either in the FERC's prior orders or that of any other similar federal regulatory body. It noted that the FERC has not claimed the authority of such a precedent. The court agreed with the plaintiffs that the agency "simply has no authority to do such a thing."[42]

In assessing the scope of the FERC's authority, the court started with a "fundamental proposition" of federal law:[43] "As a federal agency, FERC is a creature of statute, having no constitutional or common law existence or authority, but *only* those authorities conferred upon it by Congress."[44] Therefore, the court added, "if there is no statute conferring authority, FERC has none."[45] The court continued this line of analysis with this quotation from the US Supreme Court: "[A]n agency literally has no power to act ... unless and until Congress confers power upon it."[46]

The court stated that it is "therefore incumbent upon FERC to demonstrate that some statute confers upon it the power it purported to exercise in its replacement of the governing board of the regulated utility."[47] The best the FERC could do in this regard was point to two sections of the Federal Power Act giving it authority to issue orders in connection with a "practice ... affecting a rate." The agency's claim was that the composition of the governing board

---

[40] *Id.* at 398.

[41] *Id.*

[42] *Id.*

[43] *Id.*

[44] *Id* (internal quotes omitted). The court cited to Atlantic City Electric Co. v. Federal Energy Regulatory Commission, 295 F.3d 1, 8 (D.C. Cir. 2002), which quoted from Michigan v. Environmental Protection Agency, 268 F.3d 1075, 1081 (D.C. Cir. 2001) (emphasis in *Atlantic City Electric* Co.).

[45] *Id.*

[46] Louisiana Public Service Commission v. Federal Communications Commission, 476 U.S. 355, 374 (1986).

[47] California Independent System Operator Corporation v. Federal Energy Regulatory Commission, 372 F.3d 395, 398 (D.C. Cir. 2004).

of a utility and the method of its selection was such a "practice," and because the FERC believes the selection method to be discriminatory the agency has the "authority to determine a just and reasonable practice and to place such practice in force" by means of an order.[48] The court, having reviewed those sections, wrote that "it is not immediately apparent that either has anything to do with the authority claimed by FERC to discharge and replace the governing board of a utility with governors chosen by a process of its own choice."[49]

The court stated that Congress, in these sections, "set forth the power of the Commission with respect to rates and charges, and entered certain legislative directions concerning determination of cost of production or transmission."[50] The court added: "It therefore remains FERC's task to show how those provisions somehow empower it to make the unprecedented invasion of internal corporate governance it has undertaken in the orders under review."[51]

The court, in reviewing the FERC's construction of the word *practices* in the context of the sections, applied the *Chevron* formula.[52] It stated that it is therefore "our task to determine whether Congress, when it used the word 'practices' in [one of these sections], was intending to empower FERC to re-make the corporate governance of regulated utilities, or, if Congress did not plainly so intend, if it was reasonable of FERC to so interpret the words of the statute as to vest it with such power."[53]

In considering "clarity and specificity" of congressional intent expressed in the word *practice*, the court recalled that '[a]mbiguity is a creature not of definitional possibilities but of statutory context."[54] The court continued: "The issue is not so much whether the word 'practice' is, in some abstract sense, ambiguous, but rather whether,

---

48 *Id.* at 399.

49 *Id.*

50 *Id.*

51 *Id.*

52 See Chapter 2, text accompanied by notes 94–120.

53 California Independent System Operator Corporation v. Federal Energy Regulatory Commission, 372 F.3d 395, 400 (D.C. Cir. 2004).

54 *Id.* The second of these quotations is from Brown v. Gardner, 513 U.S. 115, 118 (1994).

read in context and using the traditional tools of statutory construction, the term 'practice' encompasses the procedures used to select CAISO's board, that is, in the words of *Chevron*, 'whether Congress has directly spoken to the precise question at issue'."[55] "On this point," the court concluded, "Congress's intent is crystal clear, and we therefore need not reach *Chevron* step two."[56]

At the first step of *Chevron*, the court said that it began with a "plain language" analysis of the statutory text. That is, the court assumed "that the legislative purpose is expressed by the ordinary meaning of the words used."[57] Thus, the court wrote, the word "practices" is a word of "sufficiently diverse definitions that the only realistic approach to determining Congress's 'plain meaning,' if any, is to regard the word in its context."[58] It added: The canon of statutory construction "*noscitur a sociis*, i.e., a word is known by the company it keeps ... is 'often wisely applied where a word is capable of many meanings in order to avoid giving unintended breadth to the Acts of Congress.'"[59]

The court observed that the plaintiffs in this case argued, "with considerable convincing force, that the intent of Congress in [the FPA section involved] is actually quite plain: the grant of authority to regulate rates, charges, classifications, and closely related matters."[60] Therefore, the plaintiffs' argument was that FERC's "interpretation of the section should fall at the first stage of *Chevron* review, as the statute is not ambiguous on the point at issue."[61] The court stated that, "[c]ertainly, the plaintiffs "accurately describe[d] the context," adding that "[n]one of the words surrounding the word

---

[55] California Independent System Operator Corporation v. Federal Energy Regulatory Commission, 372 F.3d 395, 400 (D.C. Cir. 2004), quoting from *Chevron*, 467 U.S. at 842.

[56] California Independent System Operator Corporation v. Federal Energy Regulatory Commission, 372 F.3d 395, 400 (D.C. Cir. 2004).

[57] *Id*. The quotation is from Security Industries Association v. Board of Governors, 468 U.S. 137, 149 (1984).

[58] California Independent System Operator Corporation v. Federal Energy Regulatory Commission, 372 F.3d 395, 400 (D.C. Cir. 2004).

[59] *Id*. The quotation is from Amgen, Inc. v. Smith, 357 F.3d 103, 112 (D.C. Cir. 2004).

[60] California Independent System Operator Corporation v. Federal Energy Regulatory Commission, 372 F.3d 395, 400 (D.C. Cir. 2004).

[61] *Id*.

'practice' in the statutory section suggest a congressional concern with corporate governance or structure."[62] The court continued: "By its terms, the section only comes into play when the Commission has had a hearing and finds that a 'rate, charge, or classification' employed by a regulated utility in its jurisdictional transactions is 'unjust, unreasonable, unduly discriminatory or preferential'."[63] The court reasoned: "It is quite a leap to move as FERC has from that context of transactional terms to an implication that [,] by the word 'practice,' Congress empowered the Commission not merely to effect a reformation of some 'practice' in a more traditional sense of actions habitually being taken by a utility in connection with a rate found to be unjust or unreasonable, but also to empower the Commission to reform completely the governing structure of the utility on the Commission's assertion that it is 'obligated not only to remedy past discrimination but also to take all reasonable steps to prevent possible undue discrimination from occurring'."[64]

The court noted that another section of the FPA delegates to the FERC limited authority to regulate conflicts of interest among the directors of public utilities and market actors who deal with these utilities.[65] It stated that "were FERC's reading of [the principal section of the FPA at issue] correct, [that section] would be superfluous, as [the section] would already give FERC plenary authority to resolve such conflicts by altering the corporate governance structure of public utilities, so long as FERC concluded that the change would remedy unjust discrimination of some kind."[66] The court concluded that "[t]raditional principles of statutory construction counsel against reading acts of Congress to be superfluous" and thus that Congress's "specific and limited enumeration of FERC's power over corporate governance in [the

---

[62] *Id.*
[63] *Id.*
[64] *Id.* at 400–401.
[65] Here is a situation where Congress granted a federal governmental agency jurisdiction to regulate in the realm of conflicts of interest. Certainly no comparable authority has been granted to the IRS in the nonprofit law context (see Chapter 1, text accompanied by notes 96 and 97).
[66] California Independent System Operator Corporation v. Federal Energy Regulatory Commission, 372 F.3d 395, 401 (D.C. Cir. 2004).

other section] is strong evidence that [the principal section] confers no such authority on FERC."[67]

The court wrote that the FERC's construction of the word *practice* in this context "is therefore a sufficiently poor fit with the apparent meaning of the statute that the statute is not ambiguous on the very question before us." It noted that the Supreme Court opined that the "poor fit" of statutory language with a construction urged by the agency charged with administering the statute made the agency's reading 'unreasonable'."[68]

The court wrote that, "[w]hile this discussion of reasonableness may sound like *Chevron* step two, the Supreme Court reminded us that where the 'text and *reasonable inferences from it* give a clear answer against the government ... that ... is the end of the matter'."[69] It stated that, as the Supreme Court did, "we are prepared to strike the agency interpretation down at *Chevron* step one, as 'this clear textually grounded conclusion in [the petitioner's] favor is fatal to the remaining principal arguments advanced against it."[70]

The court noted that, in support of the "breathtaking scope" which the FERC construes the statute as conferring on it, the FERC cited an earlier opinion of the court for the proposition that "there is an infinitude of practices affecting rates and service."[71] It stated that the FERC "apparently would have us hold that the existence of an 'infinitude' of practices supposes that there is also an infinitude of acceptable definitions for what constitutes a 'practice' to give it the authority to regulate anything done by or connected with a regulated utility, as any act or aspect of such an entity's corporate existence could affect, in some sense, the rates"; as to that, the court wrote it was "not biting."[72] This language, said the court, was

---

[67] *Id.*

[68] *Id.* The quotation is from Brown v. Gardner, 513 U.S. 115, 120 (1994).

[69] *Id.* (emphasis supplied by the court).

[70] California Independent System Operator Corporation v. Federal Energy Regulatory Commission, 372 F.3d 395, 401 (D.C. Cir. 2004). The internal quotation is from Brown v. Gardner, 513 U.S. 115, 120 (1994).

[71] City of Cleveland v. Federal Energy Regulatory Commission, 773 F.2d 1368, 1376 (D.C. Cir. 1985).

[72] California Independent System Operator Corporation v. Federal Energy Regulatory Commission, 372 F.3d 395, 401 (D.C. Cir. 2004).

taken out of context; it was written as part of a "discussion of a petitioner's challenge to features of a specific schedule for the provision of electrical service to specified customers," where the petitioner argued that the FERC had accepted findings that "were too vague in the recitation of practices."[73] The court, in the earlier case, held that the statutory requirement for the setting forth of practices "must reasonably be read to require the recitation of only those practices that affect rates and services *significantly*, that are realistically *susceptible* of specification, and that are not so generally understood in any contractual arrangement as to render recitation superfluous."[74] As to this non-precedent, the court concluded: "The discussion of the infinitude of practices was then in terms of pointing out how absurd it would have been for FERC to go beyond a reasonable construction of 'practices' in applying the text of the statute. FERC did not commit such an absurdity in the [earlier] case. In this case, it has."[75]

The FERC's citation to another case was "equally unavailing."[76] In that instance, several electric utility companies banded to form a regional power pool, which was a voluntary association the purpose of which was to promote a reliable and economic transmission grid. Inasmuch as this pooling amounted to a rate that the FPA required the utilities to file with the FERC, the utilities applied to the FERC for approval of the arrangement. In response, the FERC conditioned its approval of the power-pooling arrangement on removal of membership criteria which denied certain privileges to some but not all participants.

The court stated that this prior case "actually illustrates FERC's overreaching in this case well."[77] In that case, the FERC conditioned the approval of the power pool on removal of the membership

---

[73] *Id.*

[74] City of Cleveland v. Federal Energy Regulatory Commission, 773 F.2d 1368, 1376 (D.C. Cir. 1985).

[75] California Independent System Operator Corporation v. Federal Energy Regulatory Commission, 372 F.3d 395, 402 (D.C. Cir. 2004).

[76] *Id.* That case is Central Iowa Power Cooperative v. Federal Energy Regulatory Commission, 606 F.2d 1156 (D.C. Cir. 1979).

[77] California Independent System Operator Corporation v. Federal Energy Regulatory Commission, 372 F.3d 395, 402 (D.C. Cir. 2004).

criteria, rather than ordering the power pool to directly change those criteria. In the CAISO case, the court said the FERC took a "much more extreme step." [78] As the court stated the matter, "[r]ather than merely threatening to revoke CAISO's ISO status if it did not remove its board, similar to what it did in [the prior case], FERC has instead decided to order CAISO directly to change its board."[79] It added that it "never once hinted in [the previous case] that such an extreme measure was within FERC's ... authority."[80]

The court wrote that "[o]ur firm conviction that FERC's stretching of the authority granted it by the statute's use of the word 'practice' when it extends its authority to the structuring of the corporate governance and the choosing and appointment of corporate directors is supported both by the history of the application of this and similar statutes and by the implications of FERC's amorphous defining of the term."[81] As to precedent, the court continued, the "Supreme Court has been instructive on this issue at least as far back as 1916."[82]

The FPA section principally at issue in this case was derived from a section of the since-repealed Interstate Commerce Act. The court noted that it is "another traditional tool of statutory construction that 'where provisions of one statute have been adopted by another, the interpretation which has been authoritatively placed upon the former applies to the latter also'."[83] The court thus looked to the Supreme Court's consideration of the meaning of the word *practices* in the earlier statute.

The Supreme Court interpreted the ICA's use of the word *practices* to "refer only to a railroad's terms of service and rejected a broader construction in which 'it could be contended ... that every detail of railroad operation is a practice within the meaning of the

---

[78] *Id.*
[79] *Id.*
[80] *Id.*
[81] *Id.*
[82] *Id.*
[83] *Id.* The quotation is from Hope Natural Gas Co. v. Federal Power Commission, 196 F.2d 803, 807 (4th Cir. 1952).

Act'."[84] Subsequently, the Supreme Court considered whether the ICA, by empowering the Interstate Commerce Commission to regulate the 'practice' of carriers, conferred on the ICC the authority to regulate the number of individuals to be employed in crews. The Court, reasoning that the "Act uses the word 'practice' in connection with the fixing of rates to be charged and prescribing of service to be rendered by the carriers," rejected that proposition.[85] The court noted that the Supreme Court "[e]mploy[ed] the same sort of contextual reasoning we have already discussed";[86] the Court declared that "[t]hat word is deemed to apply only to acts or things belonging to the same class as those meant by the words of the law that are associated with it."[87]

The court then turned to the "implications" of the FERC's "claimed authority to regulate all actions or activities of public utilities including the personnel and structure of its corporate governance," under the rubric of *practices*, observing that "[w]ere we to uphold this theory, the implications would be staggering."[88] The court wrote: "If FERC can remove a board of directors and dictate the method of choosing a new one because the method of selecting the old one might have made it appear discriminatory, or have even been given cause to fear future discrimination, then it would seem that FERC could also dictate the choice of CEO, COO and the method of contracting for services, labor, office space, or whatever one might imagine, assuming FERC made the appropriate finding."[89] However, the court continued, "we really need no such parade of horribles," in that the very act attempted by the FERC in

---

[84] California Independent System Operator Corporation v. Federal Energy Regulatory Commission, 372 F.3d 395, 402 (D.C. Cir. 2004). The quotation is from United States v. Pennsylvania Railroad Co., 242 U.S. 208, 228–233 (1916).
[85] Missouri Pacific Railroad Co. v. Norwood, 283 U.S. 249, 257 (1931).
[86] California Independent System Operator Corporation v. Federal Energy Regulatory Commission, 372 F.3d 395, 403 (D.C. Cir. 2004).
[87] Missouri Pacific Railroad Co. v. Norwood, 283 U.S. 249, 257 (1931).
[88] California Independent System Operator Corporation v. Federal Energy Regulatory Commission, 372 F.3d 395, 403 (D.C. Cir. 2004).
[89] *Id.*

this case "is quite enough to reveal the drastic implications of its overreaching."[90]

The court wrote that the "same statutory terms that apply to FERC's regulation of CAISO apply to its regulation of other jurisdictional utilities."[91] The court concluded with this: "FERC has the authority not to accept something which it does not deem an ISO. It does not have the authority to reform and regulate the governing body of a public utility under the theory that corporate governance constitutes a 'practice' for ratemaking authority purposes."[92]

Commentary on CAISO Opinion

The opinion by the US Court of Appeals for the District of Columbia Circuit in *CAISO* is most instructive when evaluating the matter of the jurisdiction of the IRS to regulate the composition of boards of directors of public charities and other tax-exempt organizations. There are many parallels between the FERC's attempt to dictate the composition of the board of a public benefit corporation and the IRS's efforts to do the same thing with respect to exempt organizations.

The differences in these situations, however, are as striking as the similarities. For example, the DC Circuit had an organic statute[93] to review in assessing the scope of the FERC's jurisdiction. It quoted a prior opinion in noting that the FERC is a creature of statute, having no authority but that conferred on it by Congress. As the court stated, "if there is no statute conferring authority, FERC has none." By contrast, there is no organic statute involving the IRS; the most that can be done in this regard is extrapolate from statutory law sketching the duties of the Secretary of the Treasury and the IRS Oversight Board.[94]

---

[90] *Id*. at 403–404.
[91] *Id*. at 404.
[92] *Id*.
[93] See the text accompanied by *supra* note 6.
[94] See Chapter 1, text accompanied by note 44.

In defense of its actions against CAISO, the FERC relied on two provisions in the Federal Power Act. The IRS, by contrast, has never stated its reasoning for entry into the realm of nonprofit governance in any formal document, such as a revenue ruling or even an announcement or notice. The FERC could at least try to rely on case law within its clear regulatory mandate. The IRS, by contrast, essentially relies on one court opinion, all too often misconstruing the import of what the court held. The CAISO court invoked the *Chevron* doctrine to aid it to its conclusion; that doctrine cannot be applied to the IRS in this context because there is no statute, certainly no statute concerning nonprofit governance, for a court to evaluate.[95] Likewise, the tools of statutory construction utilized by the DC Circuit in analyzing the scope of the FERC's jurisdiction are of no utility in determining the validity of what the IRS is doing in connection with nonprofit governance.

Despite all this, the conclusions reached in the CAISO case are equally applicable to the IRS. The DC Circuit found that the FERC had "no authority" to dictate the composition of governing boards. The FERC was said to simply have "no authority to do such a thing." The FERC's interpretation of the scope of its jurisdiction was deemed "breathtaking." The FERC engaged in "overreaching." The agency took an "extreme step." The FERC undertook an "unprecedented invasion of internal corporate governance." It tried to "re-make the corporate governance" of the regulated utilities. The FERC committed an "absurdity." It "stretched" the authority accorded it. The implications of what the FERC tried to do were cast as "staggering." That is, the agency could dictate the choices of corporate executives and the method of contracting for services, labor, office space, and the like. The appellate court contemplated the "very act attempted by the FERC," observing that "is quite enough to reveal the drastic implications of its overreaching."

Each of these observations by the DC Circuit apply to what the IRS has done and continues to do in the realm of nonprofit governance.

---

[95] See *id.*, text accompanied by notes 42–48.

The foregoing essentially comes down to this: Just as the FERC has the authority to deny an organization the status of an ISO, if in the view of the agency it does not qualify as that type of entity, so too does the IRS have the authority to deny recognition of tax exemption to an organization if in the view of that agency it does not qualify for exemption. But, just as that specific grant of authority does not accord the FERC the authority to "reform and regulate the governing body" of a public utility, this specific grant of authority to the IRS does not give it plenary authority to reform and regulate the governing bodies of public charities and other tax-exempt entities.

IRS's Lack of Expertise

There is another element of the law that serves to help support this assertion of no IRS jurisdiction to engage in nonprofit governance: lack of agency expertise.

In a concurring opinion, a Supreme Court Justice observed: "This Court often has expressed concern that the scope of an agency's authorization be limited to those areas in which the agency fairly may be said to have expertise." [96] In *California Independent System Operator Corporation*, the court noted that Congress has created a Securities and Exchange Commission with "extensive powers over corporate regulation" and that "[e]very state has statutes affecting corporate governance."[97] It added that "[p]resumably the members of the federal and state commissions charged with securities and corporate regulation are chosen with an eye to their expertise in matters corporate" and that "[c]ertainly the legislative bodies have given them powers with a view to that subject matter."[98] On this point, the court concluded: "The same cannot be said of the

[96] Bob Jones University v. United States, 461 U.S. 574, 611 (1983). As to the reference to "expertise," the Justice cited to the FCC, CSC, and FPC cases, noted above.

[97] California Independent System Operator Corporation v. Federal Energy Regulatory Commission, 372 F.3d 395, 404 (D.C. Cir. 2004).

[98] *Id.*

legislative empowerment of FERC, nor presumably are its members chosen principally for their expertise in corporate structure."[99]

Earlier this year, a Court majority returned to this point, in *King v. Burwell*, when holding that federal tax credits are available in connection with federal health insurance exchanges.[100] In that case, the Court stated that the availability of these credits is a "question of deep economic and political significance that is central to this statutory scheme" and, "had Congress wished to assign that question to an agency, it surely would have done so expressly."[101] The Court continued: "It is especially unlikely that Congress would have delegated this decision to the *IRS*, which has no expertise in crafting health insurance policy of this sort." [102] The Court concluded: "This is not a case for the IRS."[103]

These observations by the Court are most relevant to the theme of this book. As discussed, this matter of the IRS's heavy involvement in nonprofit governance is also a question of deep economic significance to public charities and other categories of tax-exempt organizations.[104] Surely, if Congress wishes to assign the task of regulating nonprofit governance to the IRS, it would do so expressly.[105] Also, as discussed, the IRS lacks the expertise to craft nonprofit governance policy of this nature.[106]

---

[99] *Id.*

[100] King v. Burwell, 135 S. Ct. 2480 (2015).

[101] *Id.* at 2489.

[102] *Id.*

[103] *Id.*

[104] See Chapter 1, text accompanied by and of note 100.

[105] On December 18, 2015, a massive ($1.15 trillion) tax and omnibus spending bill was signed into law (Protecting Americans from Tax Hikes Act of 2015 (Pub. L. No. 114-113)). It contains more than a dozen provisions changing or adding elements of the law of tax-exempt organizations. The entire package of them, however, is miniscule when compared to the matter of regulation of the governance of nonprofit organizations. It is difficult to believe that Congress would place so much detail as to exempt organizations law in a measure, yet assign the mammoth role of nonprofit governance to the IRS so cryptically.

[106] See the text accompanied by *supra* notes 96–106.

IRS's Demonstrated Lack of Expertise to Regulate Nonprofit Governance

There are five basic elements in support of the proposition that the IRS lacks the necessary expertise to regulate in the realm of nonprofit governance: (1) its incorrect interpretation of and reliance on the private benefit doctrine; (2) its use of the annual information return to ask questions about governance policies and procedures that go beyond what is permissible, using the standard of relevancy; (3) its inability to articulate sensible good governance principles; (4) the mistakes made in designing and implementing its agents' governance check sheet; and (5) the lack of correlative data in support of the IRS's proposition that good governance practices leads to tax law compliance.

IRS's Incorrect Reliance on Private Benefit Doctrine

When the IRS decided to embark on its regulation of nonprofit governance, it had no statutory (or regulatory) authority on which to base its actions. At that time, there was only one court decision remotely on point.[107] The IRS still repeatedly cites this opinion in its private letter rulings on nonprofit governance, all too frequently, however, distorting or even wrongly construing the *Bubbling Well Church* decision. Here are some examples of the IRS's misconstruction of the text of the *Bubbling Well Church* opinion:

- A small and related governing board "creates greater cause to believe [an organization is] operated for private, rather than public, interests."[108]

---

[107] Bubbling Well Church of Universal Love, Inc. v. Commissioner, 74 T.C. 531 (1980). See Chapter 3, text accompanied by notes 94–102. On this point, the *Church of Ethereal Joy* opinion (see *id.*. text accompanied by notes 103–111) essentially parroted *Bubbling Well*.

[108] Priv. Ltr. Rul. 201232034 (May 16, 2012).

- Private inurement is "indicated by the fact that the board members consist of the same family and control all aspects of the program."[109]
- The "undue control of the organization by a related board causes the organization to serve private interests."[110]
- A "small group of individuals ... have [sic] exclusive control over the management of [an organization's] funds and operations" and "as a result of this exclusive control [the entity's] founders benefit."[111]
- An organization controlled by related individuals must "clearly demonstrate" that private interests are not being served."[112]
- An individual, by being an organization's president, executive director, sole employee, and incorporator (and one of three directors) has "complete control" of the organization's operations and thus was engaging in acts of private inurement.[113]

Lacking any statutory standard to follow when regulating in the realm of nonprofit governance, and in the absence of any guidance from the Treasury Department in the form of a regulation, the IRS was, having decided to embark on this new regulatory focus, forced to find a standard on its own. At this point, the agency had two basic choices: invent a standard or exploit an existing one. This was not a difficult choice, however, because there was no existing standard on the point. (That remains the situation.) The path chosen by the IRS, then, was to utilize an existing body of law, albeit then concoct a new application of it.

The body of law selected by the IRS to bear the burden of supporting a basis in law for its newfound interest in nonprofit

---

[109] Priv. Ltr. Rul. 201302040 (October 19, 2012). *Bubbling Well Church* is a private benefit, not a private inurement, case. See Chapter 3, text accompanied by notes 28–53.

[110] Priv. Ltr. Rul. 201325017 (March 28, 2013).

[111] Priv. Ltr. Rul. 201421022 (February 27, 2014).

[112] Priv. Ltr. Rul. 201452017 (October 2, 2014).

[113] Priv. Ltr. Rul. 201540019 (July 7, 2015). See the comment in *supra* note 109.

governance was the private benefit doctrine.[114] It was a poor choice, inasmuch as the doctrine really had no particular relationship to the governance of tax-exempt organizations (and that state of affairs continues). There was, however, no other existing doctrine to apply. Thus, the IRS had to make do with the private benefit doctrine because that was all it had with which to work.

The private benefit doctrine, as noted, is essentially a common law doctrine. It has been in Western law for centuries, primarily as applicable with respect to charitable trusts. The doctrine basically means that these trusts must be devoted to charitable, rather than private, ends. The doctrine is not reflected in US statutory law (except to the extent it is somewhat represented in the private inurement doctrine[115]). It is the subject of one sentence in the tax regulations regarding tax exemption for charitable organizations. There, the doctrine is little more than a restatement of an age-old common law principle.

Therefore, there is nothing in the traditional private benefit doctrine expressly applicable to nonprofit governance. The IRS position, that the existence of a small board and/or a related board is private benefit per se, thus has no basis in precedence and is completely an invention conjured by the agency. This construction of the private benefit doctrine, while noteworthy as to its inventiveness, set the stage for a series of actions by the IRS that laid bare its lack of expertise and competence in the realm of nonprofit governance.

The IRS took the (obvious) centuries-old common-law principle that a tax-exempt charity may not be primarily operated for private ends and quickly flipped it to mean its opposite: a tax-exempt charity must be controlled and operated by unrelated parties as a matter of required "public oversight" so as to prevent the possibility of or appearance of private benefit. This, however, is clearly not an element of the federal tax law.

Based on this misguided view of the law, the IRS began taking the position, as articulated by its examining agents (who initially were wholly untrained in this area), that it had the authority to determine a public charity's board size, to determine when a

---

[114] See Chapter 3, text accompanied by notes 28–41.
[115] See *id.*, text accompanied by notes 42–53.

charity's board is too small, to determine when a charity's board is too incestuous, and to force a charity to expand its governing board to include unrelated parties as a condition of obtaining recognition of, or retaining, tax exemption.

The IRS's decision to embark on the regulation of the governance of public charities and certain other categories of tax-exempt organizations coincided with its decision to substantially revise the basic annual information return, the Form 990. This revamping of the annual information return afforded the IRS the opportunity (and the platform) to integrate nonprofit governance into and throughout the return. The result was many questions about nearly all aspects of governance.

Then, the IRS embedded in these questions references to all manner of policies, procedures, processes, and protocols. It did not take long for IRS agents to insist (incorrectly) that these policies and the like were mandatory as a condition of tax exemption. In general, IRS agents, whether reviewing applications for recognition of exemption or examining the operations of tax-exempt organizations, integrated their faulty understanding of the private benefit doctrine into their insistence on various policies and procedures.

Thus, to reiterate, the private benefit doctrine does not prohibit small boards or related boards of tax-exempt organizations, nor does it mandate that exempt organizations adopt and adhere to various policies and procedures. The most that the private benefit doctrine has to say in the realm of governance is that, in the case of a nonprofit organization with a board of related individuals, a court should give greater scrutiny to the entity's operations before agreeing that it is tax-exempt.[116]

The following are some specific positions taken in IRS private letter rulings that illustrate the agency's lack of expertise in the area of nonprofit governance:

- As early as April 2008, the IRS was taking the position, with the private benefit doctrine as its sole authority, that, to be tax-exempt as a charitable organization, an entity must have board

---

[116] Bubbling Well Church of Universal Love, Inc. v. Commissioner, 74 T.C. 531 (1980).

members who are representative of the community.[117] That, however, except for health care providers,[118] is not the law.

- An organization had three directors, which the IRS used as one reason for denying recognition of tax exemption.[119] The IRS was critical of this arrangement, stating that the entity's board of directors had "unfettered control" over the organization; that is true, however, for any nonprofit organization (with the possible exception in the case of some membership entities). Also, the IRS applied the private benefit doctrine because the organization did not establish that the entity will not be operated for the "personal benefit" of its directors; this was incorrect because the doctrine applies when there has been a violation, not when there might be a violation.
- The IRS ruled that an organization could not be tax-exempt, in part because it lacked an "independent" board.[120] There is nothing in the federal tax law that imposes such a requirement. Also, this board of related individuals was said to have an "inherent conflict of interest." The federal tax law addresses the matters of private inurement, private benefit, excess benefit transactions, and self-dealing but is silent as to conflicts of interest. This is an area where the IRS lacks jurisdiction.[121]
- An organization applied to the IRS for recognition of tax exemption on the ground it was a synagogue. Although there were other reasons for denial of this recognition, the IRS stated that there was unwarranted private benefit because the entity lacked a "system for public oversight."[122] This aspect of the ruling is absurd on its face; there is no requirement in the federal tax law that an exempt church

---

[117] Priv. Ltr. Rul. 200828029 (April 18, 2008).
[118] See Chapter 3, text accompanied by note 82.
[119] Priv. Ltr. Rul. 200845053 (August 11, 2008).
[120] Priv. Ltr. Rul. 201252021 (September 13, 2012).
[121] See Chapter 1, text accompanied by notes 96 and 97.
[122] Priv. Ltr. Rul. 201325017 (March 28, 2013).

must have such a system and such a rule would be blatantly unconstitutional if it existed.

- The IRS's position is that one-person boards are per se instances of unwarranted private benefit.[123] If state law permits, boards consisting of one individual are lawful; the IRS lacks the authority to, in effect, preempt state law.[124]
- An organization was precluded by the IRS from tax exemption as a public charity, in part because there was no "public control" of or "public involvement" in the entity.[125] There is no requirement in the federal tax law that a charitable entity, to be tax-exempt, must be controlled by the public and there likewise is no requirement (except in connection with the facts-and-circumstances test[126]) that there be public involvement.
- An organization failed in its effort to be recognized as an exempt business league.[127] One of the reasons provided by the IRS for the denial of recognition in this instance was that there was "no oversight of an independent board."[128] There is no requirement in the federal tax law that an exempt

---

[123] Priv. Ltr. Rul. 201242016 (July 27, 2012).

[124] One of the oddities in this context is that, in the glossary that is part of the Form 990 instructions, the IRS defines the term *governing body* to mean the "group of 1 or more persons authorized under state law to make governance decisions on behalf of the organization and its shareholders or members, if applicable."

[125] Priv. Ltr. Rul. 201429027 (December 12, 2012).

[126] As discussed, some tax-exempt charitable organizations are publicly supported charities (see Chapter 3, text accompanied by note 29). These charities are generally required to normally receive at least one-third of their financial support from the public. An exception, however, is available for certain types of publicly supported charities (those described in IRC § 170(b)(1)(A)(vi)); this exception, which is known as the facts-and-circumstances test, enables a charity to be considered publicly supported even though its public support ratio is as low as 10 percent (Reg. § 1.170A-9(f)(3)). One of the set of facts and circumstances that is taken into account in this regard is whether there is public participation in an organization's programs or policies (Reg. § 1.170A-9(f)(3)(iii)(D)).

[127] This is a type of noncharitable organization referenced in IRC § 501(c)(6); these entities are usually trade or professional member-based organizations.

[128] Priv. Ltr. Rul. 201349021 (July 2, 2013).

business league, which usually has a membership-elected board, have outside oversight or an independent board.[129]

- An organization failed in its efforts to qualify as a tax-exempt church, in part because it had a two-person board of related individuals. The IRS ruled that the organization must amend its bylaws to make provision for control vested in a board of directors "consisting of a majority of unrelated persons."[130] While it is unlikely that a church would have a two-individual board (related or not), the IRS has no authority to require that a board of a charity consist of a majority of unrelated individuals.
- The tax exemption of an organization was revoked because its president was found to have repeatedly engaged in private inurement and excess benefit transactions. The entity's governing body consisted of the president, his father, and his wife. The IRS stated that all of these inappropriate transactions occurred because the entity had a "family-based governing board." [131] This stance was ridiculous because these types of transactions can (and do) just as easily occur where there is a board of unrelated individuals.
- An organization was unsuccessful in obtaining recognition of tax exemption, in part because its articles of organization provided that its chief executive officer, one of three directors, cannot be removed from the board. The IRS ruled that this organization had "structured its board so that private interests are protected." [132] This is a common

---

[129] The federal tax regulations that summarize the qualifications for tax exemption for business leagues (Reg. § 1.501(c)(6)-1) say nothing about public oversight or an independent board. The Supreme Court reviewed these regulations and pronounced them reasonable; the Court did not reference any requirement of outside oversight or independent boards (National Mufflers Dealers Association, Inc. v. United States, 440 U.S. 472 (1979)). The U.S. Court of Appeals for the Seventh Circuit held that a nonprofit organization failed each of the federal tax law requirements for exemption as a business league (other than being nonprofit); it also was silent as to any requirement of an independent board or outside oversight (ABA Retirement Funds v. United States, 759 F.3d 718 (7th Cir. 2014)).

[130] Priv. Ltr. Rul. 200843032 (August 1, 2008).

[131] Priv. Ltr. Rul. 201113041 (January 7, 2011).

[132] Priv. Ltr. Rul. 201218041 (February 7, 2012).

approach, to enable founders of organizations from being removed from the boards. If this type of provision is legal under state law, the IRS lacks the jurisdiction to unilaterally state that it amounts to unwarranted private benefit and thus is a violation of the federal tax law.

- The IRS denied recognition of exemption to an entity claiming to be a charitable organization, in part because it had not adopted bylaws or a conflict-of-interest policy.[133] The reason given for the denial was that the organization lacks the "basic procedural safeguards necessary to prevent impermissible private benefits." The federal tax law of exempt organizations does not, however, include a requirement for any such safeguards. Bylaws and conflict-of-interest policies are not required as a condition of tax exemption.

There is one more illustration of the IRS's lack of expertise in the realm of nonprofit governance. This concerns application of the IRS's ruling policy as to governance to private foundations.

A private foundation is a form of tax-exempt charitable organization; foundations are subsets of the charitable sector.[134] Most private foundations have relatively small governing boards; it is common for these boards to consist primarily if not wholly of related individuals (as is the case, by definition, with family foundations). Thus, for example, the US Tax Court, having noted that private foundations are "typically subject to the control of a single individual, family, or small group of persons," observed that they are "especially susceptible to having their resources diverted to serve private rather than charitable purposes, thereby subverting the rationale for according them tax-exempt status and the benefits of being eligible to receive tax-deductible contributions."[135]

Therefore, it would seem that private foundations should be subject to the IRS position, as reflected in the agency's ruling policy, that small boards of directors and/or related boards of directors are

---

[133] Priv. Ltr. Rul. 201221022 (March 1, 2012).

[134] See Chapter 3, text accompanied by notes 20–27.

[135] Parks v. Commissioner, 145 T.C. 278, 299 (2015).

intrinsically forms of prohibited private benefit. (Were that the case, there would be no such thing as a tax-exempt family private foundation.) The stance of the IRS, however, is that its ruling policy is inapplicable with respect to private foundations. The basis for this distinction (occasionally expressed, always informally) is rarely articulated. As a matter of federal tax law, however, the private benefit doctrine is equally applicable with respect to public charities and private foundations.

The private benefit doctrine, like the private inurement doctrine, is applicable to private foundations, inasmuch as those doctrines are applicable to exempt charitable organizations generally. These doctrines are not accorded much attention in the private foundation context, however, because transactions or arrangements that are potentially the subject of attention from those law sources are instead addressed by the rules prohibiting (severely taxing and undoing) acts of self-dealing between private foundations and those who are disqualified persons with respect to them.[136]

As is reflected in the summary of the IRS ruling policy in this context, the IRS has repeatedly expressed concern with small, related boards having "complete," "absolute," "unfettered," and like control over the organization's finances (including the setting of directors' compensation) and operations.[137] Yet that is not a problem for the IRS when that type of control is exercised in the private foundation setting.

There is no principled basis for this differentiation by the IRS in its treatment of public charities and private foundations. Presumably the IRS realizes that application of its ruling policy as to governance in the private foundation setting would (if upheld by the judiciary) lead to elimination of tax exemption for nearly all private foundations. That would trigger a major uproar in the charitable community and in Congress – a reaction that the IRS is unwilling to endure. So, instead, the IRS has unilaterally and without public explanation excepted private foundations from its application of the private benefit doctrine as to governance. There is no justification for this distinction. All this policy does (other than highlight the lack

---

[136] IRC § 4941.
[137] See Chapter 6.

of expertise of the IRS in this area) is demonstrate that the IRS's ruling policy as to governance of public charities is wholly inconsistent with the federal tax law.

Form 990 Irrelevant Governance Questions

The revamping of the annual information return and the relevance of the governance questions on that return to tax administration have been summarized.[138] After the revised return was first issued (as a draft for the 2008 tax year), on June 14, 2007, the IRS received comments from the public. One commentator wrote that the proposed return "goes beyond the information required by the Internal Revenue Code" and that what a given organization does regarding "best practices" is a matter for the business judgment of the organization.[139]

Perhaps sensitive to comments such as this, the revised draft of the Form 990, released on December 20, 2007, stated in Part VI that the information being sought about policies was not required by the Internal Revenue Code.[140] This practice continues today, as to Part VI, Section B (concerning some policies).[141] The current Form 990 instructions for Part VI state that "[a]lthough federal tax law generally does not mandate particular management structures, operational policies, or administrative practices, every organization is required to answer each question in Part VI." This point is reiterated: "Even though the information on policies and procedures requested in Section B generally is not required under the Internal Revenue Code, the IRS considers such policies and procedures to generally improve tax compliance." Also: "The absence of appropriate policies and procedures *can* lead to opportunities for

---

[138] See Chapter 5, text accompanied by notes 12–49].

[139] These comments were submitted, by letter dated September 14, 2007, by the president and CEO of a tax-exempt organization by the name of Philanthropic Research, Inc., which is the current public repository of annual information returns (known as "Guidestar"). This submission is noted in the Owens Article at 288.

[140] Form 990, Part VI, Section B.

[141] The most recent version of Form 990 is for tax year 2016.

excess benefit transactions, inurement, operation for non-exempt purposes, or other activities inconsistent with exempt status" (emphasis added).

In revising the Form 990, the IRS ignored the recommendations of its Advisory Committee on Tax-Exempt and Government Entities (ACT). In a 2006 report, the ACT recommended that "[t]o ensure that the form remains focused on meeting the Service's core mission, Form 990 should be designed to determine compliance with federal tax law."[142] This ACT report added that "[e]videntiary questions should be formulated to obtain evidence or facts which will reveal whether the filer has complied with federal tax law" and that "[q]uestions regarding governance 'best practices' ... are probably insufficiently connected to the elements of any violation of the tax code to prompt the efficient use of enforcement resources."[143]

A commentator had this to say about these matters: "Clearly, the IRS is assuming a new role in charity governance, and perhaps more broadly, with other types of tax-exempt organizations;" he noted that, "[i]n doing so, it has publicly acknowledged that it is moving beyond the requirements of the [C]ode."[144] He referenced then-Commissioner Miller's speech, where Mr. Miller stated his view that the IRS has the authority to take these steps and has proclaimed that the agency has "been doing it for a long time."[145]

This commentator also observed that "[i]t does not appear ... that the IRS has ever publicly announced that the information it is compelling, under civil and criminal penalties, is 'not required by the Internal Revenue Code.'"[146] He added that "it appears that this situation is truly unprecedented."[147]

---

[142] ACT, *Policies and Guidelines for Form 990 Revision* 23 (June 7, 2006).

[143] *Id.* at 26.

[144] Owens Article at 288.

[145] See Chapter 5, text accompanied by note 4.

[146] Owens Article at 291.

[147] *Id.* Owens mused that a court challenge, in the form of an action to enjoin the IRS from compelling information about governance by means of the Form 990, "would potentially be successful," in that it would not be a violation of the Anti-Injunction Act (IRC § 7421), which basically prohibits lawsuits brought for the purpose of restraining the assessment or collection of tax. Although application of IRC § 7421 is outside the scope of this discussion, it may be said that his prediction

Consequently, the tax-exempt community is in a "truly unprecedented" set of circumstances where the IRS is compelling, on the annual information return, information that is not relevant to administration of, and is not required by, the federal tax laws – indicators that the IRS is operating beyond the bounds of its expertise and of its jurisdiction.

IRS's Inability to Articulate Good Governance Principles

The IRS's proposed good governance principles[148] were poorly received and, as it turned out, short-lived. They suffered from many flaws, two of which are common to the several sets of nonprofit governance principles that have been published. That is, first, they were designed for the larger charities, with their considerable financial and staff resources. Second, they seemed predicated on the assumption that there is a constant mass of talented individuals who want nothing more than to serve on a charity's board and who are willing to devote unlimited amounts of time to that assignment, without need for compensation or fear of liability. The IRS's proposed principles were also criticized for offering nothing innovative in this list of "best practices" for nonprofit governance, rehashing platitudes and fiduciary law summaries that appear in countless other governance standards.

Some of the elements in this IRS package were simply unrealistic and even silly. Was the IRS going to interview board members to assess whether they are sufficiently "passionate"? How many charitable boards include an individual who is an expert in "ethics"? How many boards have an expert on "compensation"? The "critical areas" of board competence did not include law. (After all, the IRS said it wanted to see a "culture of legal compliance.") Since when

---

about the inapplicability of the Act was prescient. For example, the U.S. Court of Appeals for the District of Columbia Circuit held that a case raising the issue as to whether the IRS is acting unconstitutionally in processing an application for recognition (using discriminatory standards), filed by a nonprofit organization seeking recognition of exempt status as a charitable entity, may proceed, in part because the action is not precluded by the Act (Z Street, Inc. v. Koskinen, 791 F.3d 24 (D.C. Cir. 2015)).

[148] See Chapter 5, text accompanied by notes 51 and 52.

does the board of a charitable entity have to represent a "public interest'? The IRS word police was feared to be out, checking to see whether mission statements are "clearly articulated" and "well-written." It was not clear why the referenced conflict-of-interest policy did not apply to a charity's officers.

As state attorneys general can attest, it is not true that "success at fundraising requires care and honesty." A number of observers were perplexed with the idea of "trading volunteers"; these individuals are not tradable at will and the proposal ignored why individuals volunteer in the first place. There is a total disconnect between a charity being "successful" and whether the compensation it pays is "reasonable"; a charity can pay excessive compensation and still be successful. Expense reimbursement is generally not compensation to begin with. While a document retention policy is usually a meritorious idea as an element of management, it is doubtful that it makes a charity more "effective" as a charity.

Noting that the topics and suggestions in these principles seemed to have been drawn from several nongovernmental sources and materials from states' attorneys general offices, a commentator noted the "broad departure of the proposals from matters of traditional tax administration."[149] This commentator also stated that the IRS did "not appear to have been instructed to assemble the exposure draft [of good governance principles] by law or under any other form of formal congressional or Treasury Department direction," so that the "legal import of the document is unclear; it does not fall into one of the traditional categories of Treasury or IRS guidance."[150] In any event, this approach by the IRS for advancing good governance principles was quietly abandoned, with the agency turning to the revamped annual information return as its vehicle for this purpose.[151]

---

[149] Owens Article at 287.

[150] *Id.*

[151] See Chapter 5, text accompanied by notes 12–49. Comments about the draft Form 990 have also been said by the IRS to help develop its charitable organizations' "Life Cycle" tool that has been available since 2004 on the IRS's website.

The IRS embarrassed itself in publishing this document. The exempt organizations community feared that IRS agents were going to ignore the admonition that the document contained "suggestions" and begin imposing these governance elements as law when processing applications for recognition of exemption and auditing tax-exempt organizations. Observers were chagrined that the IRS, which was and still is far behind in attending to the work it is supposed to be doing,[152] would ignore these responsibilities and wander off into an area in which it has no jurisdiction, authority, or expertise (the latter nicely illustrated by the proposed good governance principles).

Failure of Agents' Training Materials

The so-called "training materials" provided to its agents by the IRS are in fact little more than a rewrite of the IRS's proposed good governance principles.[153] They provide a rationale for the IRS's stances on nonprofit governance but little in the way of explanations and answers to questions that exempt organizations should be asking inquiring agents. It is not a document reflecting much expertise on the subject.

The materials are silent on the IRS's use of the private benefit doctrine and the agency's application of the *Bubbling Well Church* decision. There are many "shoulds" in the document, with no justification in the federal tax law for any of them. Not surprisingly, they do not reflect the inherent tension between what the applicable federal tax law is and the agency's position on nonprofit governance regulation. They certainly do not address the questions of the IRS's jurisdiction and regulatory authority in this area.

---

[152] See Chapter 8, text accompanied by notes 42–45.
[153] See Chapter 5, text accompanied by notes 53 and 54.

Failure of Governance Check Sheet

The IRS's agents' governance check sheet[154] merely reflects the questions about policies and procedures reflected in the annual information return and give no hint that the policies being requested by the agency are not required.

Probably the most illuminating aspect of these materials are statements like the federal tax law "generally does not mandate particular management structures, operational policies, or administrative practices," and the tax law "does not require charities to have governance and management policies." Yet they simultaneously state that the IRS will review organizations' applications for recognition of exemption and annual information returns to determine whether they have adopted various policies. In other words, the stance of the IRS is that, despite the fact that the federal tax law does not require these policies, the IRS is going to demand them anyway. This posture is not the mark of a federal agency exhibiting convincing regulatory expertise.

IRS and Data Correlation

With its single study,[155] the IRS strained mightily to find its touted direct correlation between an exempt organization that is governed in accordance with "good governance" practices and its compliance with the federal tax law. Yet, further analysis of this information leads to other, sometimes, contrary, positions. In many ways, all this study shows is that exempt organizations that are knowledgeable about the federal tax law are more likely to be in compliance with that body of law.

It was said that organizations that always use comparability data when setting compensation are more likely to be in compliance with the tax law. The rule of law in this context is that compensation paid by public charities and other exempt organizations to their executives

---

[154] See *id.*, text accompanied by notes 55 and 56.

[155] See *id.*, text accompanied by notes 57–60.

must be reasonable. The process of determining the reasonableness of compensation is akin to valuing an item of property; to do so, the appraiser assesses the value of comparable properties. Thus, the principal way to determine whether an individual's compensation is reasonable is to compare the amount paid, or to be paid, to individuals in comparable positions with comparable responsibilities at comparable organizations (collectively, *comparability data*). Thus, what this portion of the study shows is that an organization that complies with the law is in compliance with the law. This conclusion is underscored by the finding that organizations that never or rarely use the comparable-data approach are not necessarily out of compliance with the tax law.

The same can be said for the finding that organizations with procedures in place for the proper use of charitable assets are more likely to be compliant. Experience testifies to the fact that a procedure in place is not necessarily a procedure that is followed. All this aspect of the study seems to show is that the IRS's preference for having a procedure in place for the proper use of charitable assets is satisfied (and thus qualifies the organization as compliant) when an organization has a procedure in place for the proper use of charitable assets.

The other two findings that the IRS deems favorable to its conclusion that there is this direct correlation are rather astounding. One finding is that an organization with a written mission statement is likely to be more law-compliant. It is hard to believe that such a statement, often developed on a one-time basis and frequently only a sentence in length, has any influence on the actions of a governing board. Week-to-week, month-to-month, these statements are rarely invoked. These mission statements are usually prepared by staff, vetted by lawyers, and placed in the minute book so the organization can truthfully annually report to the IRS that it adopted a mission statement.

The other finding is that an organization is often more law-compliant where its board has reviewed the Form 990. The IRS's requirement is that the Form 990 be *provided to* the board members, not that it be *reviewed by* them. (There is no mandatory advance provision period.) The Form 990 may be provided by board members electronically; the IRS's requirement is satisfied if one or more recipients hit the delete button one second after the document arrives. Even if there is board review of the Form 990, that does not mean there is board discussion of the document; even if the board met to discuss the draft Form 990, the document is so monstrous and technical it would likely contribute more to board confusion and despair than good governance.

The IRS has greatly played down the portion of its report that shows no statistically significant correlation between law compliance and certain practices. But there are two stunning findings. One finding is that there is no correlation between adoption and enforcement of conflict-of-interest policies and law compliance. In its push to regulate nonprofit governance, the IRS has made no greater effort than its insistence that public charities and other types of organizations have these policies. Private letter rulings reflect denial of recognition of tax exemption, at least in part, because the organization refused to adopt a conflict-of-interest policy. An inquiry about use of these policies is the lead-off question in Form 990, Part VI, Section B, concerning hoped-for policies in this "crown jewel" (as the IRS sees it) in the annual information return. The IRS has prepared a prototype of a conflict-of-interest policy to make it as easy as possible for organizations to adopt one – the only type of policy accorded this emphasis. It is difficult today for a charitable organization to obtain recognition of tax exemption without first adopting and submitting a conflict-of-interest policy; these policies are often now submitted as a matter of course, along with articles of organization and bylaws. It has become common for public charities and other exempt entities to adopt and enforce conflict-of-interest policies.[156] One would think with recent years' emphasis on conflicts of interest and their resolution by tax-exempt charitable organizations that there would be a huge positive correlation

---

[156] As an illustration, as part of its compliance check of a sampling of the nation's tax-exempt colleges and universities, the IRS asked (by means of its Form 14018 (September 2008)) these private institutions whether they had a conflict-of-interest policy governing members of the institutions' "ruling body" and their "top management" officials, and perhaps fulltime faculty. The resulting interim report indicated that most of these institutions have these policies (IRS's Interim Report on Nonprofit Colleges and Universities Compliance Project (May 7, 2010 (IR-201058)). The final report was silent on the matter.

between this governance practice and law compliance.The other astounding finding was that there is little, if any, correlation between law compliance and family and/or business relationships on the governing board. Here, in fact, is a fertile field for abuse, particularly in the case of business relationships on the board, with the potential for excess benefit transactions, self-dealing, and other forms of private inurement.

The IRS, since its entry into the realm of nonprofit governance, has been vociferous in its insistence that boards containing related individuals are inherently forms of private benefit, are to be avoided, and are a basis for denial of recognition of tax exemption. This finding, of itself, is sufficiently dazzling to undercut the IRS's efforts to bootstrap itself into the role of regulator of the governance of public charities and other exempt organizations.

The final finding, that organizations controlled by one individual or a small board are likely to be noncompliant with the law, is merely reflective of what the law has recognized for nearly 50 years. Organizations like this, by their very nature, tend to have little or no staff, and accounting and legal services. It is the view of the IRS that organizations with small boards are hotbeds of private benefit and thus not entitled to recognition of tax exemption; it has issued many private letter rulings to that effect. [157] This likelihood of noncompliance may be due more to ignorance than malevolence. In any event, the law on this point is well-settled: A nonprofit organization with a small board, while it needs to be subject to a more intense level of scrutiny when ascertaining its qualification for tax exemption, is not automatically precluded from exemption.[158]

It may be noted that, in a 2008 report, the committee stated that there is "little or no empirical evidence to date that supports the efficacy of any specific governance practices by nonprofit organizations, much less compliance with the requirements for maintaining tax exemption."[159]

---

[157] See Chapter 6, text accompanied by notes 10–66.

[158] Bubbling Well Church of Universal Love, Inc. v. Commissioner, 74 T.C. 531 (1980).

[159] ACT, *The Appropriate Role of the Internal Revenue Service with Respect to Tax-Exempt Organizations Good Governance Issues* 1 (June 11, 2008).

Summary of Analysis

The governance of nonprofit, tax-exempt organizations has traditionally been the subject of state law, such as by enforcement of nonprofit corporation and trust statutes, charitable fundraising regulation, and the oversight role of states' attorneys general. With two narrow exceptions, Congress has never evinced any interest in creating federal statutory law on this topic. This state of affairs in the law has existed since the creation of the United States and the enactment of various elements of the federal law of tax-exempt organizations (the latter beginning in 1913). There is nothing in the statements of IRS jurisdiction that remotely justifies the great leap of the IRS into nonprofit governance regulation, starting in 2007.[160]

It is difficult to overstate the enormity of the consequences of the IRS's entry into the realm of nonprofit governance.[161] This development is the most important one in the evolution of the law of nonprofit organizations since enactment of the Tax Reform Act of 1969. The IRS's presence in the realm of nonprofit governance has directly affected the behavior of innumerable trustees, directors, officers, and executive employees of public charities and other tax-exempt organizations, plus the practices of exempt organizations' lawyers, accountants, and other consultants. Indeed, a new industry of consultants advising nonprofit organizations on governance matters has been born, directly in the aftermath of the IRS's entry into this field. The amount of fees paid by exempt organizations to educate boards and staff, have policies developed, and put various protocols and practices into place is incalculable. In the overall scheme of things, the IRS's efforts to regulate nonprofit governance may not quite rise to the level of the *Brown & Williamson* standard of

---

[160] Although the topic of preemption is outside the scope of this book, there is an element of that topic here. For example, the IRS has in effect preempted the laws of some states by taking the position that the concept of the one-director nonprofit corporation, permissible in those states, is private benefit per se precluding tax exemption as a charitable entity.

[161] A description of some of these consequences is in Chapter 1, text accompanied by note 100. In general, see Chapter 8, text accompanied by notes 49–55.

"economic and political significance"[162] but, within the nonprofit organizations' universe, what the IRS has done is enormous (and, from a law standpoint, troubling).

If one case were to be selected in support of the arguments in this chapter, it would be the opinion concerning CAISO.[163] In that decision, the court rejected the notion that the FERC had jurisdiction to dictate the composition and manner of selection of the governing board of a nonprofit organization. No statutory authority for that attempt exists; the court stated that the FERC "simply has no authority to do such a thing." That is the case here; in trying to regulate nonprofit governance, the IRS simply has no authority to do such a thing.

The court in the CAISO case did not mince words. It portrayed what the agency was doing in the realm of nonprofit governance as "breathtaking," "overreaching," "stretching," and commission of an "absurdity." It explored the "implications" of the FERC's order, referring to them as a "parade of horribles." The court stated that the FERC has the authority to not accept something which it does not deem to be an ISO. This authority is akin to the IRS's authority to determine (at least initially) whether a nonprofit organization is tax-exempt. The court stated that the FERC does not have the authority to "reform and regulate the governing body" of a nonprofit organization. Neither does the IRS.

As discussed, the IRS lacks the requisite expertise to regulate in the field of nonprofit governance.[164] To reiterate, its position to base its regulatory authority on the private benefit doctrine is arbitrary, capricious, and otherwise contrary to law. Its draft of "good governance" principles was poorly done and had to be jettisoned by the agency. Its training materials for agents manifest the IRS's ignorance when it comes to nonprofit governance. The IRS's efforts to correlate "data" to prove that "well-governed" charities are more tax-law compliant is speculative at best. The only aspect of this that favors the IRS is that there is no other federal agency that has

---

[162] Federal Drug Administration v. Brown & Williamson Tobacco Corp., 529 U.S. 120, 160 (2000).

[163] See the text accompanied by *supra* notes 39–95.

[164] See the text accompanied by notes 96–159.

nonprofit law governance expertise either.[165] This more likely proves that the preexisting system of leaving nonprofit governance to the states was sound.[166]

Congress knows how to define an agency's jurisdiction and can do so with great precision when it chooses to do so.[167] Indeed, the lack of IRS jurisdiction in this context can be seen in what the agency should have done: participating with the Treasury Department in drafting a regulation on nonprofit governance or otherwise announcing its interest in regulating in this area, such as by revenue ruling. In the interim, the IRS should have declined jurisdiction, just as the FCC did,[168] over nonprofit governance.

The Supreme Court's sentence in *King* v. *Burwell* can be paraphrased to read: It is especially unlikely that Congress has

---

[165] When the then-TE/GE Commissioner announced the entry of the IRS into the realm of nonprofit governance in 2007, he conceded that the agency would be going "beyond its traditional spheres of activity" but asserted that there was a "vacuum" that needs to be filled in this area and that the IRS was going to fill it (see Chapter 5, text accompanied by note 1). Even if there was (or is) such a vacuum, the filling of it is the responsibility of Congress, not the IRS. As a dissenting Supreme Court Justice wrote, "social policy in the first instance is a matter for legislative concern" (Alexander v. Americans United, Inc., 416 U.S. 752, 774–775 (1974)). In dissent, the Chief Justice stated: "We do not leave it to the agency to decide when it is in charge" (City of Arlington, Texas v. Federal Communications Commission, 133 S. Ct. 1863, 1886 (2013)).

[166] As another example of this point, during the period that proposed regulations concerning limitations on political campaign activity by tax-exempt social welfare organizations were extant (they were subsequently withdrawn), four U.S. senators wrote to the Commissioner of Internal Revenue, asking that the regulation project be suspended (letter dated February 19, 2014, reproduced in Bloomberg BNA, *Daily Tax Report*, Feb. 20, 2014). In this letter, the senators stated: "The IRS is not the appropriate agency to regulate political activity as the proposal delineates given its lack of subject-matter expertise and role as impartial administrator of our nation's tax laws."

[167] For example, a court of appeals read the federal election law to read that the FEC had jurisdiction to regulate contributions to political committees but not to groups attempting to draft candidates (because, in the case of the latter, the individuals benefiting from their efforts were not yet "candidates") (Federal Election Commission v. Machinists Non-Partisan Political League, 655 F.2d 380 (D.C. Cir. 1981)). To be sure, the court was narrowly construing these definitions out of free speech concerns but this case still illustrates precise line-drawing when it comes to describing agency jurisdiction.

[168] See Chapter 2, text accompanied by notes 32–42.

delegated the matter of nonprofit governance to the IRS, which has no expertise in crafting nonprofit governance policy. This, too, is not a case for the IRS. The agency, in this regard, is operating outside the scope of its jurisdiction. Its acts in this regard are ultra vires.

8

IRS Lacks Authority to Regulate Nonprofit Governance

> Paraphrasing the US Supreme Court, "it is plain that Congress has not given the IRS the authority that it seeks to exercise here."
>
> *Federal Drug Administration v. Brown & Williamson Tobacco Corp. (2000)*

A second approach, for a court, in framing the scope of an agency's jurisdiction (in this context, authority) is review of the agency's construction of a statute that is part of the overall statutory construct defining and comprising the agency's jurisdiction.[1] The construction by the agency at issue usually is manifested in the form of a regulation. This exercise is generally accomplished by adherence to the *Chevron* principle.[2]

The US Supreme Court has cautioned, however, that not every agency action is within its authority, in that agencies may stretch the authority they have beyond its lawful bounds; agencies sometimes overreach. When this happens, the Court stated, the result is an "incorrect application of agency authority."[3] In an instance of this nature, an agency's action is "ultra vires."[4]

The *Chevron* analysis approach is not particularly helpful when assessing the lawfulness of the IRS's efforts to regulate nonprofit governance. This is because, as discussed, there is no statute – organic or otherwise – that explicitly accords the IRS jurisdiction with respect to the matter of this type of governance. It cannot even be

---

[1] See Chapter 2, text accompanied by notes 1–10.
[2] *Id.*, text accompanied by notes 94–120.
[3] City of Arlington, Texas v. Federal Communications Commission, 133 S. Ct. 1863, 1869 (2013).
[4] *Id.*

said that a statute is ambiguous on the point; the statutes are silent on the point. Moreover, the IRS's construction of its authority is not manifested in a regulation but is confined to a batch of private letter rulings, as to which there cannot be judicial deference.[5]

Further, the IRS's regulation of nonprofit governance is arbitrary, capricious, an abuse of discretion, and is otherwise not in accordance with law.[6]

Application of *Chevron* Standard

The ultimate purpose of the *Chevron* approach to determining the scope of an agency's regulatory authority is to enable Congress to legislate in an environment where it knows, if it chooses to leave gaps in a statute to be subsequently filled, by regulation, by an agency with jurisdiction over the statute, that the gap-filling will be tolerated (by the judiciary) only if the terms of the implementing regulation are reasonable.[7] A concomitant element of this principle is that, if the gap involves matters of major economic or political significance, the courts will not lightly presume that the legislature has implicitly delegated these decisions to the agency.[8] All of this is part of the overriding admonition, issued by the Supreme Court, that courts should take seriously and apply rigorously, in all cases, statutory limits on agencies' authority.[9]

Even though the ultimate test may well be whether an agency's interpretation of a statute expressed in a regulation is reasonable, the *Chevron* framework presupposes a model. After all, the Supreme Court's admonition speaks of *statutory limits* on an agency's authority. Thus the model presupposes two elements: a

---

[5] See Chapter 2, text accompanied by notes 130-141.

[6] See the text accompanied by *infra* notes 27–45.

[7] City of Arlington, Texas v. Federal Communications Commission, 133 S. Ct. 1863, 1868 (2013), referencing AT&T Corp. v. Iowa Utilities Board, 525 U.S. 366, 397 (1999). See Chapter 2, text accompanied by notes 102-105.

[8] Federal Drug Administration v. Brown & Williamson Tobacco Corp., 529 U.S. 120, 160 (2000).

[9] City of Arlington, Texas v. Federal Communications Commission, 133 S. Ct. 1863, 1872 (2013).

statute that an agency is charged with administering and a regulation that the agency has issued in (ostensible) advancement of the purposes of the statute.

These elements are reflected in many cases. One example involves the check-the-box regulations, where the courts involved rejected the argument that the Treasury Department exceeded its authority in promulgating the entity-classification regulations.[10] In this case, a court of appeals adhered to the "perimeters of [*Chevron*] and its directive to courts to give deference to an agency's interpretation of its statutes that the agency is entrusted to administer and to the rules that govern implementation, as long as they are reasonable [and] are clear."[11]

By contrast, although the IRS is authorized to regulate the practice of representation of persons before the Department of the Treasury, courts have held that the IRS was not, by reason of this statute, accorded the authority to regulate tax-return preparers or regulate the preparation and filing of ordinary refund claims.[12] As to the former, an appellate court stated that the IRS's statutory authority "cannot be stretched so broadly" and that the IRS "may not unilaterally expand its authority through such an expansive, atextual, and ahistorical reading" of the statute.[13] As to the latter, a court concluded that the "traditional tools of statutory interpretation unambiguously foreclose the IRS's interpretation," in that the regulation involved failed *Chevron* step one because the statute was not ambiguous.[14]

But suppose there is no statute reasonably framing the range of an agency's regulatory authority. Or, suppose that, in addition to the absence of such a statute, the agency's policymaking is done in the absence of a regulation. That is the case here, involving the IRS

---

[10] See Chapter 2, text accompanied by notes 184–189.
[11] Lattriello v. United States, 484 F.3d 372, 377 (6th Cir. 2007).
[12] See Chapter 2, text accompanied by notes 191–202.
[13] Loving v. Internal Revenue Service, 742 F.3d 1013, 1015, 1022 (D.C. Cir. 2014). In this case, it was noted that, although the statute involved was enacted in 1884, the IRS did not take its position, by regulation, until 2011. As to the matter of regulation of nonprofit governance, the relevant statute was enacted in 1913 and the IRS did not announce its policy, by private letter rulings, until 2007.
[14] Ridgely v. Lew, 55 F. Supp. 3d 89, 98 (D.D.C. 2014).

and its policy determinations with respect to nonprofit governance. There is no statute on point, much less one that is ambiguous. Without a regulation for a court to examine, there cannot be application of the *Chevron* principle, whereby a court is likely, having found the controlling statute to be ambiguous on the topic, to give deference to an agency's interpretation. Without the presence of a regulation, there can only be, at most, *Skidmore* deference.[15]

Although the *Chevron* principle cannot apply in this context with respect to the IRS's efforts to regulate in the field of nonprofit governance, it should be noted that the Supreme Court stated, as to application of the *Chevron* second step, courts may not disturb an agency rule unless it is "arbitrary and capricious in substance, or manifestly contrary to the statute."[16] Here, the applicable statutes are silent on the matter of the regulation of nonprofit governance, so it cannot be said that the IRS's stance is "contrary" to a statute. The stance, however, does not find any support in a statute. The IRS's unwarranted invocation of the private benefit doctrine in this context, coupled with its erroneous application of that doctrine[17] and its lack of expertise as to the topic[18] (plus its failure of the other *Skidmore* elements), demonstrates that the IRS's regulatory efforts are arbitrary and capricious in substance.[19]

The Court has also stated that it has "applied *Chevron* where concerns about agency self-aggrandizement are at their apogee: in cases where an agency's expansive construction of the extent of its own power would have wrought a fundamental change in the regulatory scheme."[20] The IRS's stance as to nonprofit governance is an "expansive construction of the extent of its own power" and that the agency's actions have "wrought a fundamental change in the regulatory scheme." The Court cited as an example the assertion by

---

[15] Skidmore v. Swift & Co., 323 U.S. 134 (1944).

[16] Household Credit Services, Inc. v. Pfennig, 541 U.S. 232, 242 (2004), quoting United States v. Mead Corp., 533 U.S. 218, 227 (2001)

[17] See Chapter 7, text accompanied by notes 107–137.

[18] *Id.*, text accompanied by notes 107–159.

[19] See the text accompanied by *infra* notes 27–45.

[20] City of Arlington, Texas v. Federal Communications Commission, 133 S. Ct. 1863, 1872 (2013).

the Federal Drug Administration that it had jurisdiction to regulate tobacco products. That position was seen by the Court as posing a question of "economic and political magnitude." [21] For the tax-exempt community, the IRS's leap into the realm of nonprofit governance and its subsequent regulatory efforts are matters close to, if not constituting, considerable "economic and political magnitude."[22]

Application of *Skidmore* Standard

There is almost no federal statutory or regulatory law pertaining to the subject of nonprofit governance. The IRS's position as to nonprofit governance is not expressed in any form of document that is formally entitled to even *Skidmore* deference. Thus, presumably a court could basically decide, on its own, whether the IRS's position, based as it is on a series of private letter rulings resting largely on the private benefit doctrine, has any basis in the law. But *Skidmore* offers some guidance.

Pursuant to *Skidmore*, the weight accorded an agency's interpretation depends on an alchemy involving five factors: (1) the degree of the agency's care, (2) the agency's consistency, (3) the agency's formalities, (4) the agency's "relative expertness," and (5) the persuasiveness of the agency's position.[23]

Analysis of *Skidmore* Factors

As to the matter of an agency's "care," in the context of guidance as to nonprofit governance, the IRS certainly could have taken more care, as that term may be construed, than it has so far. It could have elevated its policymaking on governance to one or

---

[21] Federal Drug Administration v. Brown & Williamson Tobacco Corp., 529 U.S. 120, 133 (2000).

[22] See the text accompanied by *infra* notes 50–56.

[23] United States v. Mead Corporation, 533 U.S. 218, 227 (2001).

more revenue rulings or even a notice.[24] Instead, the IRS is using only a blend of private letter rulings, forms of annual information returns and instructions, and officials' speeches.

The quality of IRS private letter rulings in the exempt organization's context these days is notoriously low. These documents all too frequently are poorly written, with inconsistent facts, citations of irrelevant or misconstrued law, and often shaky legal conclusions. The IRS has prepackaged paragraphs containing its view on various bodies of law (such as the private benefit and commerciality doctrines) that are often inaccurate or at least overstated. Many of these rulings emanate from cases where the organization's officers are representing the entity pro se and they cannot or will not stand up to agents' pressures (such as to adopt policies).

As to the factor of consistency, it may be conceded that most of the IRS's private letter rulings concerning nonprofit governance are consistent – albeit consistently erroneous. There are some private letter rulings on the subject of nonprofit governance, however, that are inconsistent with the majority of them.[25] Thus, the IRS has not been consistent in its issuance of private letter rulings as to governance that are based on the private benefit doctrine.

This absence of care being taken in this context by the IRS also speaks to the IRS's lack of formality in this process. The fact is reflected in the GAO's Regulatory Guidance Processes Report.[26] The IRS's lack of expertise as to the law aspects of nonprofit governance is summarized above.[27]

The IRS's positions on the matter of application of the federal tax law in the realm of nonprofit governance are certainly not persuasive. First, they are not predicated on the basis of any statutory or regulatory set of standards. Second, these positions are based on the private benefit doctrine, in the total absence of any support in the case law for the agency's position. Third, the

---

[24] As discussed (see Chapter 9, text accompanied by note 18), one approach is promulgation of a regulation. That, however, the IRS cannot do on its own. Tax regulations are issued by the Department of the Treasury, albeit in conjunction with the IRS.

[25] See Chapter 6, text accompanied by notes 113–121.

[26] See Chapter 1, text accompanied by notes 89 and 90.

[27] See Chapter 7, text accompanied by notes 107–159.

application of the private benefit doctrine in this context is predicated on the reading of one private benefit doctrine case that is often a perversion of what the court actually decided. Fourth, the IRS has used the promulgation of a revised annual information return as an opportunity to force (or at least try to force) tax-exempt organizations to adopt a battery of policies, procedures, and the like, which it does not have the authority to do (and admits as much). Fifth, the IRS has repeatedly demonstrated (in its draft good governance principles package, its agents' training materials, and positions taken in private letter rulings) that it lacks the expertise required to support ruling in this area. Sixth, the IRS does not have any meaningful data to back up its rationale for intervening in nonprofit governance, which is that a properly governed tax-exempt organization will be in compliance with the federal tax law.

The IRS's policy as to regulation of nonprofit governance fails, in terms of form and substance, all of the *Skidmore* factors. Even though these factors cannot technically apply, they provide considerable guidance leading to the conclusion that the IRS lacks the authority to regulate in the realm of nonprofit governance. Its acts in this regard are ultra vires.

IRS's Policy is Arbitrary and Capricious

Pursuant to the Administrative Procedure Act, a court must "hold unlawful and set aside agency action, findings, and conclusions" that the court finds to be "arbitrary, capricious, an abuse of discretion, or otherwise not in accordance with law."[28] A court's review under this "standard is narrow and a court is not to substitute its judgment for that of the agency."[29] A reviewing court, however, must ensure that the agency "engaged in reasoned decisionmaking."[30] To engage in this requisite reasoned decisionmaking, the agency "must examine the relevant data and articulate a satisfactory explanation for its action

---

[28] 5 U.S.C. § 706(2)(A).

[29] Motor Vehicle Manufacturers Association of the United States v. State Farm Mutual Automobile Insurance Co., 463 U.S. 29, 43 (1983).

[30] Judulang v. Holder, 132 S. Ct. 476, 484 (2011).

including a 'rational connection between the facts found and the choice made.'"[31]

In reviewing an agency action, a court must determine "'whether the decision was based on a consideration of the relevant factors and whether there has been a clear error of judgment.'"[32] The Supreme Court stated: "Normally, an agency rule would be arbitrary and capricious if the agency has relied on factors which Congress has not intended it to consider, entirely failed to consider an important aspect of the problem, offered an explanation for its decision that runs counter to the evidence before the agency, or is so implausible that it could not be ascribed to a difference in view or the product of agency expertise."[33]

Chevron step two[34] incorporates the reasoned decision-making standard of *State Farm*.[35] Under either standard, the "analysis would be the same, because under *Chevron* step two, we ask whether an agency interpretation is 'arbitrary or capricious in substance.'"[36]

A court generally will not override an agency's "reasoned judgment about what conclusions to draw from technical evidence or how to adjudicate between rival scientific [or governance] theories."[37] However, "where an agency has articulated no reasoned basis for its decision – where its action is founded on unsupported assertions or unstated inferences – ... [a court] will not 'abdicate the judicial duty carefully to "review the record to ascertain that the

---

[31] Motor Vehicle Manufacturers Association of the United States v. State Farm Mutual Automobile Insurance Co., 463 U.S. 29, 43 (1983), quoting from Burlington Truck Lines v. United States, 371 U.S. 156, 168 (1962).

[32] Motor Vehicle Manufacturers Association of the United States v. State Farm Mutual Automobile Insurance Co., 463 U.S. 29, 43 (1983), quoting from Bowman Transportation, Inc. v. Arkansas-Best Freight System, Inc., 419 U.S. 281, 285 (1974).

[33] Motor Vehicle Manufacturers Association of the United States v. State Farm Mutual Automobile Insurance Co., 463 U.S. 29, 43 (1983).

[34] See Chapter 2, text accompanied by notes 99–101.

[35] Judulang v. Holder, 132 S. Ct. 476, 483 (2011).

[36] *Id.*, quoting Mayo Foundation for Medical Education and Research v. United States, 562 U.S. 44, 53 (2011).

[37] Tripoli Rocketry Association v. Bureau of Alcohol, Tobacco, Firearms and Explosives, 437 F.3d 75, 83 (D.C. Cir. 2006).

agency has made a reasoned decision based on reasonable extrapolations from some reliable evidence."[38]

As an illustration of the foregoing, the US Tax Court struck down tax regulations that required entities entering into qualified cost-sharing agreements to share stock-based compensation costs.[39] The court had earlier held that the sharing of these costs need not be required because parties operating at arm's length would not do so.[40] These regulations were found to lack any basis in fact because the Treasury Department failed to (1) engage in any fact-finding and therefore failed to examine the relevant data, and (2) support its belief that unrelated parties would share stock-based compensation costs in the context of a qualified cost-sharing agreement with any evidence in the record. The regulations were found to be invalid as a matter of law because, in part, the Department failed to rationally connect the choice it made with the facts found and it failed to respond to significant comments when it issued the final regulations.[41]

It is submitted that the IRS's actions in (1) rationalizing its position that its role in regulating nonprofit governance, including its private letter ruling policy, is properly based on the private benefit doctrine, and (2) concluding that small governing boards of public charities and other exempt organizations and related boards of these organizations are per se violations of that doctrine are arbitrary and capricious.

First, these actions and policies have never been articulated in a regulation, revenue ruling, notice, or any other formal type of IRS

---

[38] *Id.*, quoting from American Mining Congress v. Environmental Protection Agency, 907 F.2d 1179, 1187 (D.C. Cir. 1990)).

[39] Altera Corporation and Subsidiaries v. Commissioner, 145 T.C. 91 (2015). The regulation at issue was Reg. § 1.482-7(d)(2).

[40] Xilinx, Inc. v. Commissioner, 125 T.C. 37 (2005), *aff'd*, 598 F.3d 1191 (9th Cir. 2010).

[41] An article takes the position that the Tax Court's reasoning in *Altera*, that the Department of the Treasury failed to satisfy the reasoned decisionmaking standard and thus was arbitrary and capricious, may serve as a basis for attack on other Treasury and IRS regulatory actions (McManus, "'Altera' Decision Casts Shadow Over Proposed, Adopted Rules," Bloomberg BNA, *Daily Tax Report* J-1 (Oct. 27, 2015)). Likewise, Kantowitz, "Some Thoughts on the 'Altera' Case," Bloomberg BNA, *Daily Tax Report* J-1 (Dec. 30, 2015).

guidance. The IRS's rationale (or rationales) underlying these positions in these regards has never been articulated. Thus, there is no evidence that the IRS, in this setting, has ever engaged in "reasoned decisionmaking." There is no public record that the agency has examined any data concerning charities' board size and composition in relation to acts of private benefit. Thus, there has not been provision of any explanation (let alone a "satisfactory" one) for its action, so there has never publicly been offered a "rational connection between the facts found and the choice made."

Instead, the IRS has based its policies and other positions on a blatant distortion of the little case law guidance there is. The rule developed in the cases, principally *Bubbling Well Church*, is that organizations with a small board and/or a related board are to be subject to a higher level of scrutiny by the IRS and the courts.[42] The agency, however, has, without any principled basis for doing so, converted this jurisprudence into a rule that small boards and related boards are automatically substantial evidence of private benefit (or sometimes private inurement) warranting denial of recognition of tax exemption or revocation of exemption. This is a "clear error of judgment."

The fact that regulation of nonprofit governance is outside the IRS's jurisdiction has been discussed. Thus, its actions in this regard are arbitrary and capricious because the agency has "relied on factors which Congress has not intended it to consider." The agency has "entirely failed to consider" "important aspect(s) of the problem," which include a lack of data in support of its position and case law that is inconsistent with that position. The agency's position is implausible because it is incorrect and borne of a lack of expertise.

Even if the IRS's positions as to the regulation of nonprofit governance were the subject of a formal rule, that rule would be struck down by a reviewing court because, as was the case in *Altera*, the agency's positions lack a basis in fact and are invalid as a matter of law.

As to the Administrative Procedure Act standards, for the foregoing reasons, the IRS's policies and positions as to its

---

[42] See Chapter 3, text accompanied by notes 94–108.

regulation of nonprofit governance constitute an abuse of discretion and development of policy that is not in accordance with law.

There is another aspect of this prospect of an agency's regulatory action being arbitrary and capricious (particularly the latter). The IRS undertook the self-assigned task of starting to regulate nonprofit governance at a time when it was far behind in its work in the tax-exempt organizations' field that it was supposed to be doing. Much of this delay was due to a large inventory of pending but unprocessed applications for recognition of exemption. This backup has largely been resolved. Yet the IRS remains far behind in its exempt organizations work.

The Department of the Treasury and the IRS annually publish a compendium of their current guidance projects; this publication is termed the "Priority Guidance Plan." The current version of this compendium[43] reflects 21 projects (for the most part, issuance of final regulations) in the tax-exempt organizations area. One project has been on this Plan list since 2008, another since 2009, another since 2011, and another since 2012;[44] as to one project on the list, pertaining to the promulgation of regulations relating to a statute that was enacted in 2006, proposed regulations have yet to be issued. The IRS has been entangled in what some are labeling a "scandal" over discriminatory processing of exemption applications for over three years;[45] it should be striving to rebuild its stature and infrastructure in the exempt organizations area legitimately within the bounds of its jurisdiction instead of devoting time to matters that are beyond the range of its authority. It is capricious (as well as irresponsible) for a government agency to ignore work that should be in progress that is within its jurisdiction while simultaneously embarking on an "expansive construction of the extent of its own power"[46] that is outside the scope of its authority.

---

[43] Treasury-IRS Priority Guidance Plan for 2016–2017 (August 15, 2016).

[44] There were two projects that have been on the Plan list since 2012; in one of these instances, final regulations were issued on September 23, 2015 (T.D. 9740), three years to the day the proposed regulations were published.

[45] See Chapter 5, text accompanied by note 60.

[46] City of Arlington, Texas v. Federal Communications Commission, 133 S. Ct. 1863, 1872 (2013).

Summary of Analysis

The *Chevron* principle cannot be applied to this matter of IRS authority to regulate in the realm of nonprofit governance for the simple reasons that there is no statute for a court to consider and no regulation for a court to examine. In short, there is nothing in this context to which a court could affix deference, or even seriously contemplate it. Moreover, it is questionable how far a court might go in applying *Chevron* in this circumstance where the IRS has "wrought a fundamental change in the regulatory scheme."[47]

Likewise, *Skidmore* deference is unavailable in this setting. Nonetheless, the five *Skidmore* factors lead to the conclusion that the IRS does not have the authority to regulate nonprofit governance. Just as is the case with respect to its lack of jurisdiction,[48] the acts of the IRS are outside the scope of its authority and thus are ultra vires.

But there is more. In establishing its policies and implementing its enforcement efforts in connection with nonprofit governance, the IRS has not "engaged in reasoned decisionmaking."[49] First, the reasoning underlying the IRS's actions has never been articulated in written guidance, formal or informal. Worse, the IRS has relied almost entirely on the private benefit doctrine as the legal underpinning for its stances that small governing boards and related boards of nonprofit organizations are per se violations of that doctrine – positions that are arbitrary and capricious if only because of the IRS's distortion of the doctrine to fit its viewpoint. In this regard, the IRS has clearly made an error of judgment.

These circumstances are compounded by the fact that the IRS is far behind in the exempt organizations work it should be doing. With unfinished projects stretching back as far as 2008, it is capricious for the IRS to be embarking on an "expansive construction of the extent of its own power" that is beyond the scope of its authority.

---

[47] See Chapter 2, text accompanied by note 110.

[48] See Chapter 7.

[49] Judulang v. Holder, 132 S. Ct. 476, 484 (2011).

Concept of the Extraordinary Case

As discussed, deference under *Chevron* to an agency's construction of a statute that it administers is premised on the theory that a statute's ambiguity constitutes an implicit delegation from Congress to the agency to fill in gaps in the statute.[50] In this context, however, the Supreme Court has written that, in "extraordinary cases," there "may be reason to hesitate before concluding that Congress has intended such an implicit delegation."[51] Although *Chevron* is inapplicable in the context of the IRS's attempt to regulate nonprofit governance, the concept of the *extraordinary case* is not.

In the face of the Federal Drug Administration's effort to regulate the use of tobacco products, the Court stated that "[t]his is hardly an ordinary case."[52] The Court noted that, "[c]ontrary to its representations to Congress since 1914, the FDA has now asserted jurisdiction to regulate an industry constituting a significant portion of the American economy."[53] The IRS has not made any representations to Congress concerning its authority over the regulation of nonprofit governance, its assertion of this authority beginning in 2007, in relation to statutes it has been administering since 1913, pertains to a significant portion of the nonprofit sector and thus the American economy.

The Court explained: "Owing to its unique place in American history and society, tobacco has its own unique political history. Congress, for better or for worse, has created a distinct regulatory scheme for tobacco products, squarely rejected proposals to give the FDA jurisdiction over tobacco, and repeatedly acted to preclude any agency from exercising significant policy-making authority in the area."[54] Admittedly, this matter of IRS authority has not been placed

---

[50] See Chapter 2, text accompanied by notes 102–105.

[51] Federal Drug Administration v. Brown & Williamson Tobacco Corp., 529 U.S. 120, 159 (2000).

[52] Federal Drug Administration v. Brown & Williamson Tobacco Corp., 529 U.S. 120, 159 (2000).

[53] *Id.*

[54] *Id.* at 159–160.

squarely before Congress and admittedly Congress has not acted to any appreciable extent in connection with the governance of tax-exempt organizations.

Still, it is important to note that the Court stated that, "[g]iven this history and the breadth of the authority that the FDA has asserted, we are obliged to defer not to the agency's expansive construction of the statute, but to Congress's consistent judgment to deny the FDA this power."[55] It may be asserted that a court would say the same with respect to the IRS's expansive construction of the scope of its authority.

The Court concluded that, "[r]eading the [Federal Food, Drug, and Cosmetic Act] as a whole, as well as in conjunction with Congress's subsequent tobacco-specific legislation, it is plain that Congress has not given the FDA the authority that it seeks to exercise here."[56] Similarly, it is asserted (even in the absence of any congressional intervention or interaction) that a reading of the federal tax law makes it plain that Congress has not given the IRS the authority that it is exercising in connection with the regulation of nonprofit governance.

---

[55] *Id.* at 160.
[56] *Id.* at 161.

9

Concluding Thoughts

This chapter of the book includes a review of the central issue addressed in it, the two central arguments made in the book, and the reasons in support of these arguments. This chapter also identifies several other related issues, including the need for revision of current procedures concerning determinations as to deciding the types of guidance the Treasury Department and the IRS produces, development of policies as to when non-regulatory guidance should be considered a rule for purposes of the CRA, and the need for formal law in the field of nonprofit governance.

Review of Central Issue

The central issue addressed in this book is whether the IRS has, as a matter of law, jurisdiction and authority to regulate in the area of governance of public charities and other types of nonprofit, tax-exempt organizations. The answer to the question inherent in that issue, as the reader will have deduced by now, is no.

The backdrop for this issue is that, from the first days of the functioning of the United States government and since enactment of the first constitutional federal income tax statute in 1913, the regulation of nonprofit governance had been almost wholly the province of state government – until 2007. In that year, the IRS announced that it was asserting jurisdiction and regulatory authority over nonprofit organization governance.

This assertion was not the consequence of legislation enacted by Congress or a regulation promulgated by the Department of the Treasury based on existing statutory law. The IRS did not publish a revenue ruling on the point. There was no court opinion serving as a trigger for this development, nor was there any scandal in the nonprofit community. There was no call from Congress for IRS action in this area. The announcement of the IRS's entry into this field of regulation was made by an IRS official at a tax law conference as part of a speech. The policies of the IRS in this regard are, to date, stated only in private letter rulings. The IRS has never provided any public explanation as to the reason or reasons for this major policy shift, or the basis in law for it.

Review of Central Arguments

One of the oddities surrounding the current setting as to this matter of nonprofit governance, from a federal law standpoint, is that, as noted, there is no relevant statute or tax regulation. As discussed throughout, and particularly in Chapters 7 and 8, this state of affairs precludes conventional analysis as to federal agency's jurisdiction and regulatory authority.

Nonetheless, as Supreme Court jurisprudence makes clear, there are two approaches to this type of analysis. One approach has the courts directly determining whether an agency has jurisdiction over a subject matter by analyzing the content of one or more statutes pertaining to the agency's formation and purpose. The other approach is for a court to evaluate the lawfulness of a rule promulgated by an agency and, as part of that exercise, evaluate the scope of the agency's regulatory authority. Either approach, as discussed in the beginning of Chapter 2, can lead to the conclusion than an agency's action is ultra vires.

The two central arguments are that the IRS (1) lacks the jurisdiction to regulate in the field of nonprofit governance and (2) lacks the authority to regulate in the realm of nonprofit governance.

Review of Reasons in Support of Arguments

IRS Lacks Jurisdiction

The efforts of the IRS to regulate the governance of public charities and other types of tax-exempt organizations are what the Supreme Court has, as discussed, termed an "assertion of authority not conferred." There is little in the way of a statutory framework by which to assess the IRS's jurisdiction in this instance. Thus, it is difficult to apply the Court's test in this context, which is "whether the agency has stayed within the bounds of its *statutory* authority." Nonetheless, many Supreme Court and other court cases, reviewed primarily in Chapter 2, provide guidance on the point.

Collateral aspects of this type of analysis, derived from Supreme Court jurisprudence, are also discussed in the book. This includes the enormity of the consequences of the IRS's assertion of jurisdiction and the lack of expertise within the IRS as to nonprofit governance. Further, the IRS's position to base its regulatory authority on the private benefit doctrine is arbitrary, capricious, and otherwise contrary to law. Its draft of "good governance" principles was poorly done and had to be jettisoned by the agency. Its training materials for agents manifest the IRS's ignorance when it comes to nonprofit governance. The IRS's efforts to correlate "data" to prove that "well-governed" charities are more tax-law compliant is specious at best. The only aspect of this that favors the IRS is that there is no other federal agency that has nonprofit law governance expertise either. This more likely proves that the preexisting system of leaving nonprofit governance to the states was sound.

Overall, the actions of the IRS in regulating nonprofit governance are and continue to be ultra vires acts because the agency lacks jurisdiction as to that area.

IRS Lacks Authority

The efforts of the IRS to regulate the governance of public charities and other types of tax-exempt organizations are what the Supreme Court has termed an "incorrect application of agency authority." Again, because there is little in the way of a relevant statutory framework, and the absence of a regulation to evaluate, it is not possible to properly apply conventional analysis in this area, which entails application of the *Chevron* standard. Nonetheless, the book reviews and applies some of the law in this area, particularly the fact that the IRS regulatory action is arbitrary and capricious. The case law lends support to the argument that the IRS's stance as to nonprofit governance is an "expansive construction of the extent of its own power" and that the agency's actions have "wrought a fundamental change in the regulatory scheme."

Thus, the principles of *Chevron* deference are inapplicable in this context. Moreover, because the IRS's position as to nonprofit governance is not expressed in any form of document that would give rise to analysis under the *Skidmore* principle, that path of analysis cannot be formally followed either. Nonetheless, the five *Skidmore* factors are applied, with the book concluding that the IRS policy as to regulation of nonprofit governance fails, in terms of form and substance, all of them.

Overall, the actions of the IRS in regulating nonprofit governance are and continue to be ultra vires acts because the agency lacks the requisite authority to regulate in this area.

IRS Guidance Document Types

An important byproduct of the IRS's clumsy efforts to regulate in the field of nonprofit governance – in the absence of jurisdiction, authority, expertise, and lack of competence to understand and apply the fundamental law it is trying to utilize (the private benefit doctrine) – is the highlighting of the IRS's basic approach to begin with. This matter of nonprofit governance is inherently a significant and meaningful component of nonprofit law. This matter of IRS entry into the field of governance – what the US Court of Appeals for the District of Columbia Circuit characterized in *CAISO* as an "unprecedented invasion of internal corporate governance" – is of enormous significance to the exempt organizations community (not to mention the evolution of administrative law generally). Thus, the question is: Why did the IRS select the type of guidance documents it did – speeches, the Form 990 and its instructions, and private letter rulings – in launching this important initiative?

Before exploration of an answer to that question, it is critical to, once again, simultaneously contemplate the basis of law the IRS has been and is using in asserting its role of nonprofit governance regulator. The plain fact is: There is no such law. That is, aside from the fundamental issues of jurisdiction and authority (or, more precisely, in this instance, the lack thereof), why did the IRS choose to invoke the private benefit doctrine as the legal basis for its position? The simple answer is: There was no other body of law from which to pick. But that simple answer distorts this basic truth: The IRS had to stretch, and in some instances distort and misconstrue, the doctrine in its effort to make it fit. The fundamental point is that the private benefit doctrine does not support, as a basis in law, the IRS's campaign to make nonprofit governance a proper matter of federal tax law. The IRS had to invent its current version of the private benefit doctrine by reconstructing the doctrine – some would say mangle it – to make it conform to its entirely absurd positions that there must be "public oversight" of public charities (including churches), that these entities and other types of tax-exempt organizations must have "independent" boards or boards that are "representative of the community," and/or that there must be "public control" of exempt charitable organizations. How it has been able to do these things, unchecked and not corrected, is based in large part on this matter of guidance document selection. That is, it has been able to hide what it is doing from the public and Congress by employing techniques and documents that are not formally *authoritative*.

Consequently, as to this matter of IRS selection of guidance documents, we know that the agency picked guidance forms that are so low in the guidance forms hierarchy as to escape the need for disclosure to and solicitation of comments from the public. It may be stipulated that the subject of nonprofit governance and the IRS's role in it (if any) deserves a higher degree of attention, exposure, and guidance than has been accorded. Thus, this development has highlighted this issue: What can be done to prevent this kind of extreme agency overreach from recurring and to curb the IRS in this regard?

Some of the answers to this question are provided below. Before getting to them, however, a look at two short-term solutions is warranted. It is unlikely that the APA will be amended to require federal agencies to issue authoritative guidance in certain circumstances. (Again, in the case of the IRS, such guidance would entail regulations, revenue rulings, revenue procedures, notices, and/or announcements.) Thus, we will not, any time soon if ever, see a statute mandating that the IRS, when contemplating a move such as entry into the realm of nonprofit governance, first issue a revenue ruling or an announcement (ideally coupled with a requirement of making the document available as a draft for public comment).

A fallback solution is proposed in the GAO's Regulatory Guidance Processes Report.[1] There, the GAO recommended that the Commissioner of Internal Revenue take action to cause the IRS's current policies and procedures for drafting guidance (interpretation of the federal tax law) to be amended to include factors to consider when deciding what *type* of guidance to issue. If properly designed and implemented (and enforced), this upgrading of the procedures could force the IRS to come out from the darkness of nonprecedential private letter rulings and forms and expose radical policy changes, such as the IRS's entry into nonprofit governance, to the light of public disclosure and opportunity for public comment. These factors would presumably resemble those that are used to determine when a regulatory proposal is *significant* or *economically significant* or adhere to the *Brown & Williamson* formulation.[2] Certainly, the case can be made that the IRS's policies and demands in the realm of nonprofit governance have had and are having enormous economic and other consequences in the exempt community.

Not only would public exposure bring abuses by the IRS like this to light, there should be a formal procedure for getting this type of agency overreach to Congress early in the process, to cause the power grab to be nipped while budding or otherwise resolve the issue. As it happens, the GAO offered a most relevant proposal in this regard: Development of policies and procedures to help guidance-drafting IRS personnel assess whether, and presumably in some cases when, non-regulatory guidance may be considered a rule for purposes of the Congressional Review Act.[3]

Collaterally, the GAO further recommended that the Secretary of the Treasury and the Director of the Office of Management and Budget develop ways to solicit public comment on the potential effects of non-regulatory guidance, including measures of economic

---

[1] See Chapter 1, note 51.

[2] See Chapter 8, text accompanied by notes 50–56.

[3] See Chapter 1, text accompanied by notes 88–90.

impact. This reform may require a slight expansion of the role of the Office of Information and Regulatory Affairs.

Unanswered Issues

An exhaustive exploration of solutions to this matter of the IRS's ultra vires acts in the field of nonprofit governance is outside the framework of this book. Certainly one approach to resolution of the current dilemma is litigation in an appropriate federal court. There are two approaches in this regard.

One of these approaches is to file a request pursuant to the Freedom of Information Act, which generally requires federal governmental agencies to release requested agency records to the public,[4] seeking production of documents and other records relating to the development and execution of the IRS's policy regarding the regulation of nonprofit governance.[5] *Records* are agency records subject to the FOIA if the agency created or obtained them and the agency controlled them at the time the FOIA request is made.[6] If the FOIA request is denied by the IRS or, as is more likely, the IRS refuses to adhere to the request, a lawsuit can be filed seeking the production of documents and records improperly withheld by the IRS in response to the request.[7] The information sought would generally correspond to the information contained in the record required by the US Tax Court in the *Altera* case.[8]

---

[4] 5 U.S.C. § 552(a)(3)(A).

[5] For FOIA purposes, the IRS is an "agency" within the meaning of 5 U.S.C. § 552(f)(1). Cf. Chapter 1, text accompanied by note 36.

[6] U.S. Department of Justice v. Tax Analysts, 492 U.S. 136, 144-145 (1989).

[7] For example, a lawyer made a FOIA request seeking all documents maintained by the IRS relating to proposed and final regulations (albeit issued in 1982). After expiration of the required deadline, the lawyer sued the IRS, seeking the desired records (Judkins v. Internal Revenue Service, Civil Case No. 1:16-cv-01794 (D.D.C., complaint filed on September 8, 2016). Thereafter, the Department of the Treasury was sued on the same basis (Judkins v. Department of the Treasury, Civil Case No. 1:16-cv-01811 (D.D.C., complaint filed on September 12, 2016).

[8] See Chapter 8, text accompanied by notes 39–41.

The other approach in this regard, certainly the more direct one, would be to contest the IRS's acts, relating to regulation of nonprofit governance, in federal court. To date, however, no nonprofit organizations have elected to sue. This matter is compounded by the fact that, in the two instances where a federal court (the US Tax Court) has addressed the governance issues, from a tax law standpoint, the court incorrectly ruled.[9] A major part of this problem is that other law issues were involved in these cases, as well as many "bad facts" from the standpoint of the nonprofit organizations involved.

A test case focused solely on the issues of board size and/or board composition, in the context of application of the private benefit doctrine, is overdue. A nonprofit organization seeking tax exemption as a charitable entity, and denied exemption on the basis of one or more governance issues, could seek a declaratory judgment from the US District Court for the District of Columbia.[10] With the CAISO case[11] as precedent, a substantial likelihood exists that the organization would prevail in that court and/or on appeal.[12]

The most conventional solution to bringing clarity (and solid legal underpinning) to this matter of nonprofit governance law at the federal level is enactment of statutory law on this subject by Congress.[13] Congress, however, has not shown much interest in acting in this area. Indeed, the most recent flurry of activity in this

---

[9] See Chapter 3, text accompanied by notes 109–141.

[10] IRC § 7428.

[11] See Chapter 7, text accompanied by notes 39–95.

[12] Should such a case be won against the government, with one or more courts finding that the IRS's issuance of private letter rulings in the realm of nonprofit governance (other than the correct ones) are ultra vires acts (pursuant to either theory), the issue of retroactive application would arise. It is not clear, as a matter of law, how many years of IRS rulings would be adversely affected. A parallel situation when a court invalidated an IRS church inquiry (United States v. Living Word Christian Center, 2009-1 U.S.T.C. ¶ 50,199 (D. Minn. 2009); as a practical matter, it appears that at least examinations occurring in years prior to the running of the applicable statute of limitations were adversely affected. (A corrective regulation was proposed later in 2009 (REG-112756-09); it has yet to be issued in final form.)

[13] This approach would, of course, put in place a type of "organic statute" that is needed for *Chevron* or *Skidmore* analysis. See Chapter 2, text accompanied by notes 106-120, Chapter 8, text accompanied by notes 7–19.

regard occurred in 2004. In that year, the Senate Finance Committee held a hearing on a range of subjects, including governance, pertaining to tax-exempt organizations.[14] In connection with that hearing, Committee staff prepared a paper as a discussion draft that contained a variety of proposals, including a section on "strong governance and best practices" for exempt organizations.[15] Nothing has come of these recommendations. The Committee lost interest in this subject, turning the matter over to a public charity, Independent Sector, which devised "Principles for Good Governance and Ethical Practice," most recently updated in May 2015, which, of course, are not law.[16] In any event, the tax-exempt organizations community should consider whether it really wants Congress to authorize the IRS to regulate in the realm of nonprofit governance. An alternative, of course, is to cause Congress to prohibit this type of regulation by the IRS, along the lines of Congress's ban on development of guidance by the IRS concerning the extent of allowable political campaign activity by tax-exempt organizations.[17]

Another solution would be promulgation of a tax regulation on nonprofit governance matters by the Department of the Treasury. One problem with this approach is that the Treasury Department may lack jurisdiction or regulatory authority in this area for the same reasons that current IRS actions in this area are ultra vires. A second problem is that the Treasury Department is facing a backlog of regulations inventory in connection with projects already commenced (some as far back as 2008 and 2009) or that should be underway.[18] A third problem in this regard is that the Treasury Department, emulating Congress, has shown no interest in this task.

---

[14] "Charity Oversight and Reform: Keeping Bad Things from Happening to Good Charities," Hearing before the Senate Committee on Finance, U.S. Senate, June 24, 2004 [Senate Hearing 108-603], 108th Cong., 2nd Sess. (2004).

[15] This paper is available at www.finance.senate.gov/hearings/testimony/2004test//062204stfdis.pdf. See Chapter 4, text accompanied by note 14.

[16] In this author's opinion, these principles, while not ideal, are the best of the sets of good governance principles produced to date. These principles are summarized in Chapter 4, text accompanied by note [20].

[17] See Chapter 7, note 166.

[18] See Chapter 8, text accompanied by notes 42–45.

Noting that the IRS has "demonstrated a desire to increase its oversight" in the area of governance of tax-exempt organizations and that there is "no precedential federal tax law guidance that prescribes the appropriate standards for nonprofit governance," a former director of the Exempt Organizations Division wrote to the Department of the Treasury, on January 14, 2009, saying that it would be "helpful to have clear direction from the Treasury Department regarding the specific standards to which nonprofits will be held." He observed that this "lack of guidance not only impairs taxpayer efforts at voluntary compliance but also creates a risk that similarly situated taxpayers may be subject to differing treatment" from the IRS.

He stated that organizations that submit applications for recognition of exemption or ruling requests "may obtain disparate and subjective interpretations of the Service's policy, depending on the agent who happens to handle the matter." He continued: "Moreover, absent published guidance on this issue, a taxpayer under examination has no context or ability to challenge the Service's findings regarding its governance practices at the examination level or within the agency's Appeal function."

To ensure "consistent, transparent enforcement of the federal tax laws," the former director of the Division requested the Treasury Department to issue guidance regarding the standards for nonprofit governance, "with appropriate notice and opportunity for comment, as soon as possible."[19] Nothing publicly has come of this request.

Still another approach would be issuance of a revenue ruling by the IRS on the subject of nonprofit governance. This matter should not be left to the IRS, however, because its history of private letter ruling policy, from 2007 to the present, shows that the agency lacks the capacity or expertise to provide correct guidance in this field (such as by revenue ruling), because that guidance would presumably be based on application of the private benefit doctrine, which, as has been explained, is a flawed and mistaken interpretation of the doctrine. Moreover, elevating this matter of

---

[19] This petition to the Department of the Treasury assumed, but did not address the point, that the Department has the jurisdiction and regulatory authority to promulgate the requested regulation.

governance to revenue ruling status would surely subject the federal government to one or more lawsuits, enabling the IRS position to be formally tested against *Skidmore* deference standards.

It is surprising that the states have been so passive in relation to the IRS's encroachments into the realm of nonprofit governance. Only California has enhanced its statutory authority in this regard in recent years, and that occurred before the IRS embarked on its regulatory initiative.[20] One of the stupendous ironies in this regard is that the California nonprofit corporation statute permits corporations with only one director. Thus, despite all of the integrity features embedded in that state's nonprofit corporation law, IRS policy precludes any entity with this size board from being tax-exempt under federal law.[21]

A larger policy issue, which is also outside the scope of this book, is whether the nonprofit governance function, if there is to be regulation at the federal level, should be the jurisdiction of a federal agency other than the IRS, including a new one. Proposals have been advanced over the years to create a form of "charities commission," modeled somewhat after the approach adopted in the United Kingdom, [22] that would assume responsibility for administration and enforcement of the federal tax law of charitable organizations and perhaps other types of exempt organizations. Whether such a commission would have regulatory authority in the realm of nonprofit governance is a matter that should be addressed.

Another suggestion that has been advanced for some time is to make the IRS an independent agency.[23] Even if the IRS became

---

[20] This is the California Nonprofit Integrity Act, enacted in 2004. In general, Silk and Fei, "California's Nonprofit Integrity Act of 2004," 7 *Int'l J. of Not-for-Profit Law* (no. 2) 66 (Feb. 2005).

[21] See Chapter 6, text accompanied by notes 38–44.

[22] E.g., Salamon (ed.), *The International Guide to Nonprofit Law* (John Wiley & Sons: 1997), Chapter 24.

[23] The most recent of these proposals appeared as part of a Senate Finance Committee report referenced earlier (see Chapter 5, note 60), reflecting Additional Republican Views, where it was stated that "[o]ne of the critical lessons learned from the Committee's investigation is the need for the IRS to be an independent agency." This portion of the report added: "Making the IRS an independent agency, like the Social Security Administration, would minimize the political influence of the Treasury Department, while at the same time allowing the

independent, the matter of the extent to which it has jurisdiction or regulatory authority in the field of nonprofit governance would have to be addressed.[24]

Consequently, the matters that are in need of further research are the contours of a proposed statute or proposed regulation, or placement of this regulatory function in another or new federal agency. In the meantime, while the nonprofit world just watches, the IRS continues to, unchecked, regulate in the realm of nonprofit governance, basing its decisions as to whether to grant recognition of tax-exempt status, or revoke exemptions, on a flawed interpretation of the private benefit doctrine.

Commissioner to be an independent voice for tax administration. In order for the American public to ever have its faith in the IRS restored, it is essential that the IRS be taken out of the political realm and put squarely where it needs to be – as an independent enforcement agency that is free from all real and perceived political influence and bias." (at 248–250).

[24] These various proposals are discussed in Mayer, "'The Better Part of Valour Is Discretion': Should the IRS Change or Surrender Its Oversight of Tax-Exempt Organizations?," *Columbia Jour. of Tax Law*, 2016; Notre Dame Legal Studies Paper No. 1523. Available at http://ssrn.com/abstract=2658325.

Bibliography

ACT, *The Appropriate Role of the Internal Revenue Service with Respect to Tax-Exempt Organizations Good Governance Issues* (June 11, 2008)

Committee on Finance, U.S. Senate, "Charity Oversight and Reform: Keeping Bad Things from Happening to Good Charities," Senate Hearing 108-603, 108th Cong., 2nd Sess. (2004)

Committee on Finance, U.S. Senate, "The Internal Revenue Service's Processing of 501(c)(3) and 501(c)(4) Applications for Tax-Exempt Status Submitted by 'Political Advocacy Organizations from 2010-2013," S. Rep. No. 114-119, 114th Cong., 1st Sess. (2015)

Hopkins, *The Law of Tax-Exempt Organizations, Eleventh Edition* (John Wiley & Sons, Inc.: 2015)

Hopkins, *Legal Responsibilities of Nonprofit Boards, Second Edition* (BoardSource: 2009)

Hopkins and Gross, *Nonprofit Governance: Law, Practices & Trends* (John Wiley & Sons, Inc.: 2006)

Hopkins and Hyatt, *The Law of Tax-Exempt Healthcare Organizations, Fourth Edition* (John Wiley & Sons, Inc.: 2013)

Ingram, speech on June 23, 2009, BNA, *Daily Tax Report*, p. G-6, TaxCore (June 24, 2009)

Kantowitz, "Some Thoughts on the 'Altera' Case," Bloomberg BNA, *Daily Tax Report* J-1 (Dec. 30, 2015)

Kurtz, "Difficult Definitional Problems in Tax Administration: Religion and Race," 23 *Cath. Law.* 301 (1978)

Lederman and Mazza, *Tax Controversies: Practice and Procedure, Third Edition* (LexisNexis: 2009)

Lerner, speech on June 19, 2008, BNA, *Daily Tax Report* (no. 119) TaxCore (June 20, 2008)

Mayer, "'The Better Part of Valour Is Discretion': Should the IRS Change or Surrender Its Oversight of Tax-Exempt Organizations?, *Columbia Jour. of Tax Law* (2016); Notre Dame Legal Studies Paper No. 1523

Miller, speech on April 26, 2007, BNA, *Daily Tax Report* (no. 81) TaxCore (April 27, 2007)

Miller, speech on Nov. 18, 2007, BNA, *Daily Tax Report* (no. 222) TaxCore (Nov. 19, 2007)

Miller, speeches on April 29, 2008, BNA, *Daily Tax Report* (no. 83) TaxCore (April 30, 2008)

Owens, "Charities and Governance: Is the IRS Subject to Challenge?," 60 *Exempt Org. Tax Rev.* (no. 3) 287 (June 2008)

Republican Commissioners, Federal Election Commission, letter to Department of Treasury and IRS, Feb. 27, 2014, Bloomberg BNA, *Daily Tax Report* (no. 41) G-2 (Mar. 3, 2014)

Shulman, speech on Nov. 11, 2008, BNA, *Daily Tax Report*, p. G-1, TaxCore (Nov. 12, 2008)

Silk, "Good Governance Practices for 501(c)(3) Organizations: Should the IRS Become Further Involved?," 57 *Exempt Org. Tax Rev.* (no. 2) 183 (Aug. 2007)

Sunstein, "Chevron Step Zero," 92 *Va. L. Rev.* (no. 2) 187 (2006)

U.S. Government Accountability Office, "IRS Examination Selection: Internal Controls for Exempt Organization Selection Should Be Strengthened" (GAO-15-514 (July 2015)

U.S. senators, letter to IRS, Feb. 19, 2014, Bloomberg BNA, *Daily Tax Report* (Feb. 20, 2014)

TE/GE Division, IRS, "Report on FY 2016 Priorities" (Oct. 1, 2015)

Table of Cases

ABA Retirement Funds v. United States, 759 F.3d 718 (7th Cir. 2014)

Abdel-Fattah v. Commissioner, 134 T.C. 190 (2010)

Alexander v. Americans United, Inc., 416 U.S. 752 (1974)

Altera Corporation and Subsidiaries v. Commissioner, 145 T.C. 91 (2015)

Amalgamated Transit Union v. Skinner, 894 F.2d 1362 (D.C. Cir. 1990)

AmerGen Energy Co. v. LLC v. United States, 2010-2 U.S.T.C. ¶ 50,600 (U.S. Ct. Fed. Cl. 2010)

American Campaign Academy v. Commissioner, 92 T.C. 1053 (1989)

American Institute of Certified Public Accountants v. IRS, 2015 BL 357465 (D.C. Cir., Oct. 30, 2015)

American Library Association v. Federal Communications Commission, 406 F.3d 689 (D.C. Cir. 2005)

American Mining Congress v. Environmental Protection Agency, 907 F.2d 1179 (D.C. Cir. 1990)

Atlantic Mutual Insurance Co. v. Commissioner, 523 U.S. 382 (1998)

AT&T Corp. v. Iowa Utilities Board, 525 U.S. 366 (1999)

Auer v. Robbins, 51 U.S. 452 (1997)

Basic Unit Ministry of Alma Karl Schurig v. Commissioner, 511 F. Supp. 166 (D.D.C. 1981), *aff'd*, 670 F.2d 120 (D.C Cir. 1982)

Benjamin Price Genealogical Association v. United States, 79-1 U.S.T.C. ¶ 9361 (D.D.C. 1979)

Bingler v. Johnson, 394 U.S. 741 (1969)

Bob Jones University v. United States, 461 U.S. 574 (1983)

Bond v. United States, 131 S. Ct. 2355 (2011)

Bowman Transportation, Inc. v. Arkansas-Best Freight System, Inc., 419 U.S. 281 (1974)

Bubbling Well Church of Universal Love, Inc. v. Commissioner, 74 T.C. 531 (1980), *aff'd*, 670 F.2d 104 (9th Cir. 1981)

Burlington Truck Lines v. United States, 371 U.S. 156 (1962)

Burrage v. United States, 134 S. Ct. 881 (2014)

California Independent System Operator Corporation v. Federal Energy Regulatory Commission, 372 F.3d 395 (D.C. Cir. 2004)

Callaway Family Association v. Commissioner, 71 T.C. 340 (1978)

Caterpillar Tractor Co. v. United States, 589 F.2d 1040 (Ct. Cl. 1978)

Chevron U.S.A., Inc. v. Natural Resources Defense Council, Inc., 467 U.S. 837 (1984)

Citizens United v. Federal Election Commission, 558 U.S. 310 (2010)

City of Arlington, Texas v. Federal Communications Commission, 133 S. Ct. 1863 (2013)

Community Television of Southern California v. Gottfried, 459 U.S. 498 (1983)

Connecticut National Bank v. Germain, 503 U.S. 249, 253-254 (1992)

Cottage Savings Association v. Commissioner, 499 U.S. 554 (1991)

Council for Education, The v. Commissioner, 106 T.C.M. (CCH) 669 (2013)

Electric Power Supply Association v. Federal Energy Regulatory Commission, 753 F.3d 216 (D.C. Cir. 2014)

est of Hawaii v. Commissioner, 71 T.C. 1067 (1979), *aff'd*, 647 F.2d 170 (9th Cir. 1981)

Exploratory Research, Inc. v. Commissioner, 95 T.C.M. (CCH) 1347 (2008)

Federal Drug Administration v. Brown & Williamson Tobacco Corp., 529 U.S. 120 (2000)

Federal Election Commission v. Machinists Non-Partisan Political League, 655 F.2d 380 (D.C. Cir. 1981)

Federal Maritime Commission v. Seatrain Lines, Inc., 411 U.S. 726 (1973)

Founding Church of Scientology v. United States, 412 F.2d 1197 (Ct. Cl. 1969), *cert. den.*, 397 U.S. 1009 (1970)

Freedman v. Maryland, 380 U.S. 51 (1965)

George v. Commissioner, T.C. Memo. 2015-158 (Aug. 12, 2015)

Glass v. Commissioner, 471 F.3d 698 (6th Cir. 2008)

Gonzales v. Oregon, 546 U.S. 243 (2006)

Hampton v. Mow Sun Wong, 426 U.S. 88 (1976)

Household Credit Services, Inc. v. Pfennig, 541 U.S. 232 (2004)

Judalong v. Holder, 132 S. Ct. 476 (2011)

Judkins v. Internal Revenue Service, Civil Case No. 1:16-cv-01794 (D.D.C.) (Sep. 8, 2016)

Judkins v. Department of the Treasury, Civil Case No. 1:16-cv-01811 (D.D.C.) (Sep. 12, 2016)

King v. Burwell, 135 S. Ct. 2480 (2015)

Littriello v. United States, 2005-1 U.S.T.C. ¶ 50,385 (W.D. Ky. 2005), *aff'd*, 484 F.3d 372 (6th Cir. 2007), *cert. den.*, 552 U.S. 1186 (2008)

Living Faith, Inc. v. Commissioner, 950 F.2d 365 (7th Cir. 1991), *aff'g* 60 T.C.M. (CCH) 710 (1990)

Loving v. Internal Revenue Service, 917 F. Supp. 2d 67 (D.D.C. 2013, *aff'd*, 742 F.3d 1013 (D.C. Cir. 2014)

Manning Association v. Commissioner, 93 T.C. 596 (1989)

Marbury v. Madison, 5 U.S. (1 Cranch) 137 (1803)

March for Life v. Burwell, 2015 WL 5139099, 128 F. F. Supp. 3d 116 (D.D.C., Aug. 31, 2015)

Mayo Foundation for Medical Education & Research v. United States, 562 U.S. 44 (2011)

Miss Georgia Scholarship Fund, Inc. v. Commissioner, 72 T.C. 267 (1979)

Mississippi Power & Light Co. v. Mississippi ex rel. Moore, 487 U.S. 354 (1988)

Motion Picture Association v. Federal Communications Commission, 309 F.3d 796 (D.C. Cir. 2002)

Motor Vehicle Manufacturers Association of the United States v. State Farm Mutual Automobile Insurance Co., 463U.S. 29 (1983)

National Association for the Advancement of Colored People v. Federal Power Commission, 425 U.S. 662 (1976)

National Education Association of the United States v. Commissioner, 137T.C. 100 (2011)

National Muffler Dealers Association, Inc. v. United States, 440 U.S. 473 (1979)

New York Central Securities Corp. v. United States, 287 U.S. 12 (1932)

Northern Pipeline Construction Co. v. Marathon Pipe Line Co., 458 U.S. 50 (1982)

Ohio Disability Association v. Commissioner, 98 T.C.M. (CCH) 462 (2009)

Omohundro v. United States, 300 F.3d 1065 (9th Cir. 2002)

Ould v. Washington Hospital for Foundlings, 95 U.S. 303 (1878)

Parks v. Commissioner, 145 T.C. 278 (2015)

Perin v. Carey, 24 How. 465 (1861)

Pharmaceutical Research & Manufacturers of America v. Thompson, 251 F.3d 219 (D.C. Cir. 2001)

P.L.L. Scholarship Fund v. Commissioner, 82 T.C. 196 (1984)

Ridgely v. Lew, 55 F. Supp. 3d 89 (D.D.C. 2014)

Robinson v. Shell Oil Co., 519 U.S. 337 (1997)

Schaefer, Estate of v. Commissioner, 145 T.C. 134 (2015)

Skidmore v. Swift & Co., 323 U.S. 134 (1944)

Smiley v. Citibank (South Dakota), N.A., 517 U.S. 735 (1996)

Texas Department of Housing and Community Affairs v. Inclusive Communities Project, Inc., 135 S. Ct. 2507 (2015)

Thomas v. United States, 22 Ct. Cl. 749 (1991)

Tripoli Rocketry Association v. Bureau of Alcohol, Tobacco, Firearms and Explosives, 437 F.3d 75 (D.C. Cir. 2006)

True the Vote, Inc. v. Internal Revenue Service, 831 F.3d 551 (D.C. Cir. 2016)

Tualatin Valley Builders Supply v. United States, 522 F.3d 937 (9th Cir. 2008)

United Mine Workers of America v. Mine Safety & Health Administration, 823 F.2d 608 (D.C. Cir. 1987)

United States v. Arthur Young & Co., 465 U.S. 805 (1984)

United States v. Boyle, 469 U.S. 242 (1985)

United States v. Cleveland Indians Baseball Co., 532 U.S. 200 (2001)

United States v. Coopers & Lybrand, 550 F.2d 615 (10th Cir. 1977)

United States v. Harrington, 388 F.2d 520 (2nd Cir. 1968)

United States v. Josephberg, 562 F.3d 478 (2nd Cir. 2009)

United States v. Living Word Christian Center, 2009-1 U.S.T.C. ¶ 50,199 (D. Minn. 2009)

United States v. Mead Corp., 533 U.S. 218 (2001)

United States v. Nixon, 418 U.S. 683 (1974)

United States v. NorCal Tea Party Patriots, 817 F.3d 953 (6th Cir. 2016)

United States v. Powell, 379 U.S. 48 (1964)

United States v. Southwestern Cable Co., 392 U.S. 157 (1968)

U.S. Department of Jutice v. Tax Analysts, 492 U.S. 136 (1989)

Virginia v. Hicks, 539 U.S. 113 (2003)

Wilkes v. United States, 50 F. Supp. 2d 1281 (M.D. Fla. 1999), *aff'd*, 201 F.3d 394 (11th Cir. 2000)

Xilinx, Inc. v. Commissioner, 125 T.C. 37 (2005), *aff'd*, 598 F.3d 1191 (9th Cir. 2010)

Z Street, Inc. v. Commissioner, 2015 WL 3797974 (D.C. Cir. 2015)

Zimmerman v. Commissioner, 71 T.C. 367 (1978)

Table of Statutes

5 U.S.C § 706(2)
26 U.S.C. § 501(a)
26 U.S.C. § 501(c)(3)
26 U.S.C. § 6001
26 U.S.C. § 6033
26 U.S.C. § 7402(b)
26 U.S.C. § 7601(a)
26 U.S.C. § 7623(a)
26 U.S.C. § 7801(a)(1)
26 U.S.C. § 7802(c)(1)(A)
26 U.S.C. § 7803(a)(1)(A)
26 U.S.C. § 7803(a)(2)(A)
26 U.S.C. § 7805(a)
31 U.S.C. § 301

Table of Treasury Regulations

Reg. § 170A-9(e)(3)
Reg. § 170A-9(f)(3)(iii)(D)
Reg. § 1.501(c)(3)-1(a)(1)
Reg. § 1.501(c)(3)-1(c)(1)
Reg. § 601.101(a)

Table of IRS Revenue Rulings and Procedures

Rev. Rul. 55-656, 1955-2 C.B. 262
Rev. Rul. 61-170, 1961-2 C.B. 112
Rev. Rul. 66-219, 1966-2 C.B. 208
Rev. Rul. 66-323, 1966-2 C.B. 216
Rev. Rul. 69-441, 1969-2 C.B. 115
Rev. Rul. 69-545, 1969-2 C.B. 117
Rev. Rul. 70-186, 1970-1 C.B. 128
Rev. Rul. 76-152, 1976-1 C.B. 151
Rev. Rul. 98-15, 1998-1 C.B. 718
2017-5 2017-1 I.R.B. 230

Table of IRS General Counsel Memoranda

36372 (Aug. 11, 1975)
36506 (Dec. 8, 1975)
38382 (May 23, 1980)

Table of IRS Private Letter Rulings

200736037 (June 15, 2007)
200737044 (June 18, 2007)
200828029 (April 18, 2008)
200830028 (April 28, 2008)
200843032 (Aug. 1, 2008)
200845053 (Aug. 11, 2008)
200846040 (Aug. 21, 2008)
200916035 (Jan. 23, 2009)
201016088 (Jan. 29, 2010)
201113041 (Jan. 7, 2011)
201203025 (Oct. 26, 2011)
201209011 (Dec. 8, 2011)
201218041 (Feb. 7, 2012)
201221022 (Mar. 1, 2012)
201232034 (May 16, 2012)
201236033 (June 12, 2012)
201242014 (July 24, 2012)
201242016 (July 27, 2012)
201252021 (Sep. 13, 2012)
201302040 (Oct. 19, 2012)
201325017 (Mar. 28, 2013)
201332013 (May 17, 2013)
201349021 (July 2, 2013)
201411038 (Dec. 19, 2013)
201421022 (Feb. 27, 2014)
201427018 (April 7, 2014)
201429027 (Dec. 12, 2014)
201436050 (June 12, 2014)
201440020 (July 8, 2014)
201443021 (July 29, 2014)
201451030 (Sep. 25, 2014)
201452017 (Oct. 2, 2014)
201507026 (Oct. 22, 2014)
201525014 (Mar. 24, 2015)

201526020 (April 2, 2015)
201540019 (July 7, 2015)
201541013 (May 29, 2014)
201543019 (July 29, 2015)
201634029 (May 26, 2016)
201640022 (July 7, 2016)
201641023 (March 2, 2016)

Index

A

Administrative Procedure Act, 5, 15, 18, 264–265, 273
Agency expertise, factor of, 67–70
American Institute of Philanthropy standards, 127–128
American National Red Cross Governance Modernization Act, 105, 139–140
Annual information return:
  irrelevant governance questions in, 235, 241–243
  policies referenced in, 24, 235
  summary of, 78–79, 159–164
Application recognition process, 85–87
Arbitrary and capricious standard, 261–266, 271
Attorney General, US, 216
Authority, agency:
  concept of, 6–7, 27–33, 213
  IRS lack of, Chap. 8, 271–272

B

Better Business Bureau Wise Giving Alliance standards, 111–113
Bubbling Well Church opinion, 3–4, 75, 94–96, 232–233
Business leagues, 238

C

CAISO opinion:
  commentary on, 228–230, 251
  summary of, 28–29, 211, 217–228, 276
California Nonprofit Integrity Act, 129–131
Charity Navigator, 152
Chevron framework, 27, 30, 49–65, 221–224, 255–259, 266, 271
Church, federal tax definition of, 79–80, 238
City of Arlington opinion, 6–7, 28, 29–31, 211–213, 258–259
Civil Service Commission, 38–41, 214
Commission for the Preservation of America's Heritage Abroad, 31
Committee for Purchase proposed best practices, 136–137
Commodity Futures Trading Commission, 51
Commonly accepted governance standards (ostensible), 2, 3, 153, 156, Chap. 4
Community benefit standard, 91, 195
Community representation, 188–189
Conflicts of interest, 23, 161–162, 223, 236, 248
Congressional Review Act, 15, 274
Consumer Products Safety Commission, 31
Control, factor of, 180–186, 189–191
Credit counseling organizations rules, 88–89

D

Data as to governance and compliance, IRS's:
  commentary on, 246–249
  summary of, 171–173
Delegations of authority:
  explicit, 267–268

implicit, 267–268
Department of the Treasury, 9–10, 13, 23, 33, 228, 233, 252, 257, 260, 265, 269, 277, 278

E

Environmental Protection Agency, 52
Evangelical Council for Financial Accountability standards, 113–120
Expertise:
agency, 68–70
IRS lack of, 230–241, 251–252
Extraordinary cases, 267–268

F

Facts-and-circumstances test, 90, 237
Federal Communications Commission, 34–38, 214, 216–217
Federal Drug Administration, 52, 259, 267–268
Federal Election Commission, 12, 13, 45–46, 214
Federal Energy Regulatory Commission, 28–29, 53, 217–228, 251
Federal Power Commission, 41–45, 214
Federal tax law rules, 76–103

G

Good governance principles:
commentary on IRS's draft of, 243–245
IRS draft of, 164–168
summaries of, Chap. 4
Governance check sheet, IRS's:
commentary on, 246
summary of, 170–171
Governance philosophy, 105–106
Governing boards:
composition, 21
related, 195–204
size, 21, 177–178
Government Accountability Office, US, 14–20, 274–275
Government agencies:
authority of, 6–7, 27–33
expertise of, 68–70
jurisdiction of, 33–48, 252–253
Guidance as to federal tax law:
authoritative, 14–17
non-regulatory, 14, 16–17
regulatory, 15–16

I

Internal Revenue Service:
authority of, Chap. 8, 271–272
data as to correlation, 171–173
Exempt Organizations Division 2009 annual report, 164
good governance principles of (draft), 164–168
governance check sheet of, 170–171
jurisdiction of, 7–13, Chap. 7, 270–271
guidance document types, 272–275
organization of, 75–76
officials' speeches, 1–3, 155–159
private letter rulings of, Chap. 6
and regulatory guidance, 13–20
role of, 7–13
training materials of, 168–170
Interstate Commerce Commission, 43, 51, 227

J

Judicial deference, 53–57
Jurisdiction:
concept of, 7, 27–31, 33
IRS lack of, Chap. 7, 271–272

K

Koskinson, John A., 11–12

L

Loving opinion, 65–66, 257

M

Major economic or political decisions, 52–53, 68–69, 256, 259, 267–268, 274
Mayo Foundation opinion, 27, 57–59
Miller, Steven, 1–3, 24, 156–157, 242, 252

N

National Security Agency, 31
Nonprofit governance:
- and annual information return, 23-24
- board composition, 21
- board size, 21
- community representation concept, 188–189
- concept of, 21–25, 87–88
- court opinions as to, 94–103
- IRS entry into, 14, 23–25, 250–251, 269–270
- one-individual boards, 187–188
- and policies, 22
- public control, concept of, 189–191
- public oversight, concept of, 191–193
- and religious institutions, 193–194
- and IRS revenue rulings, 91–94
- state law, 21, 23, 250
- and tax case law, 94–103
- and tax regulatory law, 89–94
- and tax statutory law, 88–89

O

Office of Information and Regulatory Affairs, 15–20, 275
Office of Management and Budget, 15–20, 274–275
Organic statutes, 8–9, 46, 212, 213–215, 255
Owens, Marcus S., 9, 13, 71–72, 241, 242, 244, 278

P

Panel on Nonprofit Sector:
- good governance principles, 140–151
- recommendations, 137–139

Paperwork Reduction Act, 15
Patient Protection and Affordable Care Act, 19, 33, 69–70
Philanthropic Advisory Service standards, 107–110
Policies, governance, 4–5, 22, 205–206, 241
Priority Guidance Plan, 17, 265
Private benefit doctrine:
- as basis for IRS ruling policy, 233–235
- IRS's incorrect reliance on, 232–241
- summary of, 80–83

Private foundations, 79–80, 239–241
Private inurement doctrine, 83–85
Private letter rulings, IRS:
- board size, 175–176
- discrepant, 208–210
- policies, lack of, 205–206
- related boards, 195–204

Public charities, 79–80, 89–91
Public interest law firms, 91
Public policy doctrine, 47–48, 77–78

R

Regulatory Flexibility Act, 15
Regulatory Guidance Processes Report, 11–20, 260, 274–275
Relevance, factor of, 71–73
Ridgely opinion, 67
Rules:
- economically significant, 15–18
- significant, 15–18

S

Sarbanes-Oxley Act, 106–107
Securities and Exchange Commission, 230
Senate Finance Committee staff paper, 131–134
Skidmore standard, 259–261, 266
Standards for Excellence Institute standards, 121–127
Supporting organizations rule, 89

T

Tax exceptionalism, 59–60
Tax-exempt organizations, law of, 76–87
Training materials, IRS's:
commentary on, 245
summary of, 168–170
Transportation Safety Administration, 31
Treasury Department's voluntary best practices, US, 134–136

U

Ultra vires acts, 6, 8, 27, 28, 29, 32, 53, 211, 253, 255, 270
Unanswered questions, 273–280
Unusual grants, 90–91
Urban Mass Transportation Administration, 216